e the last

WHAT PRICE CREATIVITY?

*Papers from the 28th University of Manchester
Broadcasting Symposium, 1997*

Editors:

Sue Ralph
School of Education
University of Manchester

Jo Langham Brown
University College, Warrington
University of Manchester

Tim Lees
School of Education
University of Manchester

WHAT PRICE CREATIVITY?

*Papers from the 28th University of Manchester
Broadcasting Symposium, 1997*

Edited by

Sue Ralph
School of Education, University of Manchester

Jo Langham Brown
University College, Warrington, University of Manchester

Tim Lees
School of Education, University of Manchester

Published with the generous support of Channel 4

Current Debates in Broadcasting: 7

UNIVERSITY
UP *of* JL
LUTON PRESS

British Library Cataloguing in Publication Data
A catalogue record for this book is available from the British Library

ISBN: 1 86020 553 4
ISSN: 0963-6544

Published by
John Libbey Media
Faculty of Humanities
University of Luton
75 Castle Street
Luton
Bedfordshire LU1 3AJ
United Kingdom
Telephone: +44 (0) 1582 743297; Fax: +44 (0) 1582 743298
e-mail: ulp@luton.ac.uk

Cover design by Creative Identity, Hertford, UK
Typeset in Palatino
Printed in Great Britain by Gwynprint, Haywards Heath, West Sussex

Contents

Sponsors and Committee

One of the objectives of the Symposium Steering Committee is to keep the cost of attending the event as low as possible. It is greatly assisted in achieving this objective by the generosity of its long-term supporters and sponsors. The Committee would like to express its gratitude to its 1997 supporters and sponsors, who were:

BBC
BBC North
Border Television
Channel 4 Television

Granada Television
The *Guardian/Observer*
Independent Television Commission
Manchester City Council

In organising the Broadcasting Symposium, the School of Education of the University of Manchester was advised by a Steering Committee, the members of which were:

John Gray, independent consultant (honorary president)

Sue Ralph, University of Manchester (director)
Marjorie Burton, University of Manchester (co-ordinator)
Tim Lees, University of Manchester (administrator)

1997 Committee:

Emma Barker, Carlton Television
Jeremy Barr, Ravensbourne College
Louise Bennett, Independent Television Comission
Jo Langham Brown, University College, Warrington, University of Manchester
Sue Caro, Channel 4 Television
Freda Chapman, BECTU
David Cox, independent producer
Jane Drabble, BBC
Nick Howells, Editz Ltd
Helen Hutchinson, Border Television
Jerome Kuehl, Open Media
Jane Luca, Granada Television

John Mundy, University College, Warrington, University of Manchester
Philip Radcliffe, University of Manchester
Helen Read, The *Guardian/Observer*
Clare Reynolds, Broadcasting Standards Council
Brook Sinclair, Adcomm Ltd
Veronica Taylor, British Film Institute
Janine Thomason, BBC
Stephen Whittle, Broadcasting Standards Commission
Paul Whiting, Editz Ltd
Keith Whitmore, Manchester City Council

The Symposium is very grateful to Professor Bryan Robson,
Pro-Vice Chancellor, University of Manchester, for his support
and his welcoming address.

Transcriptions by Beryl Goddard and Mary Laurie
Audio recordings by David Griffiths and Andrew Haslam

The Symposium is grateful to the following who chaired the Paper Sessions:
Jo Langham Brown, Marie Brown, John Gray,
Bryan Luckham, Sue Ralph, Brook Sinclair

The Symposium is especially grateful to
Dr Colin Lees for proofreading this manuscript.

Foreword

On the 17th of February 1997 the world changed forever ...

With this statement, Phil Redmond in his keynote lecture delivered a broadside against the traditional attitudes and concerns of British broadcasters. The ongoing debate about 'quality' in broadcasting is, for Redmond, an irrelevance: of far greater future significance and importance for ensuring creativity in the media industry is the World Trade Organisation's agreed new protocol (brokered on that date) for the global telecommunications traffic. This really heralds the arrival of the global digital information superhighway and the end of the old established hegemony. The BBC and ITV 'theological dominion' is over. Control of the software is shifting away from the antiquated terrestrial institutions to future consumers who will schedule their own programming menus with the help of navigation software tuned to their own tastes and wishes: this will be the main impetus to programme diversity and originality. However, in the world of global markets and technological innovation, Redmond emphasised that creativity still resides with the people producing the information and entertainment content, and the most important element which can effect a revolutionary transformation of the information superhighway's essential nature remains their education and training.

Redmond's focus on the revolution initiated by convergence and digitisation, together with his emphasis on the importance of education and training, was echoed on many occasions throughout the Symposium, in both the major sessions and in the presented papers. In the last two years, the Symposium has, to an extent, broken free from a British-centred agenda, and academic papers from the United States, South Africa, Israel and Kuwait all testify to the increasing similarity in the problems and concerns of those who observe the shifting media environment in the 'global village'. However, the vexed question of 'where is it all going?' continues to bemuse, and in that context, the paper which described the process of hybridisation in the dance music industry over the last decade, together with an analysis of the emergence of the 'cocktail channel', the significance of the 'filter', and the 'remix show', created considerable interest, especially when this was linked with a paper which examined fifty years of 'remixing' on prime time network television in the United States, and which had the compelling sub-title 'Spin-offs + Copycats + Rip-offs = Creative Exhaustion?'.

The Symposium is beginning, almost by default, to mirror a less-vaunted convergence, that of media practitioners and academics. There was a time when practitioners passed researchers by (except for those oriented towards quantitative audience research) and academics loftily condemned broadcasters as self-justifying puppets of the established and powerful. However, as Jane Drabble pointed out in her concluding remarks, this year's Symposium, in the report and discussion of the Broadcasting Standards Commission's 'Values in Broadcasting' research, provided a forum for broadcasters to listen to research which had a philosophical dimension and which drew attention to the idea that the audience was not just an economic entity but also a moral force. She welcomed the opportunity the Symposium provided to engage with academic activity and with young people, who were well-represented among the delegates. Many of the academics attending the Symposium, especially those involved in teaching media studies, referred to their sense of obligation to alert students to the realities of the marketplace and the impact of casualisation and multi-skilling. While it is clear that more rarefied research interests are still important, more space is being made in the academic agenda for practical analyses of industrial structures and working conditions. In this connection, the session entitled 'What About the Workers?' brought academics, practitioners and employer, union and training representatives together to reflect on the changing nature of employment in the media and the pitfalls and opportunities which await young people, who are the true creative capital of the next century. The papers about employment and issues of identity in newsrooms in the United States serve to re-enforce the sense of a high level of international concern about education and training, along with the difficulties involved in reconciling the concerns and budgets of local media in the era of global ownership. All too often, young people are underpaid and exploited; less well publicised are the worsening conditions of all employees, and especially working mothers, in an increasingly high-pressured and volatile industry.

Issues of power in the United Kingdom were explored in the paper examining the impact of 'producers' choice' at the BBC and in the sessions entitled 'Who Shapes the Schedule' and 'Values in Broadcasting'. In many cases, accepted popular wisdom was proved to be inaccurate and flawed, and the Symposium provided a forum for received perceptions to be subjected to close scrutiny and correction. This was very clear in the papers which presented current and ongoing research on the emergence of the niche market for children's programming, attitudes towards children's programming on BBC television in the 1950s, and children's own views about their viewing preferences.

As the influence of computing and telecommunications technology alters the concept of broadcasting and makes room for the era of individual choice and narrowcasting, the 1998 Symposium, entitled 'Youth and the Global Media' picks up the key themes of this year's event and welcomes scholars and practitioners from around the world.

Our thanks to everyone who took part, speakers, delegates and paper presenters; to our sponsors for their continued generosity; and a special thanks to the publishers, John Libbey Media and particularly Professor Manuel Alverado, for their support and assistance.

Jo Langham Brown
Sue Ralph
Tim Lees

The 1997 Symposium: Keynote Address

What Price Creativity?

Phil Redmond

Chief Executive, Mersey Television

Introduction

I want to start today by issuing a few health warnings. First, like everyone else, I have no claim or monopoly on the great truths of life. These are only my views and you must take them and compare them with the views of others. Second, these views are based on a career built in television. Third, I am going to be talking about the industry in ten years time – that is the future for the students going through education right now. Fourth, I will be talking a lot about technology and cash. I make no apology for this. Without an understanding of the 'tools of the trade', no artiste, in whatever endeavour, will maximise their creative potential.

What Price Creativity? Discuss ...

The theme of the symposium is – *What Price Creativity?* What does this actually mean? Does it mean, for instance, *what is it worth?* Or, *how can you put a price on it?* Or, *is it worth the aggravation?* Or, as I suspect, *will there be sufficient money to pay for any of the above?* The simple answer is 'yes'. There is no need to worry. This is the greatest time to be in the media industries. The future is wider choice – greater diversity, greater access and greater opportunity.

The debate about quality is a bogus theology preached by historical anachronisms. I will come on to this later and, incidentally, how the world changed forever on 17th February this year – *and nobody noticed.*

First, however, we need to look at some of the challenges facing us, but before we do lets consider a few statistics, which, as we all know, can usually be made to support any argument. However, I am using these only as broad indicators.

In 1997 the value of the media industries was probably:
- UK: £30 billion
- EU: £300 billion
- Worldwide: £3000 billion

By 2007 – this should multiply by factor of ten.

So what is future?

In a word – Convergence. Computers and telecommunications – with film – will continue, especially since 17th February 1997, to blur the boundaries of what we call media. At the moment everyone accepts that media, computers and telecommunications are still separate industries – with the latter two providing support services to the former – and media sub-divided into four main categories of print, radio, television and film.

Will it happen? Of course. Look at computer companies like Compaq and Packard Bell which now expect 75–80 per cent of all their future revenues to come from the domestic market; BT alone is worth, say, £26 billion. British Television as an industry is worth £4 billion, so who do you think will win the fight for consumer time?

Now let's look at the most significant 'new media' – The Internet. With almost no distribution costs, it has the potential to reshape the media world, letting new competitors in and forcing established giants to evolve or die. Already sales of the Encyclopaedia Britannica have collapsed in the face of competition from CD-ROMS; the next battlefield will be on-line.

Yet telephone companies agree that their best business prospects lie not in carrying other people's bytes – or selling their products – but in having something to sell themselves. Which is why so many of them are investing heavily in content provision.

In 1995, MCI committed up to $2 billion in News Corporation (BT now having to promise to sell that when it takes over MCI). Ameritech put $500m into a deal with Disney – US West bought a quarter of Time Warner for $2.5 billion.

In future we will not pay for telephone calls – but only for subscription to a service provider. This is because the networks are built already. Increasing competition is bringing down the cost of using these networks to the point where the marginal cost is so low that it will not matter who is using them or when or to where. The cost of calls will be insignificant. The real costs will be for maintenance and expansion, which will mean service providers wanting to guarantee their cashflow by regular flat rate monthly subscriptions.

Everyone knows that fibre optics have greater potential than copper. But consider, for instance, that our existing phone cables are capable of carrying up to six video channels – with two copper wires. Consider also how battery technology has improved over recent years. For telephones – 20 mins to 72 hours. Laptops – 20 mins to 8 hours. In most domestic electronic products the most expensive item is the power pack to step down current from 240 to 12 volts. That seems to imply a diminishing role for the National Grid. But does it? Now consider that the National Grid, using copper cables, provides three cables into most homes. How many channels could they squeeze along those?

These developments have colossal impact on the provision of services – both traditional telecoms, data and moving images, whether home shopping or video-on-demand and every single change in any media delivery system, whether television or telecoms, is linked to computers. Yet the latest Heritage Committee Report entitled *The Future of Broadcasting and the BBC*, dated 13th.March 1997, shows that out of 52 witnesses called only *one* was from the world of computers

This fact alone demonstrates the real gulf between these who are attempting to create a framework for the television industry and what is actually happening in terms of new media.

Wider Choice – Greater Diversity – Greater Access and Greater Opportunity
There is only one thing we can be certain about, in future there will be more channels. At present there are 5 Terrestrial Analogue, 30 Satellite Analogue and probably about ten original channels on Cable. Soon there could be 25 Terrestrial

Digital channels, 500 on Satellite Digital and an *unlimited* number on Cable and/or Telcoms or even the National Grid!

Too much choice?

But, someone is bound to ask, 'Is this going to offer too much choice'? The answer to that is that no one looks at a book shop and says we have too many books. Or that more book shops mean lower quality. Similarly no-one feels obliged to go into a book shop and start in the top left hand corner and read every book.

Why then is an increase in choice in television always seen as a regressive rather than progressive development? For career prospects this means many varied gateways to a career. Careers could be in text, weather or sports channels. They all need to be researched, packaged, presented, marketed, have ad-sales, graphics, be recorded, have voice-overs, intellectual and legal clearances, accounts, telesales, personnel and so on. Not everyone needs to be Chris Evans – not everyone wants to be! So my advice to anyone entering the industry now is approach cable or satellite stations. There will be greater opportunities and all opportunities offer valuable experience.

What about the quality?

Despite the career opportunities, the next cry is always the one about 'quality' – how will it be maintained? This of course should be ignored. It is a bogus argument – as it always was.

The high priests of the terrestrial television industry would have us believe that if they cannot deliver 'quality' all the time then how can new entrants? However, let's consider a few things. The first is to remember that we can produce as much crap television as anyone else. Let's not forget that the BBC puts out the National Lottery Show or that from the very citadel of Quality Commercial Television itself – *Granada* – a top peak time show is based on viewers' home movies!

So, the argument goes, with their vast resources still producing great opportunities for rubbish, how can they, let alone anyone else, produce the same level of quality, never mind more – for less? Of course these lyrics are from the same song sheet with only a slight variation in tune. It is basically a song about restricting expansion because they cannot achieve that expansion themselves.

Despite the wasted years of Producer Choice and so-called cut backs at the BBC, the reality is that they have resources coming out of their ears – but a fixed and declining income. On the other hand Commercial Television Companies, despite the years of heavier taxation, levies, bids and annual payments for their licences, still have money coming out of their ears. They could easily increase their income but they are restricted to how much airtime they can actually sell. So whilst the BBC is resource rich but cash poor, Commercial Television is cash rich but resources poor. In other words preserving the status quo has to be the only option to preserve their market domination.

Incidentally, when I started Brookie, the High Priests of quality said it couldn't be done – not with the equipment, the budget, the people or the location. Now we are in danger of becoming part of the establishment – praised not just for

3

content and style, but for training. It's not about technology or even cash, but what you do with it – we have all seen expensive failures as well as the brashy trash shows.

What about the finance?
But, someone else will say, where will the money come from? Let's consider a few more things. Have you ever heard of an ITV Licence holder demanding to be relieved of the heavy burden of raking in advertising cash? Remember the ITV companies telling us all that C4 couldn't survive selling its own air time – it was impossible? Last year it took £485 million pounds – about a third of ITV's advertising revenue – with a quarter of the audience! Remember also the hoo-hah about Sky Sports hogging all the football. There is now more football on terrestrial television than ever before – and the increased revenue to pay £15m for Alan Shearer is a direct result. (This is an economic point – not cultural!)

Before we move off money – consider something else. Why is income from advertising so perverse? Why is the BBC in danger of losing editorial control if it takes advertising income – yet – the *Guardian*, *The Times*, the *Telegraph*, the *Independent et al* are not? Or is someone going to stand up and tell me these august journals are corrupted by ads? Could it be that press journalists can be trusted – whereas television cannot?

Why can the Tate, National, Royal Opera House *et al* be trusted to accept sponsorship and not the BBC?

How can the National Heritage Committee in this report (*The Future of Broadcasting and the BBC*) say that Channel 4 with ads is a good thing (Para 90(f)) – yet at the same time say the BBC cannot possibly consider it?

The World Changed Forever
Moving on from the theoretical to the actual. I said at the beginning that on the 17th February the world changed forever, and nobody noticed. Well, except the FT and a couple of paras in one or two of the broadsheets – but it certainly didn't make headlines like Dolly the sheep.

That weekend the World Trade Organisation brokered an agreement with 70 countries accounting for 90 per cent of global telecommunications traffic.

Why is this significant? Because with common standards, common pricing, common protocols, the global digital highway will soon move from the techno-nerds bedrooms to the family viewing area.

This is as significant a moment for the planet as the ending of the gauge war that led to the railway expansion in the mid 19th century. It means that with common protocols the transfer of knowledge and therefore the pace of tech-nological change, leading inevitably to economic and social change, will move at an ever increasing rate.

Broadcast or Narrowcast?
For the media industries this is also significant as it will wipe out another of those old media myths propagated by the hymn masters of terrestrial television, and that is that people will always want people to package channels for them, like BBC1 and BBC2 or even like newspapers.

The theologians behind this one are usually employed by BBC and ITV and do not want to admit that at the moment they control a technology with its roots in the 1930s and which is not capable of delivering anything else except large transmitters to large areas.

Their safety net is that with so much on offer there will always be a need for filters. People, organisations, systems and even channels that will sift and package. Yet, they miss the point that as the new technology competes with their structures – it will also be able to deliver the means to cope with information overload.

No one will expect to plough through a TV Guide some 500 pages thick. We will all have smart sets that will have programmable software that we will tune to our own tastes.

Of course there will always be a need for filters – people to sift out the good from the bad, like book and film reviews , and, ironically, advertisers will demand large audience channels. They will want to buy lots of people in one go – rather than have to buy 50 slots on niche channels – but, like cinema, those channels will be event led. The listed events like Cup Finals and Grand Nationals may survive on recognisable scheduled television – as will world premieres of things like Cracker – but Cracker 3, 4 and 5 will be available only on-line!

BBC, Microsoft or BT Network?

Does this mean everything will be Pay per View and/or Video on Demand? The simple answer is yes, but these are merely current marketing slogans. The reality is that we will all pay for what we watch – just as we do now – but in future it will be more transparent and depend upon the bundle of programming we buy. We may opt for pay per showing – or subscribe to a particular distributor's output.

All this is being researched aggressively, not by television companies, who see it as a threat to their terrestrial theology, but by the telecoms industries world-wide who not only have networks to deliver but, most crucially, the empirical historical research on usage. They know exactly:
- when people want to make calls
- when they don't
- when they are at home
- when they are out
- when they are available not only to make calls
- *but to take them*
- *and* – anything else the Telecoms want to send them!

Will it all happen? Let us consider a very inconvenient but simple fact – and that is that television is a second choice activity for most people.

If something better is going on they will do it. A sporting event, a wedding, or even the clocks going forward meaning people going out into their gardens more – will result in a drop in ratings. The most precious commodity we all have as viewers is our own time.

Couple this with the fact that as the major channels pick up an average 30 per cent share for their prime time programmes, this actually means that 70 per cent of viewers reject every programme, regardless of type, slot or channel. They have made an active choice to go elsewhere.

Put that together with the fact that most people will only go out to shop – if they have to. They will wait for a TV programme, if they have to. But when they can call both shopping and TV on demand, allowing them to do something else – they will do so.

The model for the future is not terrestrial scheduling – but more akin to publishing and retail book sales outlets.

Challenges That Lie Ahead

What does all this mean for the future? The first thing required is a psychological shift to embrace new technological change as a force for good. We should ignore the siren carpings of outdated theology from BBC and ITV and take an objective view of three key areas that technology will dramatically affect:
- regulation
- training
- creativity

Regulation

This will always be necessary but no more so than as an extension of the general law of the land. Our current regulatory framework for broadcasting has its origins in monopoly power and fear of technology. I think it is now generally assumed that the population en masse is not a bunch of impressionable, malleable fools who will immediately rush out and buy baked beans if a celebrity tells them to or go out and saw people in half – or even vote for a political party.

Unfortunately it is still *not* generally assumed that most of the population are also capable of making the intellectual leap from disliking a programme's content to reaching for the off button or channel remote. Fortunately, a multi-channel video-on-demand environment will make the *taste and decency* nanny-state attitude unworkable. People will be free to choose – or not – with the same freedom they have in any reputable book shop

Also fortunately, by making our so-called policy makers concentrate not on the easy and available scapegoats of controlled information channels like those of the BBC, ITV, Channel 4 or Channel 5, they will realise that with a multiplicity of information outlets, social problems – at all levels – also have a multiplicity of causes.

The increase in *reported* crime might have something to do not just with social conditions like poverty, but the way such figures are *reported* to and by the police and *reported* by the media. The same could be said about education league tables and funding.

Training

We are now standing beneath a technological waterfall. The rate of change is so fast and dramatic. Not long ago the only keyboard in production had something to do with the music, today you cannot enter a post production suite without a short course in basic word processing skills.

There is a need not just for single task or single craft skills, but an understanding of how technology makes the application of those skills differ from company to company, depending upon their rate of technological improvement. What is done by a person at one company may be automated elsewhere.

With the trend to short term contracts likely to continue, portability of skills and a system of recognised skill accreditation is vital. Employees need to know that their skill level will be recognised so they can easily move from job to job, while employers need to know that their qualifications actually imply competence.

This won't come from BBC and ITV: there is no common structure, no common aim. But it has to come from somewhere else.

For my own part, I am pleased to support the NW Training Consortium – which looks to answer the great conundrum – 'training for what?' – with industry recognised NVQs. At Liverpool John Moores University we have launched the Media Professional Studies Degree, now in its second year, to give students a better understanding of both the intellectual and business rigours that are required. We are also conducting a feasibility study into a new Television and Film School – based at JMU – that will become a national centre of excellence on new production techniques that recognises the potential of the converging industries. The working title is the *Digital Dream Factory*. We hope to have this running by 1999. In all these areas we hope to link and welcome a relationship with Skillset.

Higher education is an obvious route and within the debate about what is the role of a university – whether intellectual study for its own sake or 'ready for work' vocational training – let us not forget that the great Faculties of Engineering, Architecture and Medicine trace their roots to the demands of the industrial revolution. Similarly the future faculties of Media and Computer Studies will trace their roots back to the digital revolution.

Creativity

Yet all these formal training initiatives are fine – but anyone working in a creative field will know that the creative spark is most elusive. It often does not ignite on cue, and sometimes will bum brightly only fleetingly. It has to be captured as and when you find it.

This means casting the net wide and often – and often over the same ground as people move and develop at different rates. The trick is to find a way of making the net itself as big as possible – as wide as possible – and casting frequently.

In 1995 I wrote in the *Telegraph* that the biggest disappointment of the National Lottery was that there was no grand vision attached to its Arts Fund. It is all very well replacing Arts Centres' central heating boilers or renewing Transit vans for Touring Theatre Groups, but where was the great new idea?

I suggested that some of the Arts Council Lottery funding should be aimed at forging links between Regional Arts and Education Centres and the BBC to set up a British equivalent of the Welsh Eisteddfod. The purpose of this would be to recognise that creativity itself is nothing without exhibition. This leads to critical assessment and artistic development.

Everybody should have the right, in all age ranges, to make a film, perform, paint, draw, write, dance – if they want to. Regional Arts Boards or Local

Authorities or Higher Education establishments would combine to offer such opportunities in annual competitions open to all. The BBC would provide the exhibition space on its channels.

This would give anyone and everyone a chance to enter an annual competition that would enjoy regional and probably national exhibition. Much would be average, some would be dross, but there would be some creative sparks bouncing brightly.

Although I have already mentioned how we at JMU are hoping to establish a television and film school that will do just this – but this will only produce 20 post-graduate students a year. Taken with the National Film and Television School's 25, this won't fill the industry's expansion gap.

So the net needs to be cast wider and three publicly funded bodies already in existence could help cast that net with only a slight re-focusing of their cultural remits. These are the Arts Council, the British Film Institute and the BBC itself.

Arts Council
This is the obvious body as it is at present the main channel for funding cultural and media activity. Its present function should be re-focused and, by building onto its existing expertise, it could be more pro-active in encouraging and exploiting creative talent.

British Film Institute
On a national level I can see a role for the British Film Institute to act as a facilitator working with the BBC and Arts Council Lottery Funds to bring together arts and education centres to encourage creative convergence in digital techniques.

Exhibition should be automatic on the BBC. It doesn't have to be at 8.00pm or in peaktime – but could be on in daytime when people in education are available to view, or late night for VCR recording. The point is, that the main requirement of creative endeavour – exhibition – would be met!!

BBC
Market forces and technological change are so vast none of us can stop it, or probably influence it, except in the areas of public spending and education. We can and must influence the debate over the BBC in next Millennium, but that debate must focus on the Licence Fee itself – as a cultural fund, not on the BBC structure as a business enterprise

We don't need the BBC to be bigger and better than ITV. We need it to be innovative, responsive, relevant to and reflecting and disseminating Britain's cultural values.

How do we achieve that? I would like to see the BBC as a real public service provider linking all cultural activities to a common goal. This means linking with schools, colleges, Arts Council, lottery, BFI, etc., in cultural experiments like the National Eisteddfod idea. It should nurture tomorrow's talent through its crucial role as a catalyst for exhibition as well as creative endeavour. The BBC should be the place for that National Eisteddfod – providing opportunity for the rapid exchange of ideas and values.

Will we see it? Who knows? However, here's something else to consider. The BBC public service web site currently records between 600,000 to 1,000,000 hits a week. That's bigger than most of its radio shows and some TV programmes. Some people are interested in greater and wider communication inside and outside the BBC. Perhaps there is hope after all?

One last word on training and education. The creative industries' greatest raw material is not bricks, mortar or machines – it is its people. Funding for education and training, it is not a charitable activity – it is sound business investment.

Summary

The future is as challenging as it is bright. It's a future which will see increasingly blurred boundaries between media, computers and telecommunications. The battle for consumer time will be fought by the 'new media' and the delivery systems, be they television or telecoms, will have a colossal impact on the traditional television industry. The global digital highway will soon move into the family viewing area. Traditional terrestrial television structures will be challenged by the telecoms industry which will reshape our viewing patterns dramatically.

There is plenty of scope for choice, diversity, access and opportunity, and plenty of scope for creativity. Education and Higher Education centres should be ready to step in to the training gap. However, market forces and technological change are so vast none of us can stop it – or probably influence it, except in two areas:

1. public spending
2. education

We can and must influence the debate over the BBC in next Millennium. We must demand a say – not in any agenda set by a small privileged few but particularly in the much wider and much more important debate about what our Public Service Provider should actually be doing. That should not be trying to be all things to all licence fee payers and competing with all channels, but should have a much more focused role as the patron and protector of our national heritage.

It will not do this by aping or trying to second guess commercial enterprise elsewhere – but by building strong and permanent links to national and regional Arts Organisations, by building strong and permanent links to national and regional Educational Centres, by building effective links to organisations like the British Film Institute so that every person going through education has an opportunity, through a form of National Eisteddfodd to realise their own creativity.

In education whether formal or informal, the need is for an understanding of the impact and possibilities of technological change, how that technology will enable people to maximise or reach their own creative potential. To return to a point made earlier investment in education and training is not a charitable activity – it is a sound business investment.

That should be the joint role of the Public Service Provider and the Education Sector. That should be the price of creativity.

In other words, returning to the theme: what really matters is not the technology or even the cash – but what you do with them.

Who Shapes the Schedule?

Chair: Louise Bennett
Regional Executive, Independent Television Commission

Keith Ely
General Manager and Editor-in-Chief, Channel One Liverpool

Julia Lamaison
Director of Strategy, Granada Media Group

Adrian Moynes
Head of Schedule Planning TV, Radio Telefís Éireann, Ireland

Rob Noss
Media Associate Director, J. Walter Thompson

Louise Bennett: Ladies and gentlemen, may I welcome you to this first afternoon session of the Broadcasting Symposium. Let me introduce our three panel members. On my right here is Julia Lamaison, Director of Strategy for the Granada Media Group. For those of you who aren't aware, Granada is the licensee in the North West of England here. Julia's job until recently was as Director of Broadcasting within that North West licence area, so she was directly responsible for deciding the scheduling of Granada's output in the North West. Let me give you a bit of background on Julia. She actually started as a graduate in Landscape Design, which I only discovered yesterday. It's quite a step from Landscape Design to deciding the schedules of mainstream terrestrial television channels. Maybe she'll enlighten us on that in a moment. She has also worked with the BBC's Broadcasting Research Department, spending five years with them, and was heavily involved with research to do with *EastEnders* which, given her current position with Granada, makers of *Coronation Street*, will undoubtedly give us interesting insight into the way that folks operate within the schedule.

Moving on, to my left here is Keith Ely, who is the General Manager and Editor in Chief of Channel One Television in Liverpool, which is a very recent development – a six months old local cable operation in Liverpool. He's got a long and illustrious career on Merseyside as a journalist, a career he pursued for thirty years, most of it with the Trinity Group of Newspapers. He was Editor of the *Liverpool Daily Post* at one stage. He's been the Managing Director of the Trinity's Weekly Group of Newspapers, which covers twenty titles, and he's bringing that sort of local expertise to Channel One in its television output now. So we'll be looking to Keith to give us some insight into how a channel that's based on a single theme of news output competes in the multi-channel environment. And finally, at my far right we have Rob Noss, who is Media Associate Director with J. Walter Thompson in London. He's responsible for clients such as British Gas, De Beers and Warner Lambert. He started his career with Thames Television in Sales; he then joined the advertising agency Young and Rubicund, and after two years there he moved to J. Walter-Thompson in 1991, spent a year globe-trotting, which he describes as obligatory – and sounds ideal to me, never mind obligatory – and he now has a wide spread of clients across various portfolios.

So, I think that's enough from me, what I suggest now is that we ask Julia to start our presentation, answering the question, who shapes the schedule?

Julia Lamaison: So, where do we start? In the context of my own job with Granada Television, the 'shape' of the schedule is easy enough to determine: it's a mix of programmes that are designed to maximise the share and profile of the audience to ITV. Since when have you seen a blank screen on ITV? The schedule is filled with programmes, commercials and station-branding day by day, hour by hour, minute by minute. Rather, we should focus on the 'who' for a moment, how is the mix determined and 'who' is the mysterious person who's 'in charge'?

Thinking about this, I started with a question on everybody's lips at present. *Is it... the Government?* And in ITV terms, this also includes the regulator who ensures that the ITV system is meeting the demands of the wider Broadcasting policy. As many of you are aware, the terms of the Broadcasting Act which implemented the open bidding process for the 15 ITV licences and the subsequent legislation which set out terms for media ownership set a framework for ITV broadcasting. How does this bear on 'who' shapes the schedule? A number of criteria were set which had a very significant bearing on the shape of the ITV schedule, and which set stringent rules for ITV that neither our commercial rivals – terrestrial or in the skies – nor our public service competitors would have to match. Not only do 25 per cent of our commissioned programmes have to be from independent producers, but 65 per cent of our schedule has to be commissioned product rather than acquired, and 50 per cent has to be of European origin. These quotas are quite complicated in practice, but suffice to say that ITV will never look like Sky One or Channel 5, because we'd blow our quotas if we did.

Add to this, rules regarding the number of hours of subtitling and mandated provision of News, Religious programmes, children's programmes and current affairs and you will see that – maybe unwittingly – the Government has influenced the shape of the schedule considerably. A number of smaller criteria also apply, for example, the split of airtime in London, which means that the two biggest ITV companies compete for revenue, and, by definition, the most competitive schedule. We also have a constant review process with our regulatory body, the ITC, which ensures that the ITV schedule displays Quality, Range and Diversity. In other words, Drama has to include a variety of different types of drama.

So, mindful of our limit on acquired programming, we provide a range of high quality UK-produced drama such as *Coronation Street*, *Heartbeat* and *London's Burning*, high profile pieces such as *Prime Suspect* and *Sharpe*, as well as award winning single dramas such as *Hillsborough*, *Some Kind of Life* and *No Child of Mine*. Add to this regional initiatives such as *London Bridge* and *New Voices*, which introduces writers new to television, and you can see that the terms of our regulatory environment have a distinct influence on the shape of our schedule.

However, I really would be kidding you if I thought that the Government or the regulator was fully responsible for the shape of the schedule. So, let's ask another question... *Is it ... The TV companies?*

ITV is probably the most complicated broadcasting system in the world. It is interesting to note anecdotally that in Granada UK Broadcasting we are currently looking for a new computer system to manage our schedule process into the next century. There is not one company that can provide what we require! ITV is a network with 15 different stations with 15 different sets of regional obligations, nearly 15 different transmission centres and certainly 15 different sets of regional audiences. For example, Scottish TV has more of a problem with Channel 4, Meridian has next to no competition from Channel 5 and Granada has a worse problem than any other with satellite (a matter partly of regional pride in our outstanding Premier League football clubs!). All ITV companies have a different set of regional criteria which varies from a provision of approximately 5 hours to nearly 20.

Regional programmes demand a mix of schedule slots and these all have to be dove-tailed into the network schedule.

Apart from regional obligations the TV companies as a whole also have a considerable influence on the shape of the schedule. The ITV Council – the Managing Directors and Chief Executives – determine the overall schedule spend each year. This year this will amount to over £600m, the highest spend of any terrestrial broadcaster. However, the maxim 'invest or die' is very true and if Council were to cut the budget by 25 per cent, the shape of the schedule could change dramatically. Council are complemented by the Broadcast Board which comprises The Broadcast Directors of the companies. They determine the overall shape of the matrix and the allocation of the budget between News, Sport, Commissions and Acquired programmes. However, (back to the regulator again!) the Broadcast Board cannot be responsible for the commissioning of the individual programme strands. The choice of programming and the precise schedule mix is delegated to the ITV Network Centre, which manages the network budget on our behalf.

So how is the mix made up and what is the 'shape' that the TV companies dictate? Here are a few examples. As discussed, a certain amount of airtime has to be set aside for regional purposes. Even though, theoretically, we could schedule all our regional hours during the afternoon, this would not meet the regulator's idea of a diverse schedule appealing to all tastes, so certain regional slots have to be set aside. In Sport, broadcasting live events such as *Formula 1* and *Champions League* set rigorous demands on the schedule, and also make huge demands on the operational teams. Last Sunday's Brazilian Grand Prix was underpinned by 12 different contingency schedules and in the event over-ran by 30 minutes due to the false start.

The purchase of acquired programmes such as movies and *Home and Away* also sets certain criteria for scheduling. If you buy 3 runs on a movie, then it's cost effective to use them, even if the third run has to be used in the middle of the night. Scheduling of News is again subject to the regulator's demands for half an hour in peak. As well as daily bulletins, the schedule has to be ready to respond to major news events such as the Manchester bomb attack last June when schedules were cleared to carry important extra news bulletins.

And this leaves commissioned programmes. ITV's unique selling proposition of its quality, popular drama at 21.00, is already a schedule landmark which other channels would love to emulate. Our drama serials are the best in the UK and help contribute to the shape of our early peak schedule. In fact the drama serial producers might well be high on the list of those who shape the early peak schedule. Suppose you were Dawn Airey? Where would you schedule your new soap? If you are a soap fan you will know that you can channel-hop your way from soap to soap (apologies if I include *The Bill*, not a true serial, but still a perennial schedule element).

Virtually, the whole of the early peak schedule during weekdays is taken up with perennial serials. If I'd been C5, I too would probably have chosen 18.30... though early evidence would suggest that *Family Affairs* has yet to find much of an audience.

But, I'm getting into too much detail. Our bread and butter after all in ITV, comes from the advertisers. Maybe it's they who shape the schedule.

At Granada, we have a very close relationship with our Sales House who sell the airtime around the programmes in the schedule. For ITV, volume is still key. We capture a 37 per cent share of the audience, C4 just over 10 per cent, C5, so far, is 3 per cent with a decent movie and a following wind, and the entire satellite fraternity captures about 10 per cent. So, whatever you hear, ITV is still the key provider of volume audiences.

However, we know that our advertisers also seek a quality audience and to a certain extent the shape of the schedule is determined by them. Year-on-year comparisons of audience are key. Certain products advertise very seasonally and for most advertisers the Christmas run-up is hugely important, so this is where you will find the prestigious schedule pieces such as *Inspector Morse*, *Moll Flanders*, *Prime Suspect* and the key movie premieres.

Equally, we are constantly reviewing the programme mix to ensure that the schedule provides the audiences that Sales will require. No longer do housewives provide the main audiences sales require, but *Formula 1* for example will bring a male profile, new dramas such as *The Grand* attract upmarket viewers, and we are constantly looking for ways of attracting the elusive younger viewers.

And speaking of viewers, my thoughts turn to our audience. Maybe it is they who determine the shape of our schedule? No scheduler worth their salt would shape a schedule without analysing available audiences. Instinct might tell you that *Wheel of Fortune* would not work at 9pm at night, or *Clive James* would not work at 7pm, but analysing the audience is key to shaping our schedule. So, early evening is family, but a more downmarket audience and it is only post 9pm that the audience displays an upmarket profile that gets younger as the hour gets later.

Sundays are the most upmarket evenings, and Mondays are the youngest, since the young have blown all their pocket money partying at the weekend.

This explains why *Cracker* works so well on Monday or *Jane Eyre* on a Sunday.

Ratings are obviously important and assessing the competition is also fundamental. It's no good scheduling a male movie against the Cup Final nor soap against soap. Viewers have a choice of 4 or 5 channels or more and it's our job to shape our schedule to the best advantage. Viewers like soaps, different viewers have different tastes, and the TV is used for a variety of different reasons from information and education to entertainment and even wallpaper.

Most importantly viewers recognise quality.

However, to conclude – as Graham says on *Blind Date*, 'The choice... is yours.'

Louise Bennett: Thank you very much, Julia. If we could go to Keith ...

Keith Ely: Thank you. By a very neat trick I got Louise to expose the depths of my ignorance before I started talking by letting you know that I'm a newspaper journalist of thirty years' standing and quite new to television. I can tell you it's been a very exciting experience for me, but one, as I say, which has exposed the depths of my ignorance. Truly local television – that's sort of 'city TV', if you like – is a relatively new concept in the UK, and it's new because only now is there an appropriate delivery mechanism – that is, cable – since current technology doesn't allow for local delivery of a signal by broadcast means; and also because there is only now a viable cost-effective technology to deliver local television. By cost-effective, I mean cheap. There are really two companies in the UK who have become involved in city television and, more than coincidentally, both of them are supported by or owned by newspaper publishers. That's Mirror Group Television who own and operate Live TV, and Channel One Television, which is owned by the Daily Mail and General Trust and is a partner in Channel One, Liverpool.

It's reassuring, as I say, given the depths of my ignorance, that Julia has actually covered some of the points that I was going to make about who shapes the schedules. So I can't be that far out. But what I want to do is take you through a few elements of what I think. First of all, there's the Channel One concept and the fact that it's meant to be a sort of universal brand or universal within the UK, if that's not a contradiction. Secondly, the economics of television, in other words, operating within a tight budget. Thirdly, to what extent competition, such as Liverpool Live and other broadcast media, shapes what we do. And finally, the regulators and legislation which have already been touched on. We are totally dependent on a third party to deliver our service – the cable company, in our case – and of course on the customer, whether that's the advertiser and the provision of a schedule that advertisers like or want, or whether that's the viewer. I'll be talking a little bit about the research that we've done and the sort of qualitative anecdotal response that we've had from our viewers. So I'll start by showing you a very brief promotional video that we produced about Channel One Liverpool. It was actually produced before we went on air to try to make people aware of what the concept of local television was all about.

A short video film was shown: Channel One Liverpool: Twenty Four Hours a Day Every Day.

Keith Ely: The great thing about Liverpool is that you can always get scousers to say things, so people were prepared to give us a recommendation for Channel

One before they'd even seen it! And that brings me on to the issue of to what extent Channel One's schedule is already shaped or predicated by something that already exists: by a brand.

Channel One was born in London about three years ago and operates on the London interconnect cable network as a local TV station. They then opened a station in Bristol early last year, and then Channel One here in Liverpool – sorry, *there* in Liverpool – which opened in October of last year, so we've been on air for about six months. In fact, Liverpool is probably the biggest city in the UK that doesn't have at least a television headquarters based there. Even places like, say, Carlisle, smaller cities, have TV operations because they are the regional capitals. So Liverpool was tailor-made as a centre to launch a local television station, and for a partnership between the local newspaper publishers, *The Daily Post* and *Echo*, which are part of the Trinity Group, and Channel One Television (the other two stations, incidentally, are wholly owned subsidiaries of Channel One). The schedule, the format of what we do is actually laid down very clearly at the outset, that is, that we broadcast half an hour of news every hour. We are a news-led station and the front half of every hour is local news from Merseyside, collected by quite a small team of journalists, and the back half, the second half, is the sort of life-style programme you saw in the promotional video, which is produced by Channel One in London and sent by satellite to us in Liverpool. But the key thing is that behind all of this is the idea that Channel One should be an identifiable brand, so that if stations bearing that name were to be rolled out across the UK, you should be able to go to Newcastle or Belfast or Liverpool or wherever it is, and if you are in a Hotel be able to turn on Channel One and have a fairly good idea about what you are going to be seeing.

In order to ensure that, we have a board on which the two joint venture partners are represented. And I'm answerable to that board, so in a sense they are insuring that I am actually carrying out that sort of format and maintaining the quality of the station. But it's really the economics of local television which is the driving force that shapes the way that we actually produce things. It's a fairly low-cost operation to produce local television, and it has to be of necessity, because with a relatively small audience your advertising rates are very low, your revenue is fairly low. We have a ten year business plan for Channel One Liverpool which doesn't take us into profit until year 5 or 6, so clearly everything we do is managed within a very tight budget. Indeed, locally, when I first started this operation last year, I had no programming budget so that the cost of making programmes to me was the cost of the technology that we'd invested in and the journalists and technical staff that we employed to produce television. Those second half-hours produced by Channel One London we received in effect as a joint venture free of charge. In return for that, the supplier takes the advertising revenue that's transmitted during that period. So it's pretty difficult, I can tell you, to try to shape any kind of schedule without a budget, but we have done it, and it's interesting to see the ways that you can actually make fairly low cost relevant television. We have started a local entertainment show featuring two well-known local Radio DJs, which we actually shoot down at a local pub in Liverpool. We've started to do a series of chat shows in which local personalities, and we do insist that they're local not visitors, are involved in extensive interviews in the studio which we'll record and group together and transmit. We've started producing a local arts/what's on sort of programme, just within our normal resources. Fundamentally, we are very heavily dependent on the resources of the newspaper. I think one of the city TV stations in Birmingham, Birmingham Live, is also a joint venture, but I don't think they have the sort of relationship that we have in Liverpool where we actually attend the editorial conferences of the newspapers. We have one of their computer terminals in our News Room and we know what's happening so that's obviously a very effective way of us gathering news at little or no costs.

Thirdly, I've mentioned the competition. To what extent does the competition shape what we do? Well, it's interesting that at first we didn't take our competitor very seriously – its market pitch was quite different to ours – anybody who has watched Live TV will know that, as our research established, Topless Dancers is their most popular programme – in fact I gather that it's topless dancers on roller skates they're doing now. But what they did do and we didn't was get out and about onto the streets of Liverpool when they first went on air, talking to people, vox-popping, and we realised that we'd missed a trick here in that it's very important that local television is about local people and giving local people a platform. So they did influence what we did. In turn, we influenced what they did because they tried to move their local output up-market a little bit and renamed themselves News Eighteen Liverpool. They've dropped that since, but it certainly was a factor. And, of course, we are, to some extent anyway, influenced by what local radio is doing. We have a very successful BBC local radio station on Merseyside and to some extent, in the broadcast world, that sets the local agenda, and so we monitor very closely what they're doing.

Julia touched on the Government and the regulators and obviously to some extent they do shape what you can do, or rather what you can't do. As a newspaper man, it's been interesting to me to see the different way that we have to treat our General Election coverage or our pre-General Election coverage, much more tightly controlled than it is in the world of newspapers and, as I actually happen to believe, not to the benefit of the public. But then I would say that, wouldn't I? Clearly, the ITC is an important element in controlling what we do, and there is a practical example of how the ITC has influenced our schedule. The ITC in fact ordered us to take off air a sponsor we have for a local traffic and travel report, as a result of which we are now having to look at a much cheaper way of producing that, because without sponsorship we can't afford the sort of money that the AA wants to charge us for local traffic news. And of course masthead programming, which is the current buzzword in the cable and satellite business, the fact that regulations from the ITC will allow us in the future to produce some kind of masthead programmes, is bound to influence the sort of programming that we do over the next few years.

Telewest is the cable operator. We go out to seventy-five thousand homes on the Telewest network on Merseyside, and although I don't believe that they have in any way shaped our schedule up to now, they have indicated that they would be prepared to give us some sort of financial support for programme making, and they have also indicated what sort of programmes they might be interested in financing, so potentially they will be a factor in shaping what we do, given the fact, as I've said, that the economic constraints are forcing us to look for partners.

Finally, on to the customers, the most important part. I only left it till the end because I think it's the area of greatest concern. What we are actually doing, what we're broadcasting at the moment is predicated by a Channel One philosophy and it's interesting to me that viewers have picked up on this. Merseyside people are very outspoken and not slow in coming forward with their criticism. The market research that we've done shows that it's our local output, i.e. our news programming, this entertainment show that we produce and a local sports show that are far and away the most popular programmes and that these lifestyle programmes, which are very well made, and again on a tight budget, by Channel One in London, are not really what our audience wants. They don't hesitate to tell us: 'You're supposed to be a local television station, how come you're showing us what's on in the West End?' We have done some market research which we've undertaken ourselves while we await the results of the first BARB (Broadcasters' Audience Research Board Ltd) research and I suppose to some extent it has to be treated with a bit of caution, but we spoke to just under 500 cable subscribers on Merseyside and we asked them which channels they had watched in the past 24 hours, and the past week and the past month, and Channel One was the number one channel barring the terrestrials; that is to say for those people who were cable subscribers, Channel One had more viewers than did the satellite channels, and that seems to me to be a fairly strong indicator of the need for local television. I expect and hope that the BARB research when it's published will also confirm that.

I've had no end of ideas. I've got a drawerful of programme ideas already after six months from people who think they know what they would like to see on local television, and they all fall into a number of very clear categories and it's a bit painful for me to have to say, 'Well, great idea, but you know, we haven't got any money.' Getting sponsorship is going to be the key for our future expansion, so sponsors and advertisers clearly are an important element for us. Although we do get revenue from the cable company, carriage fee, we obviously do have to take a great note of the needs of our advertisers. The market pitch of Channel One is very much in the ABC1 category, but ironically, if you look at the social economic profile of cable viewers they tend to be very much in the C2DE range, and that's a challenge and a gap that we have to close.

O.K. That's it. Thank you.

Louise Bennett: Thank you very much, Keith. Rob, if we could bring you in here for an advertiser's point of view...

Rob Noss: Thank you.

If you take three advertisers, namely, De Beers, Kellogg's and Clorets, and briefly analyse their respective commercials, it soon becomes apparent that each commercial has very different priorities in terms of programme selection; a programme which is ideal for one advertiser is not necessarily the same for another.

To illustrate the point, an advertiser such as De Beers would look to secure programmes such as *Kavanagh QC*, or *Four Weddings and a Funeral*, whilst Kellogg's with its universal appeal would select programmes which reflect this, such as

Coronation Street and films such as *Sister Act*, whilst brands like Clorets would target the likes of *Police, Camera, Action, T.F.I. Friday* and *MTV* to correspond with their younger bias.

Against this backdrop, with each and every advertiser having different programming agendas, and therefore different scheduling priorities, it is misplaced to assume that advertisers/sponsors significantly influence a broadcaster's schedule construction.

In a multi-media environment, advertisers will migrate to those channels which offer programmes which are most appropriate to their designated target audience.

Therefore, if advertisers cannot select ideal programmes on ITV, they will look to C4/C5/satellite or cable. If television does not provide the precise media solution then the myriad of other options, namely press/radio/cinema/outdoor, etc, will be explored.

On a slight tangent, it is sometimes overlooked that advertisers spend a greater proportion of their overall budget on print Advertising than on any other media (see pichart below).

United Kingdom Advertising Expenditure by Medium 1995

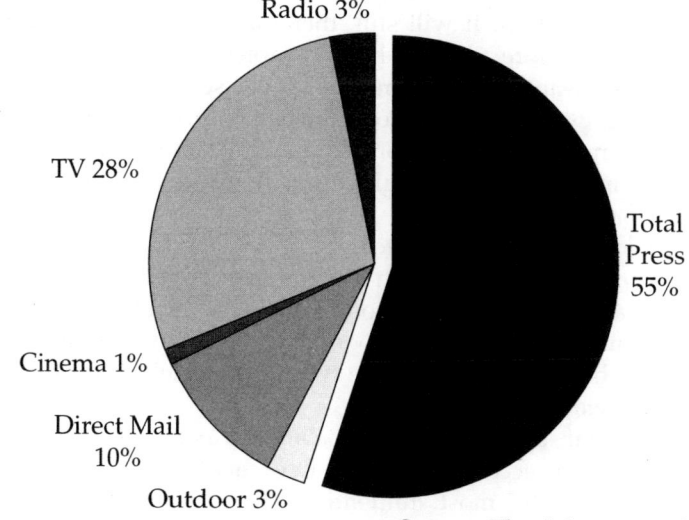

Radio 3%

TV 28%

Total Press 55%

Cinema 1%

Direct Mail 10%

Outdoor 3%

Source: The Advertising Yearbook 1996

In a television market which sees *circa* £2.4 billion invested by advertisers, it is unsurprising that opinions are sometimes publicly expressed about broadcaster's schedules. The demise of programmes such as *Man O Man*, it could be argued, was initiated by disappointing viewing levels and then accelerated by continued advertiser pressure on ITV.

On a more unified front, last year's debate about moving *News at Ten* is an example where the advertising industry, along with ITV, lobbied for some scheduling flexibility. The premise was primarily that the viewers' enjoyment of a film was considerably reduced by stopping three quarters of the way through for a forty minute news break, before returning to a now-forgotten story line!

The response, after much public debate, was a resounding 'No!', partly, it has to be said, for political reasons. Unsurprisingly, C5 have exploited this scheduling opportunity and now have uninterrupted films starting at 9 o'clock, Monday to Friday.

As with any discussion on the subject of what influences a broadcaster's schedule construction, there are numerous factors, but it's the viewer, and therefore viewing levels, which ultimately dictate whether a programme moves, or, on a more primal level, survives or dies.

As channels proliferate and audiences fragment, the challenge for advertisers is how to successfully target consumers against this backdrop.

Programmes such as *Coronation Street* in the late '60s pulled in about 60 per cent of the entire television population. That figure today, while still impressive, has been reduced to about 40 per cent. Mass rating programmes have therefore declined significantly over the last ten years.

Whilst in 1982 viewers were faced with a simple choice of four channels, with the advent of digital satellite/terrestrial, that choice could potentially expand to hundreds of channels.

As the future scenario of individuals scheduling their own programmes moves closer, it should be noted that what is currently proposed by BSkyB is near Video-On-Demand (V-O-D), a quantum leap in technological terms away from BT's interactive television trial. It will still, therefore, be some time and an estimated £15 billion later before viewers have complete flexibility to watch what they want, when they want, and become their own schedulers.

Changing viewing patterns will also influence future scheduling decisions. Just as there has been a shift away from communal family eating, the same is true of family viewing. It is increasingly difficult for advertisers to target the entire family in a one programme hit.

Where households have only one television set and a choice of only five channels, they are more likely to watch programmes together. However, introduce more choice, and the individual controlling the remote can very quickly drive other family members out of the room. This, combined with the fact that two thirds of British households now have two or more television sets, has dramatically influenced viewing patterns.

The fact remains that, by the year 2000, about 60 per cent of the UK population will still only have access to four or five channels. Mass market television will continue to be the most influential. The fact that people still enjoy discussing last night's drama/film with friends/work colleagues, should sound as a cautionary note to any over-zealous V-O-D enthusiast!

What is certain is that advertisers will continue to chase programmes which deliver large audiences, the 'must see' events, be they Sunday night dramas or critical events such as the Cup Final. As channels proliferate, the relationship between a specific channel and its viewers will be diluted, the value will be in the programme and not necessarily on which channel it appears.

The influences on 'who shapes the schedule' are therefore undoubtedly numerous, and whilst broadcasters, programme makers, governing bodies, advertisers and other interested parties all exert some influence, it is now and will continue to be the viewer who is king.

Louise Bennett: Thank you very much, Rob. We now have a speaker from the floor, Adrian Moynes of RTE, Ireland.

Adrian Moynes: I am very grateful for the opportunity to talk about a broadcasting system which is a neighbour of the United Kingdom, and which from our perspective in Ireland is closely involved in competition with the United Kingdom system in all its diversity and with all its resources. It's also funded in a way which is much more the norm for public service broadcasting throughout Europe than in the United Kingdom, as I'll explain later.

RTE is the national service broadcaster in the Republic of Ireland, where it provides services to terrestrial television channels for 1,000,000 homes. It also provides a range of four radio services. On television it makes, it commissions, it co-produces slightly less than half its transmission, and the balance is acquired. The Republic of Ireland is one of the most competitive English language broadcasting environments in Europe. Just over 70 per cent of households also receive the UK terrestrial and satellite services, as well as continental channels on a variety of distribution systems from Cable NBF and Direct to Home. Yet against that background RTE maintains a national audience share of 60 per cent in prime time, which is one of the highest audience shares in Europe. Now in the most competitive areas of the country, that is, in those cities and towns where people have multi-channelled menus, RTE's share does fall to 45 per cent, but it's still a very high figure. But naturally, like all broadcasters, RTE faces the prospect of yet more fragmentation of audiences in the way we've already heard about.

RTE's funding is dual funding. It comes from television licence fees and from commercial revenue. When the television service came into existence thirty-six years ago it was on the basis of dual funding. Last year, government approved the first increase in the television licence fee in a decade and so raised the payment for each household to £70 annually. I think by comparison in that same period the BBC had eight or perhaps nine licence fee increases. The ten year freeze on our licence fee forced us to depend more and more on advertising to pay for the service we provided. Ten years ago advertising generated 44 per cent of our income. By 1994, it was generating 51 per cent of our income, and currently it generates 58 per cent. Now clearly, we were established to earn advertising revenue. We are happy to do that. But it has to be said that an over-dependence on income from advertising is undesirable for a public service broadcaster, if for no other reason than the unreliability of advertising revenue in an increasingly competitive future. So that focuses the central challenge facing a service like ours. To secure its finances RTE must maintain audience share, or rather minimise the erosion of its audience share. As a public service broadcaster, its simultaneous duty is to provide a mainstream service, which must also embrace a diversity of programmes for a broad range of audiences, some of which are small in numbers, some of which are tiny in numbers, and this challenge of diversity has been central to a somewhat limited and constrained debate which we have been having on the future of broadcasting in Ireland.

The debate started a couple of years ago when the government published a green paper on broadcasting, in which it calls on broadcasters, among other things, to recognise an act of sturdy independent differentiated collection of publics, in other words, to treat the citizenry as a spectrum of publics and not simply as the consumer, the people you can sell stuff to. That notion of a plural audience was taken up when the main opposition party contributed to the debate on the future of broadcasting, and they made reference in their position papers to what they called 'diverse interests and opinions' in the country, and one of the most significant contributions to the debate on broadcasting and one of the few to come from outside the industry, because it has been a very introverted debate, came from the Combat Poverty Agency, and this argued the case very strongly for the equal rights of socially excluded groups and individuals to be represented and have an influence on the shape our broadcasting.

Now, all together these are reasonable expectations to lay on public service broadcasting, but you have to ask the question 'how far can the schedules be stretched in recognition of diversity?' Clearly, a public broadcaster cannot be all things to all audiences, especially when it finds itself in competition in the real world of commercial imperatives, where rival channels offer specialised services and offer them very well, and where diversity from viewers can be achieved by an affordable menu of broadcasting choices. Arguably, the recent history of broadcasting and the proliferation of channels may be read as the achievement of diversity through the offer of choice. That choice began thirty years ago with the creation of the complementary or alternative channels, BBC2 and, in Ireland, Network Two. Then came the minority remit channels, Channel Four, then it rose to theme channels: Movies, Children's, Discovery, Shopping, then Sports on subscription, then the language channels. S4C recognises an entitlement of a body of the population, and we have just established Telefís na Gaeilge (TnaG) for Irish speakers and for people interested in the Irish Language and culture in Ireland. In the United States you have something that is coming our way, the demographic channels, like the Fox Network.

Now, of course, when you mention demographic, it's the advertisers who are the people most interested in audience demographics, and they've taught broadcasters and programme makers and schedulers quite a few tricks. We schedulers analyse the viewer profile of a debut series. At the start of press conferences UTV and Radio Services declare the demographics of their target audiences, and Chris Carter, creator of *The X Files*, realised that he might just be on to something when research showed that 3 per cent of the US population believed they had been abducted by aliens.

So, how are the schedules of the public broadcasters to negotiate these dilemmas of diversity and demographics? It is, after all, an agenda of fragmentation. Faced with the possibility of on-demand programming, how do you serve your publics whilst continuing to serve *the* public, how do you make intelligent use of demographics without being used by demographics?

In Ireland, RTE has employed the strategy of maintaining the closest possible identification with the local audience, with their interests and concerns. Not surprisingly in a country where politics and sport are separate but, some would say, ultimately related obsessions, RTE wins audience share with news, current affairs and event coverage in sport. Now this is not cheap programming. Running a national newsroom and local and regional news services and providing a service of current affairs analysis and discussion does not come cheap, as anyone who has tried it can tell you, but it is cost effective. On week nights a minimum of 40 per cent, and a maximum of 60 per cent of our prime time is given over on our premier channel to information programmes which come from the News and Current Affairs sections. Now that's an average of 50 per cent a night, Monday to Friday. It's a phenomenal chunk of air time. Debate, discussion, comments are staples of our day-time radio and they regularly carry over into the running order of the chat shows and information programmes on evening television.

Another interesting difference between the UK and Ireland is this: the Irish equivalent of lifestyle programmes, which in the UK would be scheduled on BBC2 and Channel Four, play very successfully on our premier channel, RTE One. You can schedule these things at 7.30 when you're not running a simultaneous transmission of *Coronation Street*, and you can also take that 7.30 slot on a Tuesday night and you can give it to a half hour programme of current affairs in the Irish language, which is a minority language in Ireland, but nevertheless, with open English language subtitles and strong human interest stories, that programme at 7.30 on Tuesday night can regularly achieve a 25 per cent share of national viewing.

On our second channel, Network Two, where clearly we need much more domestic production, we are heavily reliant on acquired programmes. But even there, you can gain ground with a tricky sub-audience such as the 18 to 35s by offering line-ups such as *Friends* followed by *The X Files* followed by something called *Streetwise*, which is a consumer affairs magazine developed with that precise scheduling requirement in mind, and made by a young production team based in our Cork Studios.

An important challenge now facing RTE is to bring to earth a stronger schedule of homemade drama and comedy. The advertisers tell us that these improvements are essential to win the key demographics such as housekeepers with children. But, just as importantly, these genres are needed to ensure as far as possible that the public service schedule has the scope and the depth that it should have and that it speaks to its community with the full range of expression, while earning the revenue to pay for more and better programmes. Thank you very much.

Group Session Feedback
At this point, the delegates broke into groups to discuss the issues raised; a spokesperson from each group then reported back to the delegates as a whole.

Group 1:
One thing that emerged was that broadcasters know that if they've got the viewer for ten or fifteen minutes at a time, that's good going, so obviously that affects the programming; and also that the possibility for day programming for local interest groups, for instance, was something that might be explored, but so far has not shown itself to be self-supporting. So we come back all the time to this problem of costs. Channel One did give us some idea about the costings of the programmes coming in from London – and they're taking 45 per cent of programming from London at the moment – at about £2,000 for half an hour, which gives some indication of the kind of budget you're beginning to look at. We did

discover that in terms of advertising they've been more successful than they might have expected. Obviously, a question of sponsorship becomes fairly important, and the sponsorship for sports from Littlewoods, for example, does become an element in the programming.

Group 2:
We started off by thinking about the effect and usefulness of big special occasions, and *The Brits Awards* was cited as one which attracted specialist advertisers for a definite audience with a definite demographic aspect. From there we went on to what Phil Redmond mentioned this morning: are we seeing the end of scheduling, will it be entirely, as was also mentioned, that the viewer is king or even queen and can decide what he or she wants to listen to out of a wide variety of programmes? This led on to discussing how the people get and choose their programmes, do they take it from programme journals, do they take it from zapping, or how do they take it? And we've even touched on the possibility of electronic programme guides coming up in the future and their effect of steering you towards programmes. Is it really that you have this complete variety of programmes, or do the programme information aspects, which are a kind of software, steer you towards certain programmes? After that, a question I found very interesting is, do you think of your programmes strand-wise – that you always put on a drama programme, say, at nine o'clock in the evening – or do you have one evening which is a theme evening? Radio is of course a long way towards this in having certain channels on certain themes or certain days on certain themes, and this was also discussed to some extent.

But finally, we did feel that whatever form scheduling would take, and it would take different forms, that scheduling in some form is necessary, just as an index is necessary in a book. So there would never be an entire lead of no scheduling, in other words we didn't really agree completely with the idea of the viewer being absolute king, there had to be some guidance and the guidance came through some form of scheduling, although it might not be the kind of scheduling which we are used to at the moment.

Group 3:
We really began with a look at some of the technological assumptions, and there was a certain amount of scepticism from certain parts of the group about the technological determinism which was perhaps expressed this morning by Phil Redmond. There was also a discussion about the whole issue which obviously the other groups talked about, about the idea of the customer being king and whether the customer is in fact king. That bounced off into the notion of whether the customer being king did actually displace certain creative elements, then went on to one of the basic issues that always comes up, the question of access. One contributor made the point that there are power operations going on and that the new world of new systems and new provision, etc., did mean that people were being excluded from, say, sports programmes, and sports programmes have become more expensive within the new media environment. As I mentioned, there was a bit of scepticism about the dominance of consumer sovereignty and whether in fact what was happening was just more and more

of similar types of programmes, the issue of the fact that, when *Coronation Street* is on five times a week, it's no longer such a prestige sort of programme; it devalues it from the advertising point of view.

The Irish spoke up very vigorously for the fact that the British were somewhat behind the Irish broadcasters in that they're probably worrying about nothing, and pointed out that the local emphasis, the narrowing emphasis if you like, on the multiplicity of scale was already happening in Ireland. This also brought in the question of the US, where there was a lot of concern by the NBC and CBS companies that they were losing their audience; but actually it has come somewhat full circle now, and they're back to larger audience profiles – obviously not back to the sort of 1960s and 1970s huge audiences, but certainly to a situation where the big companies are less worried about the diversity of provisions taking away the mass audiences. Actually, people are going towards the concept that they want some mass participation in the audience, so again it was this issue of the big picture and also the local picture; while people get some very definite local satisfaction from their television, they also want to be part of a mass audience. Then we went on to the question of the electronic programme guide, and we did think that this was the key and that people would be much more interested in putting together some sort of menu of their own, but again the menu would be alongside the idea responding to mass programmes and texts.

Louise Bennett: Thank you all for taking part in that. Can we go to our panellists, and ask them each, in a sentence, to give their thoughts on the issues raised.

Keith Ely: I made a point in our discussion that, contrary to the last speaker, I believe that the mass market will continue to fragment, and that for individual stations the costs pressures will increase. I think, as Rob indicated, advertisers are going to migrate to those channels which are giving them what they want. I think that's going to put unbearable cost pressures on some of the large broadcasters; I produce twenty-two half hour bulletins a day and two one hour bulletins and I employ twenty-four people.

Julia Lamaison: Well, I think it's very interesting, I don't think any of us has a definitive answer to who shapes the schedule, but I am quite relieved that my group at least seemed to indicate that there'll still be a job for me in a few years' time.

Rob Noss: Finally, I would just like to say that the thing that has been demonstrated this afternoon is that you can attack this question from any perspective and any angle, and no-one has the right answer. It's a combination of factors, and to put your finger on one thing is possibly misleading.

Values In Broadcasting

A Summary of Research for the Broadcasting Standards Commission

Chair: Brook Sinclair
Director of ADCOMM Ltd

Matthew Kieran
University of Leeds

David Morrison
University of Leeds

Michael Svennevig
University of Leeds

Introduction

This paper, the result of a report prepared for the Broadcasting Standards Commission, addresses the question of the values that the British people hold, and the implications of those values for regulating broadcasting.[1] It must however be remembered that just because people hold something to be true does not necessarily make it, or that what people believe ought to be the case should automatically be taken as representing the best of all possible cases. Research, in other words, can illuminate what people think, and even why they think as they do, but it cannot, of itself, form policy. In short, it can supply facts that are useful in coming to policy judgements.

Methodology and Structure

Before any other field work was undertaken, it was decided to conduct face to face interviews with 12 key figures within the media industry (see appendix I). They were selected not because they were representative as those in the surveys were, but because they were figures who had things to say about regulation. The purpose of this exercise was to gain some idea of the circulation of ideas within the industry concerning regulation. We also wished to use the opportunity of these interviews to raise issues that we were going to address in the course of the focus groups and the surveys. A central purpose of these interviews, however, was not simply to inform ourselves of how senior media people thought about the issues under investigation, but to see how far their thinking reflected the thinking of the audience.

There were two waves of focus groups, consisting of 14 groups in total (see appendix II). The first wave consisted of 6 groups in all, and the second wave of 8 groups. The primary function of the first wave was to explore how people saw the issue of regulation, and what language was employed when discussing the moral issues that regulation entails. It was from this first wave of focus groups that we developed our notions of Neo-Aristotelian and Liberal. The second wave of focus groups was used in an intensive fashion to explore the issues that had arisen from the returns of the first survey questionnaire. The design of the study, from the outset, planned to use the focus groups in a novel manner. Given that all data require interpretation, we decided that it would be useful to present the findings of the first survey to the second set of focus groups, not only to be used as points for discussion, but to have the participants comment on what they thought the figures meant. The findings from the second wave of focus groups then fed directly into our second national questionnaire, and allowed us to make statements on the distribution of attitudes found in the focus groups.

The Project, as stated, involved two surveys. Both surveys were designed to be representative of adults (aged 16 or over) in the UK. Survey one had an achieved sample of 1,062 adults, and survey two had an achieved sample of 535 adults. The first survey was 45 minutes long and the second survey was 30 minutes long. The second survey paid particular attention to the question of the invasion of individuals' rights to privacy by the media. The absence of a moral language, however, made it difficult for people to discuss abstract moral issues. It was decided, therefore, to have respondents in this second survey act as witnesses to the scenario of an accident, and then have them decide who of those involved in the accident had the right to privacy. A complex set of moral decision situations were created so that the respondent had to think through what they themselves, if they were a regulator, would allow. By concretising moral dilemmas in this way the respondents found little difficulty in addressing moral issues. Although we can only give a snaphot of the results in a paper of this length, the full success of this approach can be seen from the report itself.

Neo-Aristotelians v. Liberals

All research is theory impregnated. Without some theory about what is being looked at, it is difficult to know what to look for. Not to have any theory means that all and every fact about the world becomes of equal importance, and since all are of equal importance, and given the many facts that exist, it is difficult to know what questions to ask. In short, there is no point asking about things that have no bearing on the research questions. Yet to ask questions that do have a bearing means that one must, ipso facto, have some theory of what does bear on the issues.

After conducting the elite interviews and the first round of focus groups we found that the most intelligible, coherent and explanatory means of making sense of the worries that arose and the different reasons for them was to conceive of the issues in terms of neo-Aristotelians and Liberals. The idea of the neo-Aristotlelian is clearly derived from Aristotelian philosophy. This would hold that the purpose of the State, and regulation, is to maintain and cultivate the character of its citizens, including the moral and social virtues required for them to lead good, flourishing lives. Thus, regulation should be informed by the right moral and social values. The State should shape and guide people's choices and characters toward what is good for them. The idea of the Liberal, on the other hand, holds that the purpose of the State, and regulation, is to protect and promote the freedom required for people to lead their lives how they choose. Thus moral and social values should not be the concern of regulation, for people have the right to do what is immoral as long as they do not infringe upon the basic rights of others.

Essentially these frameworks constitute two substantially different models which underlie people's conceptions of the nature and role of broadcasting regulation. Firstly, the archetypally liberal model takes the primary function of broadcasting regulation to ensure that people's basic needs, narrowly construed, and actual preferences are met. This is because, on the liberal model, the sole purpose of the state is to protect its citizens' basic political freedoms which ensure that people are free to lead their lives as they so choose. Essentially, society is conceived of, merely in terms of autonomous self-interested individuals who contract together in order to ensure that all are free to pursue autonomously their own particular chosen ends and goals.[2] Hence our substantive moral and social values are to be kept strictly separate from our political values in terms of governance and regulation. To do otherwise would be to undercut the very justification of the state in the first place. For the state's purpose is to protect and promote people's freedom and thus, in terms of media broadcasting, to allow for maximum individual freedom.

According to the liberal model, regulation should not be concerned with programme content as such except in a very thin, limited sense. As the broadcasting media have a duty to provide us as citizens with information required to make informed political choices and decisions clearly regulation of news programming, current affairs and investigative documentaries ought to be regulated for in terms of accuracy, fairness, bias or unwarranted intrusions into privacy. The indecency, offensiveness or immorality of what is broadcast is not and should not be the proper concern of regulation given that people are autonomous and thus should be free to choose what they want to watch and those who would wish to avoid such programmes can freely do so. Indeed, on this model, people are quite right to complain if they think that a regulator or broadcaster is modifying the content of programmes against their expectations and preferences.

Conversely, the neo-Aristotelian model construes people's needs in terms of the general moral and social values and beliefs required in order to live a fulfilling and thus good life. For the good of the individual is intimately bound up with the good of society and the state as a whole. The purpose of the state, according to this model, is to protect and promote the conditions required to cultivate and promote the well-being and thus moral good of each and every citizen.[3] The key question concerns what is in the interests of the common good. Political governance and regulation should aim to shape, protect and promote social institutions and activities so that they promote the moral and social well-being of every individual in society. Thus media regulation should ensure that broadcasting practices and programmes inform and educate people into the right kinds of beliefs, values and dispositions which are required for them to pursue their own lives in the right way.

On the neo-Aristotelian model then, broadcasting regulation should be fairly heavy and broad in scope. Even if only a few vulnerable people are 'harmed' by explicitly violent and sexual programmes, they should be banned or heavily modified for the greater good and protection of society. Moreover, even if there are no causal links between such programmes and anti-social behaviour, they may be objected to on the grounds of obscenity because some fundamental moral value is being denigrated or abused. Thus even private channels which service particular groups of people who wish to pay for such a service, and the general public have a choice whether to subscribe or not, should not be allowed to produce or broadcast such material.

The usefulness of applying these two conceptual distinctions can be seen from the report itself, especially the section in relation to the survey returns. A further advantage, in terms of policy making, is that knowing the distribution of these two types of belief systems assists not just in explaining the responses to regulation found in our study, but also in predicting likely responses to changes in regulation.

Of course, although our survey returns showed roughly half were neo-Aristotelian and half liberal, many people will tend to be liberal with regard to one issue and neo-Aristotelian with regard to another. This is, in part, a function of the lack of intellectual reflection most people tend to take in relation to such issues but it is also partly a function of the fact that, in contemporary British society, there is no real agreed consensus about just what the function of the state and regulation is with regard to such matters. However, if it was the case that those talked with are representative of the industry at large, then it would be the case that thinking on issues of regulation moved towards a Liberal rather than a Neo-Aristotelian position

Social and Media Concerns

We found, both from our focus groups and survey returns, that the overwhelming issue people were worried about was violence in society. Many people in the focus groups had had first hand experience of being a victim of crime, most usually, burglary or theft of cars. Of those who had children there was a general concern for their safety, with many parents considering that in order to protect their children they had to place restrictions on their freedom of movement. This fundamental worry about violence was, in part, linked to a major dislike for the increasingly common use of bad language in everyday life. For there was a general concern over what can best be described as uncivil behaviour – lack of politeness and respect for others. Thus it was clear from the focus groups that people are concerned at all levels – at home, at work, at leisure – about antisocial and unsocial behaviour in their everyday lives. The types of issues they were concerned about included *antisocial acts* – theft, violence drug-related crime – and *unsocial behaviour* – swearing and rudeness, especially from the young.

These concerns are equally prominently displayed in the survey results. Over eight in ten (82 per cent) of the first survey sample felt that standards of behaviour in this country have got worse. Only one in a hundred (1 per cent) felt that standards had improved. As can be seen from Table 1 below, while the main focus of concern is violent crime, sexual attitudes and swearing and bad language – unsocial rather than antisocial behaviour – also feature for the majority of people.

Table 1: Concern with Antisocial and Unsocial Behaviour

	Very concerned	Fairly concerned	Not very /not at all concerned /don't know
How concerned, if at all, are you about violent crime in this country?	64	27	9
How concerned, if at all, are you about current sexual attitudes and standards of behaviour in this country?	36	35	29
How concerned, if at all, are you about swearing and bad language in this country?	36	34	30

Survey 1

Just as people were concerned about the level of violence in society, so too they were worried about the levels of violence on television, but they were also particularly concerned with the level of bad language used in programmes. Many people did not like the promoting of life styles of those groups that they objected to and parents often objected to programmes that they perceived as showing behaviour that might set a bad example to their children. Similarly, programmes were objected to where children were portrayed showing a lack of respect for authority figures. Sex, although a concern, tended to be age related – older people were more bothered by explicit displays of sex than younger people. Generally, though, some of the most fundamental worries concerned acts and the portrayal of actions which were violent and thus anti-social or, more interestingly, behaviour which though not harmful was deemed to express deeply unsocial attitudes.

Anti-Social Acts – these are acts which, as the term suggests, are against society or community. This would include acts involving violence. People did not consider the media as an important contributor to anti-social acts. Rather, structural factors such as unemployment and social deprivation were considered much more important in making for criminal behaviour than the media.Indeed, personal factors were considered much more important in making for criminal behaviour than the media – this included such things as discipline in the home, schools, legal system, and friends. Hence it tended to be structural and personal factors when taken together that were seen as key to understanding anti-social behaviour rather than any influence the media might have.

The main factors which people believe to be the root cause of these key forms of unwanted behaviour are essentially social and economic – lack of parental discipline, unemployment, 'weak' courts, school discipline – rather than attributable to the media. The results in Table 2 below come from asking the sample to rank a number of possible causes of violent behaviour.

Table 2: Causes of Violent Crime

	% saying this has the most effect on violent crime (rank of 1)	Average rank of effect on violent crime	% saying this has no effect at all on violent crime
Lack of discipline in the home	32	3.5	7
Unemployment	17	5.5	18
Lack of tough sentencing by the courts	17	5.2	13
Lack of discipline in schools	9	4.7	11
Poor housing/ poverty	7	6.1	19
Video films	5	7.0	24
TV programmes	4	7.6	28
Break-up of old communities	3	8.4	36
Lack of willpower	3	8.7	33
Cinema films	2	8.3	32
The decline of religion	2	9.7	50

Survey 1

While people do have a marked tendency to draw attention to perceived media deficiencies – in focus groups, or in more vaguely-worded surveys – in terms of themes and content which they might object to, they did not rank the mass media as *strong* influences to any real degree. For a very small group of people, though, the media are seen as the main factor underlying violent crime.

There were minor differences in opinion between the values groups, and between other demographic groups. These are small-scale and do not affect the overall relative ratings of importance of the factors shown below. These beliefs about causation are shared between the great majority of the public. However, when we come onto considering unsociable acts peoples attitudes were, interestingly, rather different.

Unsociable Acts – these are acts that are not against society, but break the conventions of social exchange between people. This would include acts such as swearing. In contrast to anti-social acts, the media were held to be much more responsible for influencing unsociable behaviour, although other facts were also held responsible. There was a general concern that children were being influenced by the media in their attitudes towards authority. It was considered that the media encouraged a lack of respect for adults. Indeed, the media, but television in particular, was commonly seen to encourage an anti-authority attitude in the young and foster toughness as a style – this was even seen in the way young people copied 'street tough' styles of clothing worn by characters in programmes. People's central concern was that television was fostering a set of attitudes and values that ran counter to that which parents wished the young to have.

As can be seen from Table 3 below, although parents and friends are believed to be the main causes of children swearing, the media is much higher up with regard to such behaviour than it was with regard to anti-social behaviour. Among the media asked about, television is thought to be the most influential, closely followed by video films. Again, the same overall relative levels of importance of the factors was the same across demographic subgroups, and across the three value groups.

Table 3: Causes of Children Swearing

	% saying this has the most effect on children swearing	Average rank of effect on children swearing	% saying this has no effect at all on children swearing
Parents	32	4.3	14
Friends	30	3.6	8
Lack of respect for other people	11	5.9	15
TV programmes	8	5.7	17
Other people in the neighbourhood	6	6.0	18
Video films	5	5.8	14
Brothers and Sisters	2	5.3	16
Cinema films	2	6.9	23
Teachers	1	9.5	65
Pop and youth magazines	1	8.8	47

Survey 1

Although people were more worried by anti-social behaviour than by unsociable behaviour, and held television more responsible for fostering unsociable behaviour than they did for fostering anti-social behaviour, concern was expressed that unsociable behaviour might lead to anti-social behaviour. The manner in which unsociable behaviour might lead to anti-social behaviour was seen to be through the undermining of traditional authority. Television was held responsible for this – it was considered to accomplish this through the encouragement it gave to the sets of values documented above.

Moral Concerns and Values
A striking finding of the study was that people were concerned about the cultural influences of television. This is important in that most political attention has been given to the question of whether or not television influences the level of violence in society. People were concerned about the views of the world that television presented, and concerned about the moral framework that it presented. What is interesting in light of the concern over culture and moral performance was that people themselves did not have a totalising moral belief system by which to readily address moral issues. People certainly had a worked out set of values by which to live, but they did not have a worked out language by which to argue for the values that they held. This made, at the intellectual level, the management and regulation of culture a confused area for people to come to clear and consistent decisions.

In both surveys, core moral values appear to play a key role in determining people's responses to regulatory issues and judgements of other people's behaviours. On balance, and within the limits set by survey methods, the majority of people appear to be somewhat authoritarian rather than liberal in these matters. This puts them at variance with most media professionals. Overall, an individual's value orientation is unrelated to sex or age. However, there is a link to social grade – most likely reflecting educational background. Values are mainly thought to be derived from social and parental sources. At the same time the majority believe that their own moral standards are in fact different from those of their parents.

In contrast, the media are not felt to be prime movers in moral development or in causing anti-social behaviour. However, when asked to compare their own childhood with the present, the media are seen as somewhat more influential than in their past. The decline of religion – once a major source of moral belief – is not widely seen as a cause of changing values in society. Nor, for the great majority, was religion a significant influence on their own development, or a major influence on current children.

Media Regulation
Viewers' opinions are split over whether terrestrial TV, cable and satellite services should have greater freedom to show violent or sexually explicit content. These types of judgement are strongly linked to each individual's value orientation. Those high on the values scale created from the survey results tend to disapprove of relaxation of broadcast regulation, while those low on the scale tend to approve.

The surveys also contained questions about specific instances – for example, the publication and/or broadcasting of full details of a murder as revealed during a court case. Regardless of the medium – terrestrial news, cable/satellite news, press, magazines, radio news, or TV documentary – those with high value scores were consistently likely to disapprove of such details being made public. Similar reactions were found for a scenario where a best-selling book including graphic descriptions of torture was to be more widely publicised. Again, the two groups of people with opposing values came to different conclusions about the acceptability of coverage on any medium – TV, satellite, or print.

In cases where a TV programme is likely to cause offence to individuals in the audience, the dominant view is that such material should be toned down rather than not be shown at all. While the balance of opinions on this type of judgement does vary according to individual values, the broad pattern was the same across the samples. Strongly opposed views compared to the majority. Opinions did not differ when the particular form of offence was religious rather than political or generally offending. Only among those who said they were themselves religious held views which were clearly opposed to the majority view.

Opinions about whether or not certain types of content should be shown on television are highly sensitive to the state of expert opinion about possible effects. In the case where experts believe that scenes would definitely trigger violent behaviour in 'a few unbalanced people', a clear majority felt such scenes should not be shown at all. Whether or not such material is restricted to pay channels makes very little difference to this view. Where expert opinion is divided, this effect is weakened, but virtually everyone still wants some form of limitations – either banning, on-screen warnings, or time restrictions on transmission.

As can be seen in Table 4, the desire for the existence and maintenance of broad safeguards for media consumers is widespread: relaxation of regulation is widely felt – by a majority in all cases – to make the all of the available television services get worse or, at best, remain as they are. Virtually no-one believed that removal of regulation would improve things, regardless of the actual medium or channel under consideration.

Table 4: Media Regulation
If there was no regulation at all over ... would that make it better, worse or the same as it is now?

	Worse	No change/don't know	Better
Cinema films	65	34	1%
Video material	61	38	1%
BBC1	58	42	1%
ITV	59	40	1%
BBC2	57	42	1%
Channel 4/S4C	60	39	1%
Satellite and Cable channels	55	42	2%

Survey 1

Further analysis of these results showed clearly how individuals' underlying value structures have a direct effect on their opinions about media regulation. Those who fall into the Liberal values group are much less likely than their high score opposites (Aristotelians) to believe that the removal of any of the forms of regulation asked about would have a negative impact.

Invasion of Privacy
A unique feature of our research was that both surveys approached the issues of people's rights to privacy and the ethics of intrusion by the media. In the first survey, the right to privacy – the degree of control a specific person should have over being shown or mentioned in television news or documentaries – was studied in detail. 19 different types of person were asked about, including a witness to a crime, criminals themselves, the Royal Family, a disabled person, and authority figures such as a politician and a senior civil servant. Broadly speaking, there are very large differences in perceived rights to privacy which depend upon the social and moral position of the fictitious person involved. Criminals – rapists, drug dealers, shoplifters – have no effective rights to prevent TV coverage of themselves. 'Ordinary' members of the public – Lottery winners, children, disabled, parents of crime victims, Alzheimer's sufferers – are awarded full rights to prevent coverage if they wish. In between these two extremes fall those with public positions – religious leaders, business men, police and teachers, politicians. These have limited rights – not the power to prevent, but fairly wide rights to consultation and editorial input.

The second survey concentrated upon a single scenario – a child is hit by a drunk driver, the ambulance which arrives has a documentary film crew on board, and they wish to film various people and situations arising from the accident and the death of the child in the ambulance on the way to hospital. At each stage in the scenario, the sample was asked to judge specific dilemmas and decisions and courses of action on the part of the film crew's need to record events and the rights of the individual members of the public involved. The two tables below (5 and 6) detail the results from two stages in the scenario we developed:

Table 5: Accident Scenario Part 1

I would like you to imagine that a drunk driver has knocked down a neighbour's child playing in the street. You are the first on the scene to help. You go with the ambulance to comfort the child.

The ambulance crew has agreed to be filmed in action for a documentary about everyday life in the ambulance service, and there is a film crew inside the ambulance. You are shown comforting the child, but the child dies on the way to hospital. You are very upset and are crying.

You are so concerned about the child that you are not aware that the whole scene is being filmed.

In the confusion and rush, should the film crew have asked your permission before they started to film inside the ambulance?

	%
YES	77
NO	19
Don't know	4

Survey 2

Here there is a fairly clear consensual starting point for most people: permission should be sought by programme-makers, even under times of stress and confusion. Apart from a slight tendency for older people to say 'Yes' (85 per cent among the over 55s) there are no real deviations from this view. One in five, though, did not see the need to ask permission under the circumstances.

Table 6 Accident scenario Part 4

The drunk driver involved in the accident does not wish to be shown in the programme.

What should the programme-maker then do?

	%
Ignore the driver's request	43
Show the scenes with the driver's face blanked out, although this would reduce the impact of the programme	30
Show the scenes in full, but give the driver the chance to explain himself	21
Agree to the driver's request, which means cancelling the entire programme	4
Don't know	1

Survey 2

As the driver is the guilty party, he loses most rights of privacy in the sample's judgements. The most frequently-given answer was that the programme maker should simply ignore the driver's views. This fits closely with the general picture of shifting rights according to status illustrated by the findings shown in Table 25. Taken together with the proportion who chose the 'blanking out' option, three in four believed that the driver's rights should be over-ruled.

Although the above can only provide a snapshot of a very complex scenario that we developed, involving the progressive development of 7 scenarios, overall it can be seen that a clear picture emerges whereby the *informed and considered* participation of most parties to such an event – particularly the innocent parties – should be sought as an *a priori* rule by programme-makers. Where there is an obvious clash between public interest and private rights, the most preferred resolution is that of anonymising individuals – through using blanking sections on-screen. Importantly, these protections do not apply in full to the 'guilty'. In this scenario, the most widely-given judgement was that the drunk-driver's wish not to be shown should simply be ignored.

Many people appear to hold somewhat jaundiced views about the ethics of programme-makers. While virtually everyone felt that children should not be interviewed without permission from parents or teachers, far smaller proportions felt that this was what programme would actually do in practice. Broadcasters are believed to be willing to flaunt accepted rules of conduct as far as privacy is concerned in order to make their programmes.

Conclusion

Our surveys show, supported by the findings from the focus groups, that when it comes to discussing moral issues relating to the performance of the media, much depends upon the values that people hold. The absence of a common moral language was a problem since many people in the focus groups found it difficult to articulate the underlying basis of their worries and judgements. This can, in part, be accounted for by the decline in religious belief as an organising point for reality. We found that totalising belief systems, such as Christianity, have declined. There is no mystery to this decline. The reasons for it are to be found in the rise of industrialisation and urbanisation that produced new forms of rationality, along with the fracturing of communally held values. The splitting of society into classes and sub-groups has meant that no single group can expect their values to hold sway over any other group. In short, one can no longer appeal to a single standard by which to judge cultural performance – this, of course, has direct implications for regulation. Similarly there seems to have been a decline in politics, where it is understood as a moral force – to how it has moved from moral purpose to a technical rationality of management. In the realm of politics no moral language exists by which to address social and cultural moral issues.

However, the notions of neo-Aristotelian and liberal help to explain the distribution of our findings and in explaining the attitudes towards regulation, neo-Aristotelians favouring more regulation than the liberal. The usefulness of these two notions means that having identified the distribution of these 'types' of people in contemporary British society, we are in a much stronger position to predict the regulatory desires of people in an era of changing values. What the research also shows is that even though people may have difficulty in expressing themselves in moral terms in relation to moral issues, they have no difficulty whatsoever in doing so when it comes to the morality of the invasion of privacy.

It is important to point out that the mere existence of preferences and desires does not, of itself, justify them. Our research shows and explains what people think and why. But it does not follow that that because people think something that it is therefore right. Indeed, except on privacy, there is a marked disagreement over ethical, social and regulatory matters explained by the liberal and neo-Aristotelian models. But even if there were a uniform consensus, to assume that this should determine policy, as many of our focus groups did, is to leave unexamined the whole question of the purpose of culture and how it should be governed, if at all. For culture is thus, by default, conceived of as having no moral and social implications at all in terms of how we ought to see the world, represent its social order and conceive of ourselves and others. It is to push aside the very kinds of questions that need to be addressed.

References

1. Kieran, M., Morrison, D. and Svennevig, M. (1997) *Regulating for Changing Values: A report for the Broadcasting Standards Commission*, research Working paper No. 1, London, BCC, 1997).
2. The classic contemporary articulation of liberalism is to be found in John Rawls, *A Theory of Justice* (1972), Oxford, Oxford University Press.
3. Aristotle, *Nicomachean Ethics*, trs. J.A.K. Thomson, revised by Hugh Tredennick, 1976, Harmondsworth, Penguin, 1. 1097b7–11, p. 74.

Appendix I: Face to face interviews with key media and related figures.

Roger Laughton – Executive Director of United Broadcasting and Entertainment.
Will Wyatt – Chief Executive of BBC Broadcasting.
Colin Stanbridge – Managing Director, Carlton Broadcasting.
Professor ACP Simms – Professor of Psychiatry, St. James University Hospital Trust.
Phil Redmond – Chairman of Mersey Television.
Ms. Angela Eagle – Member Of Parliament, Labour Party.
Mr. John Whittingdale – Member Of Parliament, Conservative Party.
Cynog Dafis – Member Of Parliament, Plaid Cymru
Dr. Shaikh Abdul Mabud – The Islamic Academy.
Ray Gallagher – Director of Public Affairs, BSkyB.
Jim McDonald – Catholic Media Association.
Nick Pollard – Head Of News, BSkyB.

Appendix II: Focus Groups
In total 14 Focus Groups were conducted.

Stage One

Town	Sex	Age	Children	Satellite/ Cable	Social/ Grade
Leeds	Women	55+	none living at home	no	BC1/C2
Leeds	Women	45—64	no children under 16	no	C1/C2
Redditch	Women	25—44	all with at least 1 child aged 8—14	no	C1/C2
London	Men	45—64	no children under 16	no	C1/C2

Stage Two

Town	Sex	Age	Children	Satellite/ Cable	Social/ Grade
Bristol	Men	55+	none living at home	3 with satellite	BC1/C2
Walsall	Men	under 55	children aged between 10—16	mixed	BC1/C2
London	Women (Complainers)	35—65	mixed	mixed	BC1/C2
Leeds	Men	18—24	no children	mixed	BC1/C2
London	Men	under 55	at least one child under nine at home	no	BC1/C2
Bristol	Women	under 55	at least one child under nine at home	no	BC1/C2
Walsall	Women	under 55	at least one child under nine at home	mixed	BC1/C2
London	Women	18—24	no children	mixed	BC1/C2
Redditch	Men (Complainers)	35—65	mixed	no	BC1/C2

Values in Broadcasting

Chair: Colin Shaw, C.B.E.
Former Director, Broadcasting Standards Council; Honorary Professor, University of Manchester

Lady Howe
Chair, Broadcasting Standards Commission

Colin Stanbridge
Managing Director, Carlton Broadcasting

Colin Shaw: Before I introduce Lady Howe and Colin Stanbridge I just want to say a few words about standards. There is a very useful phrase which Alan Bennett coined the other day. He said about standards: 'Of course they are old fashioned, otherwise they wouldn't be standards.' I think there is a good deal of truth in that, as there usually is in things that Alan Bennett says.

I have just come back from six months in the United States looking at the question of content regulation and comparing it with content regulation in this country. It is very curious that American network television, despite the first amendment, is actually a good deal more puritanical than British television, certainly after 9.00 o'clock in the evening. In both countries lines are drawn but in America they appear to be drawn by the networks on commercial grounds. The commercial pressures and the fears of what the advertisers may do (the fact that they may boycott the networks) are very strong. It may be stronger than public opinion but public opinion makes itself felt in America much more through pressure groups than it does in this country. We really have only one noisy pressure group and that's the National Viewers and Listeners Association which comes from a fairly profound Evangelical Christian viewpoint. There is nothing like the Christian coalition that is so powerful on the American Right in both political and religious terms.

Taste and decency in this country really didn't become an issue until 1954. In 1954 the Conservative Government introduced a Bill into the House of Commons to bring in an alternative service to the BBC in television. The BBC had enjoyed the monopoly from 1927 when the old British Broadcasting Company became a Corporation. There were many fears both on the Conservative side and on the Opposition side, the Labour side, as to what would happen once commercial television came in. It's a curious thing that, whereas Americans, by and large, are fearful of what the Federal Government may do to free expression (hence the first amendment and a clause in the 1934 Communications Act which says there should be no censorship) Britain, on the whole, has been far more fearful as to what commercial interference would do. The BBC itself was set up as a reaction to what was thought to be happening in the United States and the way in which American broadcast radio in those days was going commercial and was going to have all the horrors of commercial exploitation which was so much feared in this country. So in 1927 the BBC came in as a non-commercial broadcaster as a bulwark against all the perils that were seen to exist on the other side of the Atlantic.

In the same way the Government in 1954 got cold feet about the nature of what they were doing in setting up commercial television and, really rather late in the day, put into the draft of the Bill a clause which said in effect, but I can't quote it exactly: 'The Authority' – that was the Independent Television Authority the first name of the regulator – 'shall, as far as possible, do everything it can to ensure that nothing offensive to taste and decency appears in programmes.' It is a pretty meaningless clause, because nobody has ever taken a case to court and, indeed, once you start defining taste you are in great, great difficulty.

The last person you want to trust to define taste, I suggest, is a judge. Nevertheless it is there and the words were put in by an enterprising and public spirited civil servant: I suspect without anyone noticing. It is the great escape clause, and it wasn't until 10 years later that the BBC was pressurised, I think, really quite shamelessly by the Government into accepting obligations towards taste and decency which it had never been required to observe before.

The fact is that the conscience of the country, the mood of the country, was such that there were really very few examples between 1927 at the start of the Corporation and the 1960's when the BBC did give offence of that kind. There was a flurry of activity during the war when the BBC was doing a lot of entertainment and variety programmes designed to boost the morale of the nation (but in many ways doing the opposite because some of the programmes were so bad). At that time there was a great deal of concern at the heart of the BBC at the level of the vulgarity and if you go, as I have been recently, to the archives of the BBC outside Reading you will find many files which are actually called *Vulgarity, Vulgarity I, Vulgarity II, Vulgarity III*! [laughter]

For the Americans among us there may be some comfort in the fact that, round about 1942 which was a period when the BBC censored, they actually had someone called the dirt censor. There was also a security censor and he looked at manuscripts after they had been passed by the dirt censor. I didn't know until I recently went to the archives that the dirt censor was a man whom I knew when he was much older. Actually, he was by then rather the last person I would have entrusted with any responsibilities for dirt at all. But 1942 was just after the Japanese had overrun Singapore and sunk some of the British battleships and there was a general mood of gloom and despondency, and the BBC was very worried about the effects of all this vulgarity on the population so they tightened up. A particular concern was that America was in the war and troops were coming over from America in order to fight with the allies in Europe and elsewhere and they were receiving BBC programmes. There was a worry that reports would go back as to the appalling state of British broadcasting and this wouldn't play very well in the United States where standards, they said, were so much higher. So this is a curious inversion of what generally we have been taught to think in this country about American broadcasting.

A little bit of history: at the end of the 1950's there was a Committee, a government Committee of Enquiry set up under Sir Harry Pilkington (who was a glass manufacturer and so well qualified to chair an enquiry into broadcasting!). The Pilkington Committee was very scathing about the standards of commercial television. Political pressures were such that, if you were worried about the standards in commercial television then you had to be worried about the standards of the BBC. So, in 1964, the BBC was persuaded to sign up to undertakings which meant that, in effect, they were also bound by the same taste and decency considerations that bound independent broadcasting or ITV.

The trouble with standards, once you begin to think about them and begin to codify them, is that you can run into the trouble of regarding standards as being *the* standard you should attain. The great thing in regulating broadcasting, from somebody who was in the game for a long time, is to encourage the broadcasters to do better. I am not sure about standards which the idle will say simply means fulfilling a minimum. I think you need to give people targets to aim at which are actually those you know they can do if they try. When they get there they are pleasurably surprised and they think they have thought about it all by themselves and you haven't actually pushed them towards it. If you codify, you lay down too many strict standards and you may actually be in danger of deflating standards. The same Pilkington report contained a long, very good chapter, which I commend to any of you who want to look back at the history of those times, on what good broadcasting is. The last sentence in that Chapter, Chapter 3, is: 'Good broadcasting is a practice and not a prescription.'

I believe that to be profoundly true. In the early days of the Broadcasting Standards Council we tried to write a code that would encourage people to understand the climate in which good programmes are made. There were, I think, no prohibitions in it. Once you say 'thou shalt not', it is a standing invitation, quite properly, to any enterprising producer, to circumvent it. I think always you have to find ways in which a producer can be encouraged to do things which are unexpected. Huw Wheldon, a great man in British broadcasting, used to say you can make an obscene programme about butterflies if you wish and some enterprising fellow will come along and do it if you say you cannot make an obscene programme about butterflies. Huw Wheldon also said that he would challenge people who went to him with a half-baked idea. He would say, 'In the name of what do you want to make this programme?' *In the name of what* is, I think, a profoundly useful question to ask in all sorts of circumstances. You can even ask it if you are really frustrated, '*In the name of what* is this train late?' But *in the name of what* is particularly relevant to broadcasting.

Broadcasting is full of good intentions and bad intentions and it is really sorting out the good intentions from the bad intentions that we are concerned about this morning. We are going to begin by asking Lady Howe who is the Chair on (I was about to call this her first public outing as Chair of the Broadcasting Standards Commission and I was told that 'outing' was perhaps not the word I should use) ... on her first public *appearance* as Chair of the new Broadcasting Standards Commission. The Commission was put together, for the benefit of the ignorant, by merging the Broadcasting Standards Council and the Broadcasting Complaints Commission. The Commission has moved into the offices of the Broadcasting Standards Council, Westminster, rather splendid last century offices I have to say, and there Lady Howe sits. She came to the Council with a background as the Deputy Chair of the Equal Opportunities Commission and a great many other things as well. Having got used to William Rees Mogg, to change two Chairs is always a little difficult for the Director, but I have to say it was an extraordinarily happy relationship – an extraordinarily happy time. William Rees Mogg used to say that he and I worked well at the Broadcasting Standards Council because he knew the ambushes down one side of the trail and I knew the ambushes down the other. I suspect in some cunning way it happens with Lady Howe and me as well. Anyway, Elspeth, would you like to talk to us?

Lady Howe: Well it is a great pleasure to be here on, not only my first outing as far as the Broadcasting Standards Commission is concerned, but also of course up here and, incidentally, the first time I think I have sat under your Chairmanship – that is very naughty indeed. Well, I think that we were briefed to be relatively quick and make a few general remarks so that everyone could then wade in.

I think that I want to start with a splendid platitude that we are living through an amazing social and technological revolution certainly in the broadcasting media. Now I suppose if I am honest about this, every generation, particularly when it gets to my age, must feel pretty well like that. (How long ago was the Armada? About 400 years ago, and think how things have changed since then.) Certainly it is a very interesting time. The Director of BBC television, I think, described it as 'promiscuous' in the sense, of course, that everything is up for grabs. There is no fixed centre anymore, no received set of values or authority. Society has become more diverse and that certainly seemed to be the message echoing through the research we have just heard about and which I must admit I find absolutely fascinating. As indeed is most of the research which we commission, and I will come back to that later on, but which has been essential to the work that we have done, on the Broadcasting Standards side, anyhow.

I think what we have learned a lot about over the years is the fragmentation of audiences. But we have also come to appreciate their sense of judgement about what is problematic. Their attitudes to issues of values and ethics certainly have changed and will continue to do so. In some areas there has been a relaxation, the portrayal of sex for example, but there are limits to that also: go too far and you will get an explosion. In others, for example, the portrayal of violence or even bad language, attitudes have hardened.

I will add my own particular thoughts on the question of bad language about which we have an enormous number of complaints, I have to say. It's just that one feels that it has been the sheer volume of the increase. No doubt we've heard some of the reasons why. It's been happening over a relatively short time and across most programmes and it is that which seems to have irritated and offended quite a large proportion of the audience, particularly when you mix sexual swear words with religious swear words.

But we have also noticed increased anxiety over issues of privacy and fairness both from the perspective of the viewing audience and of those directly involved. This, of course, is the side which the Broadcasting Complaints

Commission, now part of us and we are part of them, looked at. There is a growing desire to respect and protect vulnerable groups especially children.

Now the fortunate fact to be set against the sense of fraying is that the audiences do have high ethical expectations of their broadcasting system – certainly in this country. They expect broadcasters to tell the truth. The credibility of broadcasters depends, in turn, on being able to provide a place where people can recognise their reality and their hopes, ambitions and fears and where they can be met and dealt with honestly and fairly.

When broadcasting works best, it's because it 'connects', and I say this very much from an individual perspective as an enthusiast for *most* of British broadcasting. That's why I, and I do suspect an awful lot of people, want a broadcasting system which continues to make a contribution to social cohesion (I hope that does not make me sound too much of an Aristotelian). They want a broadcasting system which safeguards a democratic process and is an important element in sustaining our national culture; one which allows people to make choices and deals with tension – so interestingly differentiated in the research around unsocial and anti-social behaviour. (On that, I would like to pose the thought: does unsocial lead onto anti-social or is there a complete disconnection between the two?) I want a broadcasting system which by the way it is done sends out signals about good behaviour, about being truthful, treating people fairly and decently and so on.

Now where does the Broadcasting Standards Council/Commission sit in all of this area? We exist, of course, within the regulatory framework. We are a statutory body to help sharpen that debate. I think it does look at things from the interest of the consumer and I hope also from the viewpoint of the citizen. We are there because Parliament, responding to public pressure about the growing influence of the broadcasting media, wanted a body that could express the concerns of the consumers and protect the rights of citizens when the broadcasters get it wrong. But please remember we are not censors. We recognise broadcasting's important creative task and we support freedom of expression. Our powers too are limited and deliberately so, and indeed when the Bill was going through Parliament, we argued that they should remain deliberately limited. Our greatest weapon is that of embarrassment because broadcasters do not like having complaints upheld against them. So our role is advisory. Though on occasions we can, and do, champion the relative powerlessness of the consumer against the increasingly powerful media. It is quite interesting because the powers allow us, when we think that there is something that needs further explanation, whether we uphold it or not, to go direct to the broadcasters and ask for a statement about how decisions were arrived at and so on. Whether we upheld the complaint or not, there it is in black and white for everyone to see and for the complainant that is quite useful generally. But also specifically because there are a significant number of people who have got jolly fed up with, either hanging on waiting to get direct to the broadcasters or, indeed, just not feeling, when they did get through, very satisfied with what was said to them.

Now under the new Act there are a couple of changes – broadcasters are not allowed to comment on our findings and adjudications on air. Now, that does not mean to say they can't, at a later stage, say that they thought that we got it all wrong but they can not say that it was 'a lot of rubbish' alongside the adjudication, just before it, or just after it. They are also required to report what actions they have taken as a result of our upheld findings.

Even in the multi-channel interactive world to come and already, I would argue, on its way it is surely both possible, and certainly desirable, to think of broadcasting as serving a *public* as opposed to a merely *private* purpose. Which means that, broadly speaking, broadcasting supports generally agreed values, behaves fairly, and does not shock or cause offence without good reason. But increasingly it will be important to strengthen concepts of self-regulation in which producers, commissioners and broadcasters ask themselves the hard questions.

I am reminded very much of a fascinating home video interview between the then Chairman of the European Broadcasting Organisation and one Karl Popper who might be quite familiar to some of the academics around here. Popper was clearly dying to say something about broadcasting and it went roughly like this: 'I gather you are worried about violence?' 'Yes, I used to work with very seriously disturbed children when I was a young man, and I knew the violence that they came from. Today there is violence in every home on the box in the corner.' 'Right!' said the Chairman. 'You want more regulation, you want more done about it.' 'No!' said Karl Popper, with a smile, he reckoned there was probably enough of that. 'But,' he said, 'broadcasters, like doctors, are dealing on a daily basis with matters of life and death and they should take unto themselves the equivalent of the Hippocratic Oath.' I think we are increasingly moving down that sort of road.

But values to safeguard? There are clearly quite a number. The explosion of narrowcasting produces interesting dilemmas. These again were indicated by the research. The niche channel is aimed at those who can afford to indulge their particular passion. Certainly much broadcasting is already now firmly grounded in the market economy, but should money be able to purchase greater licence? Every channel is now competing even harder, at all hours of the day and night, to provide something for the many different audiences rather than continuing to make assumptions about a single audience. Is this likely to drive quality and standards down? That, certainly, is the fear of the many who worry about these things and it figures quite frequently in the letters of complaint we get, sometimes in just general letters, saying how much they appreciate *most* broadcasting but are worried about these areas.

We can also see quite marked divergence of views about privacy from the research and that was again equally fascinating as I personally, and as part of the Commission, move into this area as well as the ones we have been in before. And perhaps it is that divergence that broadcasters need to pay particular attention to. My privacy, especially if I'm involved in some public event, such as an accident or a crime, is clearly paramount. The private lives of public figures relatively, if not completely, are seen as fair game, especially if they are judged to have brought the publicity on themselves, while certain sorts of criminals are thought to have no rights at all and that was very clearly brought out. I would argue certainly that there is a need to hold the ring between these very different approaches in order to involve the *public* in the debate about what are accepted values and standards, to encourage international conversations and cooperation and at least define the outer boundaries of acceptability.

I do take very much the point that Colin made. As a latecomer to the Broadcasting Standards Council, although my initial thoughts may well have been, 'I wish there was more saying *don't do that*,' increasingly, I became convinced that the right approach was to point out where the dangers were, where broadcasters should be taking special care. Though I do think there is one prohibition, if I may remind you Colin, no hangings before 9 o'clock, no hangings please before 9 o'clock. I think there is ... but that is a slight diversion.

So how are we going to be working and how do we work? I think we are there to do a number of different things. Why we are there I have explained and we can go into it later if you want to and certainly Colin can say a great deal more about that.

But, some of the areas we are involved in are crucial and I would come back now to the research programme. That research programme takes the audiences and their attitudes very seriously and ensures that the consumer voice is heard. We very much hope to develop that role further. Indeed, I think it is perfectly fair to say that the Broadcasting Standards Council's contribution to the broadcasting debate, as it has developed, owes a lot to the research that we have commissioned. Let me make it absolutely clear, we are required by law to do the research and equally required by law to put it out to independent research organisations. But what we are actually doing is, in fact, reflecting in the questions what the audience is telling us are their concerns, or contradictions, or whatever it happens to be. So it is with this in mind that we look at whatever we can afford in ways of research. I think most people have, over the years as I said, agreed that has been a very important worthwhile contribution, not least since the Broadcasting Research Unit, which used to do some independent, everything-out-in-the-public-domain research, closed down some years ago. Everything is public, it's independent and it's published. In this particular case, I just wanted to make the point, that we wanted in the light of the changes in broadcasting, and indeed of the merger, to look at what values people want to see reflected in broadcasting and whether they saw differences between the media generally, and whether *privacy* was in fact of particular concern. Because research on privacy and fairness, which had really not been done at all up to that point, is included in those new areas brought into the new Broadcasting Standards Commission. So I thought you would want to know about that.

The complaints side: now here again, whether we are dealing frankly with the audience concerned about the portrayal of sex, violence, or matters of taste and decency or complaints by people with a direct interest in fairness, or invasions/infringements of privacy or alleged infringements of privacy – we get complaints. They are dealt with and we come to a conclusion one way or another, either through a hearing or, indeed, without a hearing.

Another area of our work is to continue to support better information for audiences, so that indeed they can make informed choices about what they want, or indeed what they want their children to see. All the research that we do points to the fact that there is a thirst for more information about what is being shown. Interestingly, they say that they won't necessarily use that information. I think one of the reasons for that is that it depends on the situation they are in. But they want research to be there and available. That is why I would argue that the current debates about the V chip and the EPG, or indeed any other information system, are important and I hope will go on. Fascinating to see the research in America – I was over there flitting around in a little bit of America when Colin was there – and they are all beginning to get quite excited about this.

We are also going to be supporting, as indeed from the beginning we have done, educational measures designed to strengthen children's understanding about how the media work. We've held, just recently, two seminars at a working level with broadcasters, one on bad language and then the latest one, again with broadcasters, on violence to which the Secretary of State and the Shadow Secretary of State came. What was interesting there was that both the broadcasters and ourselves had together commissioned the current research into the area and we shared an agreement on the complexity of this issue and the need to look even more closely at what, within the whole range of violence, offends and causes the deepest concern. Out of that too came the very clear feeling that there was going to be an increased need for media education either in schools, or to help parents understand. There was a need to help children as they move into the world not just to understand but to know how to deal with and be sceptical about, in the best sense of the word, the many things that they will be seeing.

Now just to end with John Tusa, whom you all know. He wrote about the price of separation from the good society. He noted, in an important and relevant list of juxtapositions, that the good society does not confuse ecstasy with enlightenment, self-gratification with freedom, it does not confuse atomisation with individuality, quality with value, exploitation with enterprise, reward with greed, cornucopia with riches, élitism with exclusiveness, organisation with effectiveness, structures with relationships and, lastly, noise with meaning. Now that's quite a list to think about. No small challenge in an increasingly global media market where the key players are two giants who may have cultural feet of clay. The lure and the power of money are strong and the only real antidote is a strongly developed sense of cultural, political, and ethical self-awareness in which trust and a sense of shared values have their place. Thank you.

Colin Shaw: Thank you very much. I would add just one to John Tusa's catalogue which is activity being confused with progress. But progress we certainly now get because we progress on to Colin Stanbridge, Managing Director of Carlton Broadcasting. He had seventeen years in the BBC after coming down from University. He was in current affairs for that time before running one of the BBC's regions and then moving on to Independent Television. Colin!

Colin Standbridge: Yes, three years at a Yorkshire university studying philosophy which I am not sure did prepare me for this morning. I wished that I had listened a bit more closely during some of the seminars and some of the lectures because I might have remembered the difference between Aristotelian and Platonic, but there you go!

I think what was interesting about this morning's dissertation was the confusion that is in the mind of the viewer, the consumer, about what we broadcast. One is tempted to say: 'Who would be a regulator given the divergence of opinion?' I think what it solidified for me is that, when it comes to regulation, I would like to go on the record as being wholly in favour of regulation. As a broadcaster I want to be regulated about content. I feel it is an important part of broadcasting: we don't make widgets, we make programmes that will, hopefully, affect society and give out information that will enable people to make important decisions. Therefore it is important that, when we get it wrong, we are told that we have got it wrong and we do something about it.

However, what I am worried about, and one of the first things that Lady Howe is going to be overseeing, is a new code on fairness and privacy. Seventeen years in the BBC has prepared me for codes, I had ring binders bulging with codes. When I got to ITV I had even more ring binders filled with codes of rules and regulations. It is an interesting point that ITV, a commercial broadcaster, is far more regulated than the BBC but that's an aside. What I found, and what I have to confess, is that I still find these codes helpful, they give me indications of conduct, indications of ways of dealing with matters. But almost to a one they never fit the situation I find on my desk when I am asked to make a decision.

That leads me to make one plea. When people like the new Broadcasting Standards Commission are charged with coming up with a new code, they draw it as widely as possible, that the rules and regulations are kept to a minimum. That does not mean that I want to get away with things, that doesn't mean that I want to have something so wide that I can drive a coach and horses through it – far from it. What I want to happen is that, when we make mistakes (or are alleged to have made mistakes), common sense is brought to bear on each individual case. Even if I disagree with the rulings that are made, even if I disagree with what I have to do subsequent to those rulings, I should feel that the individual cases have been dealt with individually. My experience is that each case is different.

When you are dealing with a code on, let's say 'fairness' you are drawing up guidelines – rules – whatever you want to call them for *broadcasters*.

An example: if you are going to make a programme about a particular subject and you are going to interview people, would it not be a good idea to make a regulation that broadcasters must inform the interviewee about all the other interviewees who are taking part in that particular programme? It seems unobjectionable when you are at your desk writing it up. However, there will always be a situation when you think that this is not a very good thing to do. One situation comes to mind: you are dealing with a Rachman or an alleged Rachman-type landlord, or a drug dealer/drug baron. Should the broadcaster, should the programme-maker really go to this person and say: 'Yes, and by the way, we have interviewed X, Y, Z who say you are a drug baron, that you have ruined their lives, that you have extorted, by foul means, extortionate rents.'? I would argue, as a responsible programme maker, that would not be very responsible at all because, if it is true that the person is what they say they are, then they will go round and 'deal with' the interviewees. I would have thought that was not a result that any regulator or any codifier would want.

Obviously there are going to be lots of occasions when you are going to want tell people and, on the whole, I do believe that we do that. But what I would hope is that, when one comes to draw up a code, that the concept of fairness is drawn widely so that when it comes to the actual event, the people who are charged – the people on the Commission, the people on the Independent Television Commission – are able to make their own decision about whether the broadcaster acted fairly, after hearing both sides of the story.

A problem might happen, if codes are drawn to closely. For example: if a 'public interest' part of a code is defined too closely, if you said there had to be an 'overwhelming public interest' for a broadcaster to secretly film or something like that, you would arrive at a situation where the lawyers would have a field day discussing –we all have lawyers discussing – what is 'overwhelming'. Also I don't think it would serve the public or the public interest. I think what we would rather have is a situation where those people, when assessing the facts, say that 'so and so was in the public interest'. If we do have too closely defined rules and regulations I believe it's a lawyers' charter and things will get out of hand. The public want to be served in terms of getting their complaints dealt with easily.

In my world a much more important conclusion, if it is policed (as I am sure it will be under Lady Howe) extremely rigorously, is that the programme-makers will throw their hands in the air on lots of occasions and say: 'Let's not do the dangerous thing, let's not do the innovative thing, let's just be safe and sound,' and we end up with a broadcasting that is bland, some would say, even blander than today.

I hope we are people that believe in self-regulation, I think I certainly do. But I hope more fervently that we don't turn into people who become self censors at every turn of the road. Thank you.

Colin Shaw: Right, we have come to the time when we can throw the subject open to the floor for discussion. Just one thought that I have. As is clear from what Lady Howe is saying, we have come across Karl Popper before. My objection, as she knows, is that a professional code is very difficult for a profession which isn't, for the most part, independent. If you are a dentist or a lawyer you have your peers sit in judgement on you. The difficulty with making a protest saying, 'I am not going to make this programme because I think it's obscene, it's corrupt in some way,' is that your boss will go off and hire somebody else who will. It is extremely difficult for a profession of this kind (assuming that broadcasting can be regarded as a profession), for broadcasters, in the sense of programme makers, to find the appropriate sanction which they can impose on those who employ them. The idea of somebody going up to Mr Murdoch and saying, 'I don't want to take this photograph for the front page of the *Sun*,' and being allowed to get away with it is really pretty unrealistic. Until we can find a way of bridging the gap, and I have always argued that somehow within the profession there should be a jury of peers who can offer a view that can be taken seriously, we are a long way away from that. The failure of the profession to speak up about the decline in the standard of British broadcasting, assuming there is some decline in values, is one of the more distressing features of last few years. However, there we are.

Questions? Comments? Contributions to the debate? I hope we have trailed our coats enough to tempt one of Phil's students out of the Trappist state in which they have been for most of the time. Who would like to open up? Yes! Would you like to remind us who you are?

Granville Williams (The Campaign for Press and Broadcasting Freedom): It's just a basic point. You have just referred to Murdoch and newspapers and we have heard in the last day or two the analogy being made between the kind of proliferation of magazine titles and the equivalent for digital TV – 'more channels, more choice'. It seems to me that is one of the issues. Indeed it is the genesis of the old Broadcasting Standards Council. If we take point about the way in which the Broadcasting Standards Council was set up, it was set up, because there was a fear that if you released the market, in other words if you were going to have, as the 1988 White Paper said 'more competition, more channels, more choice' and so on, you needed a backstop. It seems to me that, in a way, the real problem with regulation in this new era for broadcasting is the same problem that has existed over the years for newspapers – this idea of 'the freedom of the press'. This new commercial freedom goes right to the heart of trying to have a code on privacy. I can accept an absolute defence of the freedom of the press to investigate rigorously miscarriages of justice and all that, intellectually it's coherent to me. I can accept it being clearly earmarked in terms of broadcasting but that's not necessarily what it will be about. It will be about going into tacky tabloid type areas.

It seems to me that there are two questions: will it be an era where this analogy of 'more channels more choice' is going to make television the equivalent of the book stand at WH Smith with 'the freedom of the press' argument predominant? Also this issue of privacy raises the fundamental question: privacy for whom? What justice, in terms of the criteria used in the past? It's got to be in the 'public interest', it's got to be a *public* defence for that intrusion.

Colin Shaw: Colin, would you like to respond?

Colin Standbridge: I think that this comparison with the press is really rather interesting. I was at a session earlier this week where Lord Wakeham was talking about the differences between press and broadcasting regulation and there seems to be a completely different philosophy between the two. You could say with a small L that the Press has a much more liberal regime whereas broadcasting has much more proactive regulation. What I was saying earlier was that I think the danger of too much regulation, or too closely defined regulation, is that people give up, especially on investigations and believe that only newspapers can do this sort of investigation. I think that would be wrong because television has something to add to that. I don't believe that, in a digital age, we should throw up our hands and say: 'We are going to give up all regulation because there is too much of it.' I do however, think it is going to be a terrible problem, just to watch all the available television is going to be a terrible problem.

Colin Shaw: Just before I ask Lady Howe to respond let me just say that the Press Council, of which Lord Wakeham is the Chairman, is a non-statutory body funded by the newspaper industry. The Broadcasting Standards Commission is funded by the Government.

Lady Howe: I think two points. On the face of it one may ask why there should be a statutory code for broadcasting? As far as the press are concerned, I can make one defence. You go out and buy your newspapers: you choose your newspapers. What is beamed directly into your own home is very much on the concept of an Englishman's home – English person's home, Englishwoman's home – is their castle. It is felt, to come back to Popper, that TV is beamed into the home and, though you can turn off, there is an instinctive wish to turn on. We have to say that this business of privacy is a very emotive area and one in which the media generally (and the press perhaps particularly) and politicians dance round one another. There is quite clearly a voluntary code. John Wakeham and plenty of other people have talked about 'the last chance saloon' and so on and so forth. One wonders, however, what if anything will happen?

I come back to the points that Colin was making about codes. We are required as a statutory duty laid on us under the act to draw up codes. We will begin to consult in earnest quite soon. In doing that we don't want to fetter our discretion any more than we want to fetter the discretion of broadcasters. We want to set out where the dangers are, taking the very good example of Colin Shaw's own drafted code on standards, and where broadcasters should take particular care. But each case, whatever the test ends up by being, will know the danger area. How they deal with it is, of course, left to them. The last thing we want to do is have the 'chilling' effect that you were describing where broadcasters will just say, 'We can't do anything,' and so on. Practically, I don't think that will happen.

Don't forget that our code is *required* to be drawn up. As far as broadcasters are concerned, you are required by law to reflect the general intentions of it. It is not a set of rules, it is general guidance. I hope that when we finally get a code (of course, you will not like it all, and no doubt we will not like some of things that we have agreed to and thought good in the initial negotiations) we will all have learned in the process.

It is, interestingly, your point about the proliferation of channels. I am sure that had something to do with the establishment of the Commission. It was also a growing concern, and the growing amount of letters to parliamentarians, about these particular issues – certainly as far as the portrayal of sex, violence, indecency – which made them decide to set up Broadcasting Standards Commission. As you know the other one was set up – the Complaints Commission – when was it Colin?

Colin Shaw: It was a BBC body from about 1972 onwards then it became statutory in the '60s, '70s, sorry '80s.

Lady Howe: As tends to happen, when parliamentarians feel there is an issue that they can't deal with on an everyday basis they set up another organisation. In some ways, it is fair to say that the broadcasting industry in this country is more regulated than probably many others. It is interesting that, although we might feel we want a little bit more of this and a little less of that nobody seems to want to let regulation go completely. I think what I was trying to say was, that as we move to an increasingly fragmented situation, then we will try and keep what we regard as essential to the values we want to preserve; but the cross frontier scenario does require an increased effort internationally. It is interesting that the profile of the sort of things we are doing is being raised in Europe and across the Atlantic too.

I was mentioning what had been happening in America. From absolutely no regulations whatsoever, suddenly they are into the V chip. Now there might have been one or two steps in-between. In the UK because we are pretty well structured maybe we do not have to look at the V chip. I personally would not rule it out because, if it does provide yet another direct consumer choice at the point of *switch on, switch off*, then why not? But of course, what we don't know is how it would work, and the system by which it would decide the levels of violence. They already have trouble with this in America.

Colin Shaw: Comments?

John Gray: You mentioned the word 'professional'. I think one of the difficulties here is we like to think of ourselves as a profession, but unlike the ancient professions, we do not have a professional body with professional standards to which we work. Law, Medicine, very clearly do so. Where is our equivalent of the Hippocratic Oath, as Popper would have put it? What about the other ancient profession – religion? What we have acquired is a priesthood without a religion; we know how to do broadcasting but what is the philosophy behind broadcasting? Certainly when I came into the profession, the philosophy behind the broadcaster was, first and foremost, 'respect your audience'. If you respect your audience a lot of these questions of regulation do not come up.

At that time, culturally speaking in Britain, it was a fairly homogeneous audience, now it's not. The great difficulty is language. If I am doing a programme of rap music and heavy rock for a 16–24 year old audience, how can I say this is perfectly appropriate to them – the language, the concepts – but it mustn't offend somebody else? How do we say to other groups: 'But this is not for you; only criticise the kind of programmes that are intended for you; don't criticise the programmes which are not intended for you?' That is a concept of putting responsibility not on the broadcaster but on the audience. I think that the audience has to accept its share of responsibility on how it uses broadcast media and not blame the broadcasters when the audience is misusing the broadcasting medium. Thank you.

Colin Shaw: David Morrison – have you got any answer to that?

David Morrison: I think I have. I think it becomes a problem to put it back onto the audience, because as I was saying earlier, once you have a fragmentation of groups those groups actually carry values. For example: if you have homosexuality on *EastEnders*, whether one is homophobic or not, you are actually saying this kind of life style and sense of values are challenging your definition of the world and your authority.

Now, are you actually saying that, once you have got all the channels you don't have to watch this stuff? That is the problem of payment (pay-per view, subscription). If there are channels dedicated to the young, what are you saying? If the young actually take this language over, then that language actually symbolises something that the parents actually might object to. I don't think you can separate off groups as if these groups have nothing to do with the rest of society. That becomes a real problem. It's trying to square the circle.

Colin Shaw: Would anyone from the floor like to follow that up? Louise?

Louise Bennett (Independent Television Commission): Just to pick up on the point John Gray made. I think that it does actually inform how we go about assessing complaints we receive from the public. I don't know whether Lady Howe would like to pick up on this point. But what you are looking at is not just what the broadcaster has done. When you take a complaint you are say-ing: 'What is the *basis* for this complaint?' You are looking at what the audi-ence expectation is in relation to that particular programme. If it is a programme going out late at night, that's aimed at Channel 4, or at a particular audience that is looking for something that is off-beat or slightly different from the main-stream, then if the complaints are being raised by people to whom that pro-gramme is not being targeted, that is an element in your consideration of that complaint. What you look for is broadcasters who have been responsible and sensible in the way that they have decided to target and output that programme. If they decide to put that programme out on Channel 3 at 7.30 in the evening then that is going to raise different issues than if it is going out at midnight on Channel 4 on a Friday. Your audience is different, the expectations of your audi-ence are different at that time. If there is swearing at midnight, it's perhaps going to be more acceptable in the context of the programme than the same swearing would be at 7.30 in a different sort of programme. The audience does have some sense of responsibility. They have choices to make as well. What you are trying to do, as the regulator, is kind of hold the ring of the contract between the audience and the broadcaster.

Colin Shaw: So you respond with a postcard with the word, 'tough' on it do you?

Louise Bennett: No, we are a little more polite than that but you do have to take into consideration what the programme expectation is, and what the audi-ence can legitimately expect from a programme.

Colin Shaw: Anybody else want to come in on this before I ask Lady Howe?

Sebastian Timpson (Carlton): Louise, I was interested that you mentioned Channel 4 saying that you do not regulate them in quite the same way.

Louise Bennett: I did not say that.

Sebastian Timpson: You took into account that the programme was on Channel 4 and later at night than on ITV at the same time?

Louise Bennett: Okay. Let's keep it to one channel. Something that goes out on Channel 4 at 11.30 on a Friday night would not necessarily have a complaint upheld against it, but, if they then put that same programme out on a Tuesday night at 7.30, we may be in a position of upholding the complaints. I do not want you to go away with the impression that we are less strict on Channel 4 than we are on Channel 3. That is not the case.

Let me give you a concrete example and avoid any confusion here: *Brookside* with its incest storyline and also with its Trevor Jordache storyline when the stabbing occurred. In both those cases what you had was a situation where the programme went out at, say 8.30, on a Friday evening. The scenes that were being considered were marginal and we were looking at them very, very close-ly. The Commission came down on both cases with the view that showing the scenes in the 5 o'clock Omnibus on a Saturday, when there is a large number of children to view in the teatime audience, caused us concern and we upheld complaints. We issued formal warnings in relation to those particular instances. It's the scheduling in relation to that particular aspect. It is a question of audi-ence expectation at a particular time. What audience is available to view at a particular time?

To take a Channel 3 example: if you put a programme out at 7.30 on a mainstream channel the type of language, or the way you deal with issues such as violence or sexual portrayal, would be different from the way you would handle those particular subjects at 11.30 at night. What I was trying to say is that when we receive a complaint we are looking at what time it has gone out, what is the audience's expectation in relation to that particular programme. You take those sort of things into account when you come to a decision about a complaint.

I regret giving a Channel 3 versus Channel 4 comparison, that's what muddied the waters a little bit. We apply the same criteria to Channel 3 as we do to Channel 4 and to all our licensees. We take the complaint, we look at it in relation to the programme code and, if it has violated the programme code we uphold it. If it hasn't, then we don't.

Unidentified speaker: It's unfair but tempting to ask you that, if the *Brookside* incest had been on ITV at 8.30, whether or not the Commission would have taken the same view?

Colin Shaw: We are not going to have an ITV civil war. Anyone else want to pursue that particular issue? I don't want to be stuck on this for ever but if anyone is bursting to say something more which is useful? You will just have to decide – a piece of self-regulation!

Second unidentified speaker: I just really can't believe Louise's last point that, broadly, we regulate all our licensees in the same way. That is manifestly not the case. There is a sharp distinction in the way in which terrestrial and satellite broadcasters are regulated and some of us feel that there ought to be more convergence in the way that particular factor is played out.

Colin Shaw: At the risk of prolonging this, Lady Howe.

Lady Howe: A very quick one, this worry about the parents – people at home – their responsibility: there is very little doubt as our research shows that they want information. They know about the watershed and they do exercise quite a lot of judgement. Technology has made life more difficult, we are all worried about children and the appropriate ages at which they see and listen to things. Equally, increasingly they have all got videos in their bedrooms, not just their own TVs but videos as well so there is general concern. Equally, you may well have somebody putting on a programme when children are around who say: 'Well, the next channel is really aiming at the children at this time so therefore they should be watching this rather than the other.' I am not certain that I totally agree with that. It depends on each situation because it is still within watershed time. You have got to look at whatever it is because children do switch channels. A lot of our complaints are about this.

I think the business of channels is important. We get many fewer complaints from the satellite scenario because there are fewer people watching it or, maybe it is because they have paid for it and, if they have paid for it, they don't wish to complain quite as much. We do look rather differently at Channel 2 and Channel 4. Channel 4 was set up with a particular remit to experiment and so on. So we take the context, the expectations of the audience and so on into account. The areas that we look at are very complicated. Even at midnight or whenever it is, we look at violence, sex and whatever is gratuitous.

Peter Lewis (Middlesex University): I would like to ask a question of Lady Howe and Colin Stanbridge and explain what is at the back of it. Do you ever get people complaining at the lack of something? I am one of those people who have never rung up to complain. I get my students to ring up (and I give them the numbers) and tell them to ring up and praise programmes that are good and risky because I know those reports get on the controllers' desks.

We have heard from Hannah Davis that tendencies in the internationalisation of children's programmes are reducing the specific cultural identity of programming. We could say, I am quoting an example from radio (my specialism), that financial pressures on the BBC mean that tough Monday night radio dramas can't get repeated on Saturday afternoons because they would be too tough for the family audience. Therefore, you make Monday night dramas not so tough and the single play disappears and so on. Now it's very difficult for people to ask for something they have not got and memories are short. I remember Frank Gillard, who was an advocate of BBC local radio, saying how could people be expected to demand something of which they had no experience? It is clear to us specialists that we are experiencing a disappearance, due to structural reasons, competition, funding and so on, of quite a number of things in broadcasting. So I come back to my question, do people notice and complain about a lack?

Colin Stanbridge: All the time. I pray for the day when a regulator entertains a complaint about the fact that we have cut out the swear words in a Hollywood movie, and takes us to task for doing this. There are a lot of complaints especially when we cut Hollywood movies because people have seen them and they know what's in them. They complain when we cut the violence, which we regularly do, when we cut the bad language, which we regularly do, when we cut the sex scenes, which we regularly do. I suspect there isn't a notable film that we haven't cut. We get regular complaints from people about our doing this. We will carry on doing it, because we think it is the right thing to do.

Lady Howe: As far as that aspect of things is concerned, we do get the odd complaint: 'How dare you take out X number of swear words,' but it is very, very small.

About the fact that we should have more drama: alas that is outside our remit. We would pass those letters on to others. It's a question of certain standards as opposed to standards and balance and so on.

As far as children are concerned, we do regard them as a slightly broader remit. Quite early on in Colin's time we did research on the quality and, indeed, the range of children's programmes and found that, though numerically there was more time given over to children, the range had narrowed. That was very worrying. Of course, an awful lot of it is, as we know, cartoons. The more worrying aspect is some of the cartoons that will be on television in the future.

I went to a very interesting Australian conference on children's broadcasting. I have never seen so many people concerned about the quality of children's programmes. Particularly they were concerned about the programmes being sold in developing countries at very low rates. It is pretty poor quality stuff. Out of that there developed a very great feeling for a more cooperative effort and that the developed countries would try and 'do their bit' and encourage a better quality of children's programmes.

I think I come back really to Colin's point. He has always argued for a forum about what the general public feel broadcasting ought to be able to do and provide for them. There is no such forum other than in voluntary organisations. There are one or two organisations which take up some of these issues. Given the narrow remit that we have, we try our best to stretch it.

Colin Shaw: I proposed at one stage, very early in the life of the Council, that the Council should monitor the Government's 'experiment' with the deregulation of broadcasting and I was told very firmly by the Home Office that it was not an experiment.

Brian Luckham (British Council): I would like to ask Lady Howe about the ways in which the Commission will be working. I think the change in the law reflects a concern that there ought to be a more active role for the regulatory body. I would like to ask whether, when there are infringements, you are going to act purely in a reactive manner to any complaints that are made or whether you are going to be more proactive by presenting guidelines which might be helpful?

The second point follows on from that: I am concerned with media education programmes and in many schools of journalism (which of course is not the only route by which people come into the press and broadcasting) ethics and ethical issues are taught only in terms of what the law says – what you ought to do or what you can't do. I would hope that the Council will develop a relationship with teaching institutions to promote a better approach to the teaching values in broadcasting.

Lady Howe: On the proactivity: for a start I must reiterate again we are an advisory body within a regulatory framework but we have very few teeth, although we do have influence which can be quite valuable. Broadcasters are beginning to say what they have done in response to a complaint – discussed it with the department and so on. We, of course, do produce Annual Reports and in every Annual Report there have been overviews of some of the things which our correspondents have said to us and what we have noted as important looking at trends and so on. We do have an additional power under the new Act which is that, where we see a worrying trend emerging to do with our remit, then we can make separate reports to the Secretary of State. We actually thought we had that before but it is now clarified. Our proactivity is there in that sense. We also have the responsibility for persuading the broadcasters to think seriously about this, that or the other. I came into the Commission when this was more than well-established. The research which has been undertaken earlier by the Commission has been a tremendous debating point, has raised a number of important issues with broadcasters and has resulted in some changes. We probably influenced broadcasters in being more open in their activities, in publishing more of their decisions and the decisions of regulators. The BBC now has its own Complaints Unit which is part of the activity of self-regulation and much to be encouraged.

Colin Shaw: Right, I propose to take one more question and ask the two panellists to have a last word.

Stephen Kelly: As a programme maker and as a viewer, I am asked to have an enormous trust in these regulatory bodies such as the Commission and the ITC. And I do wonder about the democratic nature of these organisations. Are they to be trusted? How can we be sure that they are representative? Or are they another political quango full of nice, white male Anglo Saxons?

Lady Howe: All these quangos have been gathered from people in different walks of life. The current situation is that quango appointments are now more open. Anyone can apply to any of the departments to be considered for any of the public bodies. Are we, the Commission, representative? We don't have enough younger people, particularly parents with younger children because that is an important constituency. Currently we have not got anyone at all from ethnic groups. Dame Jocelyn Barrow was an absolute tower of strength in the past. So in that sense we are looking for gaps in the constitution which will help give us a better overview. The process is more democratic than it was. We keep on looking at all these areas.

Colin Shaw: That one will run and run so I am going to stop at that. I will, if I may, regard that as your last word. Colin's last word?

Colin Standbridge: I suppose broadcasters can not be represented (on the Commission)?

Lady Howe: No.

Colin Standbridge: As a broadcaster I welcome regulation. I would also like to say as a broadcaster that we always have discussed matters of fairness, privacy and issues of taste and decency. We have always done that.

What About the Workers?

Chair: Caroline Millington
Controller, Multimedia Development, BBC

Dinah Caine
Chief Executive, SKILLSET

Scott Hammond
Associate Professor, Brigham Young University, USA

Judith Jones
Lecturer, John Moores University, Liverpool, and freelance broadcaster

Ana Kronschnabel
MA student, University College, Warrington, and freelance film-maker

Peter Lewis
Lecturer in Media and Cultural Studies, Middlesex University

Gill Ursell
Principal Lecturer in Media and Course Director of Journalism Training Schemes, Trinity and All Saints University College, Leeds

Caroline Millington: On to 'What about the Workers' which I believe is the final main session of this conference. My name is Caroline Millington, I work for the BBC – in BBC Production – I've worked chiefly in radio but television as well for more than a quarter of a century. I am a worker in the broadcasting industry, but I'm also a manager, and that's the last time that we'll refer to management in this session.

We have a star cast of luminaries covering every angle of the increasingly large broadcasting industries, from broadcasting itself as well as anybody who is interested in studying it, dissecting it, preparing people to enter into it. What I am going to ask all of them to do is to think, for the end of the session, about the one action they personally believe would change the face of broadcasting in a beneficial way, and who they think should take it. That's just something to concentrate their minds. They have, of course, all prepared quite other things to say. We are going to start with three speakers from the floor who have prepared papers. They are not going to be delivering their whole papers because we will be here for longer than the already extended session, they are going to give brief synopsis of the key points.

We're going to begin with Judith Jones, who began her television career with Granada Television. Judith has worked on a large range of programmes including *World in Action* and *Coronation Street*. Judith is a freelance broadcaster, and she became freelance not least because she became a mother. Her paper is about passion and commitment – splendid titles – and the difficulties faced by working mothers in the British television industry. Judith.

Judith Jones (John Moores University): As has already been indicated, this research is only a small synopsis of a much longer study and it does not give a definitive picture, but it highlights some of the difficulties faced by women with children working in British television today, and certainly some of those problems will be picked up by other speakers later on. The dramatic changes in the British television industry over the past fifteen years have affected, not only its structure but also its workforce and it's estimated by the year 2000 some 20 per cent of the European workforce will be working in the communications industry.

What I set out to look at was how sympathetic this industry was to the needs of women. There are two specific features of the industry which create particular problems. One is the continuing male domination which has been confirmed, not least by Skillset in their research. There are serious substantial gender imbalances in specific areas. What this male culture has created is an environment of total commitment, long and unsociable hours and, because it's a highly competitive industry, little attention has been aimed at the needs of the employees with care responsibilities. Again, research by the British Film Industry Tracking Study has shown that 48 per cent of freelance workers find work through personal contacts. Movement between different programmes, between different companies, is increasingly through personal contacts and, therefore, it is important not to be labelled as lacking commitment or not being 100 per cent loyal and committed to working; job sharing, part-time working or even a career break may be considered to show divided loyalty, and that creates problems for women trying to juggle a career and motherhood.

The second feature of the industry is, I think, the casualisation of the workforce. That is what I'm going to talk about in greater detail later on. Freelance workers are being employed on different contracts and varying conditions. Now, under the 1994 Broadcasting Act, ITV licence holders and Channel 4 are required to make practical arrangements for promoting equality of opportunity. However, that is where the Act falls down. Independent companies, who may be supplying them with programmes and who predominately employ freelances, are outside the scope of that equal opportunities clause, so there's not necessarily any monitoring going on of what independent companies are doing in relation to their employees.

In December 1994, the BFI published some early reports from its tracking study which Nick is going to talk about in more detail later, but one of the results at that early stage was that 53 per cent of women over the age of forty working in television do not have children, compared with 15 per cent of men. This issue was taken up at the 1995 Edinburgh Television Festival where, in a lively debate, one of the commissioning editors of Channel 4, a woman called Sarah Ramsden, concluded that she did not know how it was possible to be 100 per cent committed to working in television and have children at the same time. That was the starting point for my research. Obviously, it was a thorny subject which created a lot of controversy within the industry.

Now the interviewees: these are mainly women working in television with children under the age of ten, generally working for large commercial companies rather than the BBC, because that's where, generally, freelance working has taken place. It's more marked in independent sectors than the BBC and the interviewees tend to be employed on contract. The feeling I had from the women was they all felt that this was a crucial issue and there were certain themes which came out. One was that, yes, there was a demanding culture within television, there was a high expectation of commitment. However, some of them differed, some of the women thought it was particularly *macho*, others felt it centred on a *young-people-kind-of* industry, but the consensus was that the culture was not conducive to the demands of family life, particularly in terms of long and irregular hours. Although television by its very nature will never involve working nine-to-five, there was a question mark over whether those hours are strictly necessary. Women felt they overcompensated in their work. One example: if the children were ill they wouldn't admit that was the reason for their absence, they didn't want to show any sign of weakness which could affect their future employment prospects.

The women interviewed had a variety of employment patterns but they didn't seem to indicate that freelance working had necessarily brought them any benefits. Rather the contrary. Factors such as insecurity and lack of eligibility for particular benefits were emphasised. In a market where there are increasing numbers of young people, a career break was seen as imprudent. They felt that if they took a break of more than a couple of months then it would be extremely difficult to break back into that industry.

Two women I interviewed had actually started their own companies, and this seemed to be a more advantageous position for those with children because they are able to structure their work around their position as mothers and impose certain parameters – such as not filming abroad. But, even these very conscientious employers conceded that tight budgets would make it very difficult for them to instigate all the benefits that they would like. They regarded equal opportunities as their responsibility and they both wanted to follow good working practices, they were responsible conscientious employers. I'm not sure that would go for all the independent sector.

In terms of alternative working practices – job share, part-time working – these were viewed favourably by the respondents, but did not seem to be common practice. One woman who did work part-time found it invaluable but she felt the attitude of the company was that she should be even more grateful for the opportunity that had been given to her. This raises the question of how committed companies actually are to those kind of practices. Theoretically, employers seem sympathetic but, in practice, it is not necessarily the case. I would argue that television in general doesn't seem to have embraced alternative working practices.

Women interviewees also were concerned about the notion of promotion because that would involve working longer hours. They all argued that becoming a mother had actually improved their capacity as a programme maker improving such skills as time management. They also emphasised the contribution they could make, as mothers, to programmes in which they were involved both through the contacts they had made and the fact that they felt more in touch with the real world. One example is perhaps the recent *Panorama* programme on mothers.

At the end of the research I felt the situation was fairly bleak – increasing numbers of young people opting for media courses and a career in television, more job opportunities but an absence of defined wage structures so it is only for those who are young and childless, who will often accept a lower rate of pay – a consequence of the more competitive employment market. Several organisations are proposing improvements, and I think Roy will look at what BECTU is trying to do in terms of more predictable working hours, not only for women but for everybody working in the industry. The group, *Women in Television* has also looked at the notion of the long-hours culture and is making suggestions such as giving a kind of kite mark to companies which adopt family-friendly policies. The campaign, *Opportunity 2000*, which aims to improve women's employment opportunities asserts that British business is not taking full advantage of the economic potential of women in the workforce and is arguing that women-friendly initiatives could be advantageous to the employer as well as the employees. I think in the end that it's the economic argument more than any other that's going to prove must attractive to the employers and to bring about the change in British television which will encourage more working mothers to remain active within the industry. Thank you.

Caroline Millington: Our next speaker is Scott Hammond, from Brigham Young University in the States and he's addressing a particular group of workers. Judith just took 52 per cent of the potential workforce – the women; Scott is going to talk about newsrooms and the changing demands of the industry and changing working practices. Newsrooms in the UK at least tend to be very male-dominated.

Scott Hammond (Brigham Young University, Utah): Thank you. We looked at individual identity in the newsrooms and we looked at several professional newsrooms as well as at our students, who have an emerging identity in an integrated newsroom. We define an identity in a conceptual way by looking at it as symbolic of value of the self or the semiotic of the self. I'm just going to be very brief here but we looked at seven different issues that seem to emerge in our interviews. These were areas where worker identity is changing in a new technology environment. We looked at tools and technologies, how people identify around tools and technologies. For example, in a traditional newspaper newsroom in the United States you may not see a typewriter in use but you'll see typewriters around the newsroom on display, on people's desks, as if they are an artefact or a symbol of their profession. We looked at those kind of things. We looked at the message that people are dealing with, I'll say more about that in a few minutes, we looked at the conception of audience, space and time, style of representation, the timeliness issue and then also work style. Let me say just really briefly what we found – the sort of before and after kind of things.

On tools and technologies: with print and broadcast journalists there was a strong identification around either the printing press, the typewriter or the technology of video tape. Some people we interviewed had artefacts around their desks that were old technologies that they liked to use to identify themselves. The new identities seem to be emerging around information and not around a particular symbol or tool but around information of some kind – around a message. The old identities seem to be focused on a delivery system or the medium – 'I am a newspaper person, I am a radio person, I am a television person.' The new identity seems to be moving towards a content identity – 'I am a political reporter, I am an environmental reporter.'

The old identity around the audience seems to be a mass media, broadcast notion; the new identity seems to be more specific, target-focused – 'I work for a specific audience and I have a sense of who that audience is.' In the United States there seems to be a movement towards a less geographically defined audience and a more topic-focused audience. It is not focused necessarily on: 'I work in this particular market or this community,' but rather, 'I serve a young audience, an MTV audience or a senior audience.' It seems to be more focused on that.

In terms of air time it used to be that people would identify themselves around their column or where they printed things or what newscasts they appeared upon. Now it seems to be, with the abundance of ways to communicate with your audience, moving away from where the actual communication takes place. In terms of style of representation it seems to be moving away from a textual notion to a more visual notion. That doesn't mean that text is not important it is just that the identification prior to this seemed to be text with some visual but now it seems to be visual with some text.

The last two points – timeliness; we talked a little bit about this yesterday in our presentation. There is a movement towards accuracy over time. In the new media environment timeliness – deadlines – seems to be the overall identity. So 'move quickly' is where people are identifying.

Finally, the last point, in the new media environment we are seeing a movement away from individual work, the individual by-line, to the team. Thank you.

Caroline Millington: Wonderful, thank you very much for that synthesis, I think there are a lot of things in common with what's going on here. I'm terribly grateful to the speakers for actually synthesising well-thought through, well-researched, lengthy papers and to a nice tight deadline. Peter Lewis I know will do it equally tightly. Peter is a Lecturer in Media and Cultural Studies at Middlesex University who has worked in broadcasting in a variety of roles over the years. Peter.

Peter Lewis: *(first few sentences were unrecorded but referred to the training and education of media students and the mismatch of expectations)* ... Well, the four groups whose expectations don't fit are students, people like myself who teach the students, our bosses – the academic administrators – and the media industry. A lot of this came out in the Skillset survey of media studies which I only read coming up on the train and I find that I am very much in agreement with the research. I feel this talk is supported by that research.

First then, let's take these four groups in turn – us, the lecturers; the ivory tower attitude about universities may have gone but there's a vocational/non-vocational distinction that remains and ought to be challenged. Just a bare majority of media studies courses was found in the Skillset survey to be non-vocational and around 48 per cent or something of those surveyed were vocational. Of the half that aren't vocational, I would say the justification is that the media are studied because they are a significant part of modern life.

Now if you take students, the competition in Britain for jobs means that students inevitably regard their course choices in a vocational light. That's been happening for ten years, or more, fifteen years. Media studies courses are popular and students are attracted to them partly because they perceive that social significance I mentioned and partly (whatever disclaimers are made by academic planners and the administrators) because the students think that taking media studies will help them find a job in the media.

The third group are the managers, academic administrators, who are sweating at the moment in Britain. They are in a bad state with very tight budgets, they are constrained within these budgets and meeting intake targets for specific courses is absolutely crucial and is directly related to the funding of universities. If you fail to meet the target you are penalised, so academic administrators are looking to media studies, offered in conjunction with the less popular courses that are under-recruiting, to make up the shortfalls in their targets. It is called a *honey pot* factor in the jargon of the trade.

The fourth group, the media industry, and this came out in the Skillset survey, are understandably concerned about standards of practical courses and they're burdened by demands generated by those courses for work placements and job applications of a speculative kind – general letters and CVs. The industry of old is deeply suspicious of theory courses, but what is the media industry now? Again another Skillset research study from 1994 shows that it's experiencing huge change in technology and staffing. Despite the growth in channels (already occurring) the future for most students is likely to be freelance, which actually means combining application pitches for jobs with some other form of employment altogether, or perhaps being unemployed.

So what should we be doing in the universities? Perhaps at this point I'd better just say where I'm coming from, what I'm actually doing. I've had experience in university media teaching which includes a strong practical element. In my case, I teach radio theory and practice. Currently at Middlesex, I'm in a Department called Media and Cultural Studies, so we regard media as part of culture generally, cultural consumption, cultural practice and issues like fashion and style, cultural identity, gender, race and so on, are all part of what we teach. I'm interested in putting radio on the theoretical agenda of cultural studies and media studies because in Britain it is seriously neglected. I teach courses about the economic aspect of the media and culture, media practices and structures, courses on documentary and non-fictional representation. I get in as many of my old friends from broadcasting or new acquaintances as I can as visiting lecturers plus I try to give a taste of practice, practice that is sufficient to give people the experience of issues like ethical decisions in editing and also editorial choice generally.

So I suggest that there are four things that people in my position ought to be doing. I stress that this is the proportion of the media studies sector which is not claiming to be vocational (if we hang on to that distinction at all). First we should help our students to understand the media landscape, programme genre, industry structure, global trends. Second, teach practical media skills only so far as they throw light on those issues and not to achieve some notional industry standard. By definition, we're hardly teaching practice at all but I think people ought to be given a taste of it. I think radio is very good for that. It is very quick to achieve a standard in which you can make editorial decisions. Third, we should help students market their skills and market themselves and their ideas; how to pitch their ideas, tell them how difficult it is to pitch and what the criteria are for accepting pitches. I think somebody said something like 40,000 to 60,000 documentary pitches are received by broadcasters a year across the four terrestrial channels. Fourth, work placements and co-operative ventures with those sectors that encourage volunteers – charities and public sector organisations. I try to deter my students from trying to go straight to licensed broadcasters, because they receive so many applications. There is a lot of hospital radio, there are short temporary licences we called RSLs in radio, and we hear there will be perhaps some for television, there are community channels and programming on cable, there is good community radio of a kind. There are possibilities in mainstream broadcasting provided you find a situation where the student isn't exploited.

I just want to say finally a word about community radio in Britain since I'm the author of a report for Europe on community radio called *A Gateway to Employment*. Some 2000 people are working, mostly unpaid, in community radio in this country, that's about a fifth of all radio personnel if you go by the Skillset figures from two or three years back. They work in one or two stations – I think there are less community radio stations than are claimed by the commercial sector – they work in many projects that are often funded through training schemes designed to combat unemployment among young people so that's non-broadcast, and they work in these temporary licences. We, in academia, ought to be making more connection with community radio and hospital radio and those other sectors, in order to get our students work experience of a kind that may help them go through. The research I did showed that community radio is actually providing more training than some of the more formal broadcasters, particularly given the way the BBC is being split up and training is being privatised. Commercial radio and broadcasting generally doesn't often offer training. So this sector, which has hardly begun in this country compared to other community stations in Europe, is where we should be helping our students. That's it!

Caroline Millington: Thank you Peter.

We now have a series of speakers from the platform and the first speaker has some overheads. Nick Pettigrew, British Film Institute, has the enviable task of running a five year project with some 500 people who actually work in the television industry to see how their lives are developing and, indeed, changing. His first lot of research came out last year and he's going to do a general overview of that, and he's also got some fresh stuff to share with us.

Nick Pettigrew: The British Film Institute began its longitudinal Television Industry Tracking Study in 1994 to ask questions about how changing conditions in the television industry affect individuals working in creative production jobs. As an independent organisation seeking to sustain the quality and range of production, the BFI wanted to provide useful information about the impact on individual television careers of structural, organisational and technological changes in recent years.

Respondents agreed to write a work diary and complete a questionnaire twice a year and have been guaranteed complete confidentiality. An introductory questionnaire was sent in May 1994, to obtain detailed information about education, career history, training, current job, and work values. The second wave work diary/questionnaire was sent in November 1994 and so forth at six monthly intervals until the most recent in November 1996, therefore comprising two and a half years worth of material.

Each work diary requires the respondent to write a discursive account of a nominated working day and to answer supplementary structured questions, some of which are repeated either every six months or yearly.

I am first going to describe some of the characteristics of the panel, and then go on to discuss a few of the changes that have been measured so far. Finally I am going to examine three important areas we have been looking at in the last few waves of the diary: work experience, stress in television, and working on low budget programmes.

The Panel: A sample of 532 was generated from lists supplied by broadcasters, the register of PACT, and BFI contacts. The respondents come from all sectors of the industry, from London and all regions. They are in creative production grades at each point of the production cycle: ranging from researchers and production assistants to producers and directors, and including new entrants as well as experienced executive producers.

The majority of people in the panel (62 per cent) are concentrated in the 31–40 year old and the 41–50 year old ageband. 62 per cent of the sample live in London and the South East, and 44 per cent of the sample are female, with 56 per cent male.

When examined by gender, 34 per cent of men have no children compared with 71 per cent of women. The large percentage of women with no children was attributed to the fact that the majority of women in the sample are younger. On further analysis it was found that this was not the case as 53 per cent of the over 40 year old women do not have children as opposed to 15 per cent of the men. One female freelance producer wrote: 'The same pay for twice as much work. Anti-social hours, no maternity pay or leave, or nurseries. It is becoming a young man's industry again.'

Around three quarters of the sample has had some kind of higher education. The younger the person the more likely he/she is to have received higher education, as 88 per cent of the 21–30 year olds have done so.

Just under a quarter of the 21–30 ageband who received higher education studied either media studies or a related subject. Some of the panel considered that media studies placed them at an advantage as it gave them a grounding in the basics of the business. However others felt it sometimes put them at a disadvantage, as with this young researcher: 'A producer said I was the first person she had seen who had come off one of the courses that could do the job, and she said from bad experiences in the past, if she was looking at someone's CV and they had done a media studies degree that would put her off, because a lot of producers have the idea that people come up thinking they know it all, and really they know nothing about the real business of it.'

Changes in Employment Conditions: Over the study several questions have been repeated to try and measure any changes in employment conditions of the sample. Every wave the panel are asked what methods they have used to obtain work in the past six months, and so far personal contacts have always been the most important method. In the most recent diary exactly half of the sample used personal contacts to obtain work. As one freelance director wrote, 'it's the way the whole industry seems to work.' Another researcher stated, 'Researchers get jobs because of who they know, being in the right place at the right time, and being pushy. These are the major skills required.'

Each diary wave we have asked about the employment status of the panel, and the proportion of freelances has risen very slightly every wave, with the exception of the last wave which showed a fall. A more definite picture will emerge at the end of the study but it may be that the proportions of those in freelance roles is levelling off.

When the first wave questionnaire was sent out it was found that just under a quarter of the 21–30 year olds earned less than £10,000 a year. One script editor noted: 'The company was paying £225 a week which if you are living in London and paying rent is very difficult to sustain, which is why most people who seem to thrive in the TV industry in London are people like me who don't have to pay rent because they are still living in accommodation owned by their parents.'

However we also asked about income in the fifth wave diary and the proportion of 21–30 year olds earning less than £10,000 a year had dropped from just under a quarter to 11 per cent. In fact a third now earn between £20,000 and £30,000 a year. One researcher stated that 'It depends what position you are holding. Ultimately by the time you are 30 then it essentially is a well paid job. If you were working in an ordinary office you wouldn't get as well paid. But you would get far more security and get far more pensions.'

In each diary wave several different topics are examined and I will describe three areas we have looked at – work experience, stress in television, and working on low budget programmes.

Work Experience: One of the aims of the project is to examine how people enter the television industry, and how young people are often offered work experience, usually unpaid or for travel expenses. From evidence in the study, work experience is a relatively new development, as just over half of the 21-30 year olds have done some kind of work experience, in comparison with none of the over-fifty year olds. The duration of work experience varied from a few days to several months and a couple of diarists reported being in a work experience post for a year. Most of those who did work experience were recruited on an informal basis and examples were found in different departments of the broadcasters as well as in independent companies. Some companies operated formal schemes whereas others offered work experience on a day-to-day basis.

Many of the young diarists felt that work experience was the only route into the industry as it added experience of working in television to their CV. As one freelance producer wrote in his diary: 'work experience is very useful in order to break the vicious circle of no work, no experience, no experience, no work'. In addition some respondents did more than one spell of work experience, as one young associate producer remarked: 'I would never have got my first job without several long six month placements on my CV. All employers and producers look for experience on the *right programmes.*'

Personal contacts are extremely important for getting work in the television industry but these contacts have to be made in the first place, and many of the panel thought that this was one of the main advantages of work experience: 'They're always useful for people to make contacts with those working in the industry. One contact can often lead to another.'

One of the main comments that emerged from the diaries was that work experience was useful to allow young people to see exactly what the world of TV is like. An assistant producer wrote: 'It's a way of weeding out those who are serious about what they want to do, and those who are doing it because they think it's going to be a fun career. The job being hard is something which stays with you for the rest of your career.'

The major issue facing work experience posts was the extent to which they were perceived as exploitative and replacing real jobs. In addition, it was argued that only a certain kind of person is available to do work experience, i.e. those with affluent parents or money behind them. One freelance director's comments mirrored those of many in the sample: 'If this is an important route into work in television, there is also a danger that the profession will become elitist, since only those people whose parents can afford to support them can take advantage of such schemes.'

The worst case found was from someone who knew of a company charging young people £100 a week for the privilege of working there. Similarly, other respondents talked about the absolute scandal of abuses of work experience, especially if people were budgeted for in proposals and then not paid anything. This caused disquiet among some of the sample: 'they appear to be cheap labour, filling in gaps in a depleted office.'

Stress: During previous diaries many of the panel mentioned that stress was a problem at work. However for many people in this kind of work some levels of stress are an important spur to creativity and innovation. In the fourth wave diary the panel were asked a series of questions on stress to try and establish whether this was a significant or growing problem for production staff. Forty-one per cent of the sample said their stress levels had increased in the last six months.

The three most stressful aspects of work for the panel were time, working hours, and uncertainty, and many comments relating to these areas were received. The largest group of comments referred to lack of time as one broadcaster staff editor summed up: 'Time or lack of it is probably the most stressful feature of our work. We are expected to work to very high standards in the minimal amount of time for what appears to be less money; often compromising overall standards and sometimes leading to cynicism: Oh, that'll do, we're running out of time.'

The stress caused by time was partly related to the stress of long working hours, and the following comment from a freelance director mirrored many of those in the sample when it mentioned the effect on home life: 'It is not good for relationships with people. My boyfriend, who also works in television works ten-to-ten every day and there was a month when we didn't see each other, which doesn't help your relationship on a day-to-day basis. That's when I think working in TV stinks.'

Many of the panel made comments about stress being caused by uncertainty especially amongst the freelances and independent owners, as one freelance presenter summed up: 'The general uncertainty surrounding job security is the main problem. Stress is largely down to the inability to project into the future.' Some of the independent owners mentioned uncertainty in the commissions process and the need to keep the company afloat.

Several in the panel made comments on the stress caused by not having any back up or support. As one freelance assistant producer noted: 'Very stressful period being left to research and film a programme totally on my own with a Hi8 camera, involving many late nights, long hours and heavy equipment. No support in terms of advice or additional manpower given. Too much for one person. Very cheap for them!'

Low Budget Programmes: In the sixth wave diary the sample were asked if they thought low budget programmes would be an important part of their work in the next two years and just over half thought they would be. Twenty-seven per cent of the panel stated they had actually worked on a low budget programme and went on to comment on some of the most significant effects of a low budget. Many wrote about the time pressures of low budget programmes such as this freelance production assistant: 'There's not enough time for really satisfactory research, and an inappropriate sense of rush during filming.' Several of the sample said that working on low budget programmes had increased their stress levels and left them with sense of dissatisfaction.

Another effect of low budget programmes was that the size of the crew had to be very small, be capable of multiskilling, and have no back-up. Several of the panel noted that in order to make low budget programmes, favours had to be called in and the cheapest rates possible for equipment had to be obtained. In addition, some of the panel lowered rates for their own work such as this independent owner: 'I spent a lot of time working for nothing e.g. driving at night after long days on location to save hotel bills. Reshoots using own gear and not charging, etc.' However some of the panel felt low budgets led to inventive uses of resources and led to new ways of working and thinking.

The panel were then asked what they thought were the essential skills for working on a low budget programme. Many of the older members of the panel talked of needing lots of experience to be able to work quickly and solve any problems that might arise. However a couple of the younger members of the panel thought otherwise: 'Inexperience. If you're a researcher you may be tempted to work as a producer on a low budget show. It's a better credit and the money is about the same!'

Several of the panel considered that being multi-skilled was essential to work on low budget programmes. Other important skills were the ability to preplan the shoot thoroughly to begin with and to keep the format simple. Some of the panel felt that clear thinking, working well in a team, patience and flexibility were important. An ability to work at speed was also considered important.

The panel were asked if they felt there were creative possibilities in low budget work. Several members of the panel commented that low budget programmes led to a reduction in risk and experiment. One head of department wrote, 'limited as there's not time or money to do something again, if an idea doesn't work out. So tend to play safe.' However others disagreed, and one producer went as far as to say the 'opportunity for risk taking with ideas greatest for low budget TV.'

Many of the sample talked about low budget programmes being a training ground for young people in television, and this is borne out by the fact that 41 per cent of the 21–30 year olds have worked on low budget programmes in comparison with 16 per cent of 31–40 year olds. One independent owner wrote that 'It's very useful to a company plan because it enables you to train younger producers.'

Some of the panel discussed the impact of new technology, especially the new digital cameras, on programmes. One assistant producer wrote that 'Small no crew DVC filming offer endless possibilities for documentaries which seek to follow complex stories long term and gain real intimacy with their subjects'.

Conclusions: This paper has focused on some of the data collected from five waves of the diaries and highlights some of the issues raised by the tracking study. An ESRC research grant will enable three more diary waves, and data will be analysed in terms of the relationship between changes in the industry, their impact on career patterns and the varying potentials for creative endeavour in television.

Finally, a comment from the diary of one of the freelance producers in the panel: 'I often feel like giving it up as it's so stressful and all encompassing. Wish I had more time to develop other aspects of my personality. But other times I feel honoured to be doing such a brilliant job.'

Caroline Millington: Very interesting, we are building up a picture of an industry that large numbers of people want to work in and, one way or another, then find it's either difficult or insupportable. Once they get there they find it pretty tricky but, on the other hand, it is quite enjoyable. So I thought we'd go to worker – Ana. Ana at lunchtime was confessing that she actually enjoys the media – sometimes. Can you give us your perspective? Thank you.

Ana Kronschnabl: (MA. student, University College, Warrington and freelance film maker): The question of how young practitioners view a career in broadcasting in the next decade is an important one and has to be answered, frankly, not very optimistically. Maybe I should begin by summarising my career up to this point. I grew up in Cambridge but went to college at Bulmersche in Reading to study Film, Drama and Art. After leaving college I returned to Cambridge and set up a video production company with some colleagues. After a few years I moved on to teach A level film studies and worked as an independent producer. After moving to West Wales and running my parents' pub and restaurant for a year I took on the administration of a film workshop in Cardiff. Deciding that my heart really lay in production I worked for a while at the BBC in Wales then applied to do the MA in TV Production at Warrington.

I decided to make this move because, even though it meant a slight shift in career paths and weighing myself down with the National Debt, I love film-making. Having made this move I felt very positive. Despite having some experience in production I felt that the additional qualification and the opportunity to work on broadcast productions would be extremely beneficial. As well as the practical skills I have acquired I have also become more aware of the rapidly changing global communications systems of which television is only a small part. Media corporations have moved very quickly over the past few years into the marketplace. This creates an environment in which all programmes have to compete for a share of the viewing figures on an equal basis, never mind intention or target audience.

I believe that most young people decide to opt for a career in television because they have ideas that they want to communicate with the world. They see television as one of the most powerful communication tools of this century. Being young and enthusiastic often means that you want to change what has gone before, experiment with traditional ways of doing things, push boundaries. Whilst some television still has these beliefs it is increasingly concerned with producing what it feels the 'consumer' wants. If television programming is allowed to be viewed purely as a commodity, or an export, it seems unlikely broadcasting executives will want their investment to promote controversy or experimentation. The current preoccupation of magazine type programmes based round the Loaded theme seems old-fashioned and safe, targeting an easily exploitable market, young 'fun-loving' men and women who are looking for something to reflect their lives and preoccupations. Whilst it is fundamental to television that it is entertaining, the form can not be allowed to dominate so that the content becomes subverted until it is purely formularised.

Having said all this, there is, I believe, more potential now than ever before. As the most influential medium of this century the possibilities are enormous. Yet, with the advent of cable we were given the chance to shift the emphasis away from mass entertainment to more community based programming but this didn't happen. Again, with digital television, the expansion of more satellite companies, etc., we are being given the opportunity to produce programmes that have aims other than that of making money, and reproducing tried and tested formulas.

Some sources suggest that audience viewing figures have dropped this year for the first time. It isn't enough to say that is because all potential consumers have been reached. We are being faced with another incredible technological advancement – the Internet. Individuals are being offered real, interactive communication on their own terms with (at the moment) boundaries set only by their own imagination and skill. The potential threat of this to more traditional forms of entertainment can only be imagined. If television is to survive as anything other than a large advert, programme-makers need to rethink their attitude towards their audience.

The way to foster new talent is to give it a chance. There need to be more slots on TV for programmes produced by smaller independent companies and enthusiastic people with ideas who want to make something a bit different. Instead many young creative people become disillusioned. Either because they simply can't get a job or the only jobs on offer are for subsistence wages, or because they want to produce something different and realise that there is no space for this within current programming.

I'm sure that my views must seem idealistic but they are essential to the hopes and ambitions of many young practitioners. The potential of television as we move into the new millennium is immense. We need to be given support in terms of money and space. I don't believe there will be any trouble with young people wanting to innovate and take risks but there has to be an industry out there that is interested in showing these programmes once they are produced and, equally as important, backing them financially from the ideas stage. It is not good enough to take someone's bright idea and use in-house production teams to make it. The end result will be a programme that lacks the understanding and creativity of the original idea. More faith has to be put in new, adventurous, enthusiastic people who may end up producing some pretty kooky programmes. But if their talent is allowed to be honed and grow in these ways we will produce a generation of excellent, thoughtful and creative programme-makers who can draw in an audience and compete with any innovative technology because the magic of television doesn't have to be lost! Thank you.

Caroline Millington: Thank very much Ana. Audrey Hall, who is our next speaker, has worked in both television and radio, and possibly opted for the more sensible medium of radio to get what she wants to achieve. In radio there are a lot more innovative people.

Audrey Hall (freelancer in television and radio): Thank you very much. Good Afternoon. When I met Caroline I asked her, in the introduction, to tell you that I was married with a daughter, and that my daughter is nine and three-quarters years old. The point of that is because, if you have children, you will know that age is always very important to them, they are always dying to be grown up. Age is equally as important to working mothers because, whilst we want our children to remain children, when you're working you are also looking towards them being big enough, or grown up enough, to take themselves to school, bring themselves home and hopefully look after themselves until you can get home from work. The point of saying that is that we are always aware that our 'working potential' can be hampered by the very fact that we have decided to have children.

This afternoon I'm going to restrict my comments mainly to Judith's paper, and the first thing I want to say was that it was almost like *This Is Your Life*. How did you know? It was like reading an autobiography. The first thing you talked about was when you referred to the male culture and you said it has bred environments where the general expectation is of one 100 per cent commitment to the job. All I'd say to that is, only 100 per cent? And, by the way, I've found that it's not only males who insist on this commitment, it's females too. It's anybody who basically has the power of employing you.

I'll just share something with you. My first job in television was as a researcher for *This Morning* which is one of the ITV network flagship programmes. I remember the bizarre situation when, after working there for a year, it was appraisal time. I went to the appraisal and I was told they were delighted with my work, they were delighted with my performance, they were pleased at the way I had been able to communicate and get on well with the presenters and the experts and the members of the public and so on. They were so pleased that they were going to reward me by giving me a rise in pay and also moving me into a department which we just referred to as 'strands'. Basically, this is making almost like a mini-series for the programme. It's great, you are not in on the days, and you take your time, and you do in-depth research. It's fabulous, and it really is considered as the crème de la crème of daytime television. But in that same meeting I was also told that they weren't going to extend my contract for another series because I'd made it be known that I actually wanted to work in Manchester. *This Morning* at this time was actually done out at Liverpool at the Albert Dock, and I'd made it be known that I wanted to work in Manchester to be closer to home, and also I wanted to concentrate more on current affairs. Now, the fact that I made this known, even though we were always encouraged to let people know what we wanted to do because Granada is such a big company and you're supposed to have the opportunity to move round, that was translated as less commitment than was needed for a job. I had obviously taken all that very naively as 'the truth'. In fact, I was told that I needed to live and breathe the job and the fact that I wanted to have a home life meant that my commitment was lacking. Also, at my stint over in Liverpool, we used have monthly meetings and they were kind of 'feel good' meetings where our bosses would talk to us about, you know, the programmes, and the progress that had been made and whatever. It was a kind of a very casual affair, a get-to-know-each-other affair, and these meetings would take place after work so they generally would start at seven o'clock, seven thirty and they'd go on for about an hour. When they were finished this whole idea of bonhomie carried through and people were invited to go to the pub for a drink, and I always used to say, 'No, thank you very much,' (always telling the truth) 'No, I don't want to come.' And they would say, 'Why not?' and I would say, 'No, because I want to go home.' (I had an hour's drive to get home as well.) This too was seen as less than 100 per cent commitment, the fact that I didn't particularly want to fraternise with people out of working hours. Now that was nothing against the people I was working with, they were all great, but I had a daughter, I had a husband, I had a home, and I wanted to go home. Not least for the fact that I had to get up in the morning and drive back to Liverpool the day after.

The reason I have picked up on this point is that I've always found that the working environment demands 200 per cent commitment and, more importantly, it's something that's taken for granted and never questioned or challenged. There is an old idiom that says that, as a woman, you work twice as hard as your male counterpart but I'd go even further and say that, as a working mother, you can multiply that again because you have to prove your capability and reliability in spite of what's going on at home. But, at the end of the day, I do also appreciate that the only thing that matters to the people who are making programmes, the people who are responsible for these programmes, is that the job is done, no matter how long it takes, no matter that your child care arrangements have fallen down, no matter if your child is sick. You've got a deadline, the programme has to get out and that's it and the fact that you're constantly doing 'over and above' to meet these deadlines somehow pales into insignificance.

The next point I'd like to pick up on, if I may, is Judith's comment that the long hours culture would seem to be damaging to both the family life and health and productive capacity of the employee. You know, once again, *This Is My Life*. I, as Caroline said, work in radio and television and have done so for nearly seven years now. Basically the way this worked was: I would work all day in television and then come home at night and eat my meal and then start to prepare the programmes for radio as well. When I took my first break at the end of last year when the family decided to go on holiday, I actually fell ill. When I stopped work it was almost as if my body said: 'Oh so you think you are going to have a holiday now, well no you don't!' All year I'd been drawing on whatever inner reserves I had and I spent most of the holiday in bed. That naturally had a knock-on effect, not just for me but for the family too and it was then that I sat down and reassessed what I had been doing, and of course it's great to have all of this work and earn a decent wage but the question has to be 'at what price?' I'd not only been jeopardising my health but also compromising family life as well, and what I needed to do was put my working life in perspective, which is what I've done. I've cut back on the television work. Nick talked before about the way that television is going; cable and satellite television, the five man crew which used to be the norm, down to the three man crew, down to the one man crew, the use of Hi8 cameras, one person going along and acting as producer, director, cameraman, researcher, and everything else. I didn't particularly like what I was seeing, quality in some cases has suffered, so I have decided to concentrate my efforts on radio which I love and also, importantly, there I'm in control of what I am doing.

Caroline Millington: Thank you very much indeed. You can see why broadcasters in conversation often fall to talking about 'the real world', as if they're not part of it, which only too often is the case.

Next, Dinah Caine: Dinah is Chief Executive of *Skillset*, a remarkable organisation which describes itself as the Industry Training Organisation for Broadcast, Film and Video. Dinah what is your conclusion on what you have heard so far?

Dinah Caine (Skillset): Well, many things and I am sure that we will be following them up in discussion with the audience following the presentations. If I may, I would like to concentrate on one aspect of the structural changes in the industry and the way that is having an impact on training and skill levels and what workers are experiencing or not experiencing vis a vis access to training. Incidentally, the Symposium programme speaks of Skillset and Channel Four and I would just like to make clear to you that Skillset is actually managed and funded by all the key employers and unions in the industry, we are a cross-industry body.

I'm going to focus on a couple of the surveys that we've been involved with and draw some conclusions. The main one is our freelance survey and just one statistic in relation to the women's issue is that 70 per cent of the women currently working as freelances are under forty, which begs a lot of questions.

In relation to skills and training it's true to say that the skilled workforce of today was, by and large, trained yesterday and that there is currently an above average alliance on a middle-aged workforce. Those starting work at the moment tend to be freelances or they work for independent production companies, where their skills are being developed in a much more haphazard way and, as we've already heard from Nick and others, they are being paid, or not paid, in a much more haphazard way. Even for those who are working or starting work as free-lance for broadcasting companies, it's demonstrable that they are receiving far less training then if they had entered the industry ten years ago. There's no set training period on the whole, few people are entering the industry and experiencing on-the-job development in a systematic and supervised way other than through a handful of industry-based training schemes. Freelances already within the industry are often expected to come to the job, to the engagement, with skills. Career development opportunities therefore have become much more problematic, particularly in a culture where, reportedly, commissioners are cutting budgets and where they are also starting to input directly into employment decisions on behalf of independent production companies, they are demanding proven and known skills. All of which is interesting in relation to the whole debate about the independence of the independent companies. What does one conclude from this for the existing freelances who also need access to retraining and skill-updating courses and have difficulties finding these courses and being able to pay for them? What it means is that the industry has a central challenge in relation to business planning. According to all of our research, and the soundings we take across the industry from employers and the unions, skill levels are continuing to drop and the workforce is getting older. As a consequence, and going back to the economic arguments, there is a danger now that labour costs will start to rise disproportionately for those with the proven and known skills for high budget, more specialised programmes. Freelances – and 60 per cent of the workforce are now freelance – can ultimately pick and choose who they work for and how, and that's particularly relevant at points where production levels are up. Judith's paper mentioned the issue of women with skills starting to be able to pick and choose and barter not necessarily on pay levels but on working conditions between the different employers. We'll see whether that develops. Those with less developed skills are a gamble for employers and they are less advantaged in the labour market. So, in Skillset's view, and indeed that's why we were set up, the industry demonstrably needs to invest in retraining, skill-updating courses for existing freelances and unstructured new entrance training and career development initiatives and ensure – going back to what Peter was saying – that actually there are closer and well understood links with key courses operating within higher education. I think if those issues aren't attended to, then certainly the workers will suffer in patches and certainly the industry and its cultural and competitive edge will suffer.

Just as a final point, and this is of interest and links into what Nick was saying about a shift in terms of the numbers who are freelancing. We are also now discerning a pattern of moving back from that very casual way of working. Some of the larger companies and broadcasters are starting to look at appointing freelances on longer term contracts or on first-call arrangements with an annual retainer, and some are genuinely beginning to question whether long term employment for individuals is a more sensible and economical way for them to move forward into the next millennium and into digitalisation. Thank you.

Caroline Millington: You're being very patient indeed, but in two speakers' time I expect you all to explode with statements, queries, provocative intellectual thoughts, as I'm sure you will.

Gill Ursell is Principal Lecturer in ...

Gill Ursell: Well, my other existence is as a single working mother who some-how managed to hold down a job for about twenty years ...

Caroline Millington: And is also Principal Lecturer in Media and Course Director of Journalism Training Schemes at Trinity and All Saints University College Leeds.

Gill Ursell: I have been researching television employment for the last five years in the wake of the 1990 Act, but of necessity referring back to 1986, and one of the things I wanted to touch on before I actually get into some of my data, because some of it has already been confirmed and been told by other people, is something I hope will make you laugh.

There is the problem of job insecurity in the free-lance field, but if you have the advantage of tenured employment, that does not mean you escape all the problems. You might well find yourself facing a performance appraisal, so I thought you might like to see this, which was passed around the BBC in 1994 as the workers' version of performance appraisal.

Caroline Millington: Pick out some of the points....

Gill Ursell: *Performance factors far exceed job requirement*, you score A, but you only get E if you *don't meet any of the requirements*. Adaptability, if you *can walk on water constantly*, you score an A. If you *pass water in emergencies* you only score an E. *Timeliness is faster than a speeding bullet*, A. But if you *wound yourself in the foot* then you score an E.

So, one way of dealing with stress is humour, and maybe there'll be more grounds for it. I should say I didn't replicate it, but there was a version of the organisational chart also in the BBC at the time which had the typical pyramid, and at the top were the blameless, underneath were the scapegoats and then the final level were suckers. I thought that was rather nice. Anyway, as I say, I've been looking at employment from 1986 and of course, at that time in history you're looking at the duopoly of producer broadcasters, the BBC on the one hand and ITV on the other, and if you look at the job losses from those two areas of broadcasting, what you find is roughly – and the figures are arguable because the basis on which they have been measured has varied across time and between companies – but roughly 44 per cent job losses from those producer broadcasters of BBC and ITV, a very very substantial loss indeed. But it's not a loss which has been borne equally by all sectors of occupation in broadcasting. If you take the 1986 submission by the BBC to the Peacock Committee, the BBC defined its labour markets as essentially threefold. 60 per cent of its workers were not television specific people they were clerical, secretarial, administrative, housekeepers, cleaners, porters, this sort of thing who, in a sense, could be made redundant without necessarily facing themselves terrible job losses, they could turn to other employers quite readily. But that still left you with 40 per cent of people whose work was television specific and those 40 per cent divide equally: 20 per cent into crews, set crafts, production, technical, post production, those kind of workers, and the other 20 per cent being the production teams, that means writers, directors, producers, researchers, location managers, journalists to some extent, those kind of people identified as being on the creative side, and of course, the stars, the personalities. And if you're talking about different labour forces in broadcasting you are also talking about different labour markets from which you draw those workers. The 60 per cent of non-television specific, you can talk about as being a very broad and generous national labour market, so the employers have no problems whatsoever in drawing on those kinds of people. The 20 per cent of talent and production people increasingly are now drawn on an international basis, because increasingly media productions are gearing up for international production and/or international marketing, and this is having an influence on the kinds of workers who come forward to do that kind of work. But the more problematic area is the 20 per cent who make up the production crews, the set crafts, the technical people, and it is these whom Dinah has already addressed as being the ones where you find ageing, where you find the diminution of skills, where you find a real issue of prospective job shortages, labour shortages in the next period. Some people would respond, 'Well, no, hang on a minute, new technology means that we do not need these older skills for television production anymore.' But I would advise against that view. There are a number of things developing from the mid '90's onwards which indicate that the demand for labour, and this will be good news to the unions and those who want to organise collectively in the industry to improve aspects of the quality of working life. There are signs that demands for labour will rise, and it's not merely the emergence of the cable operators and satellites as consumers of programmes, there are other things. In the United States we have have already seen to quite a substantial extent a convergence of film industry production with television industry production, and because of the increasing relatedness of the American film structures and broadcast structures with the British film and broadcast structures, we are now beginning just to see the start of that convergence over here of workers, production workers in broadcasting being also production workers in film, and with the proliferation of output media, video or other forms of on-line transmission etc., I think you have to anticipate that that will mean lots more jobs in the future. But it isn't just lots more jobs for digital technology and digital-originated material, it is lots more jobs too for people that can work in the old technologies, the film formats, because there is still a demand, if anything a growing demand, for film format material.

Dinah touched on the fact that some of the companies are in broadcasting moving away from freelancing, and that is certainly my experience from my research. The one company that I focused on in particular peaked about three years ago at a staff contract, a staff freelance ratio of 60 per cent staff 40 per cent freelance, and they've moved back from that so they are now 70 per cent staff, 30 per cent free-lance, and that does seem to be happening in other parts of the country. I should add that it might be a particular regional feature. I said that the different occupational bands are being drawn from different labour markets. You can talk broad national for one set, you can talk international for another set, but if you are talking technical staff craft skills then you're in a sense talking about a much more narrow national or even regional labour market, and the companies faced with that situation are going to have to negotiate better terms and conditions and we are beginning to see that happening, and I hope Roy's going to tell us more about it, and I think I would like to leave it at that point. I came prepared to talk for two hours but I'm obviously not going to.

Caroline Millington: Thank you Gill – particularly for that! That's what we call an effortless segue into our final formal speaker, Roy Lockett, who is the Deputy General Secretary of the industry union BECTU. Roy, you're clearly the answer to the workers.

Roy Lockett: Yes, the answer to the workers' prayer, that's me. You can trust me, I'm a full-time official!

Well, I've re-written my speech about eight times sitting here. It's quite problematic. Let's just say that it seems to me that the structural changes have been very broadly identified by lots of speakers here, they've been institutional, they've been technological, they've been legislative, they've been cultural in terms of what television was, and what television and broadcasting is now. I don't intend to rehearse all of those arguments. For us, the major impact of that inside the workforce is the shift to freelancing, the fact is that more than 60 per cent of the workforce is now freelance; and the evidence we have is that that's increasing. The BBC is still sacking permanent staff, it's still hiving off major departments. The design department has just gone from the BBC, a treasure house of talent simply gone, disappeared, and that's continuing. So, if there is a trend away from that, it's not happening in West London.

Clearly, the industry is now about the bottom line. It's about costs. We live in an industry where production is budget-led, where you go to a producer or independent commissioner and he or she says 'There's twenty thousand pounds an hour for this programme,' and that's it, you either make it or you don't, you can't come back and say 'Well, that's not enough money,' or, 'I want thirty thousand,' or, 'That doesn't allow me a lot on our schedule,' or, 'I can't have a big enough crew.' You simply can't say that because there are another five people lined up prepared to do the job. Now that has an immense impact because it has meant those kind of pressures, as people have said, crews have got smaller and smaller, schedules have got shorter, hours have got longer, and the exploitation at the bottom of newcomers to the industry has got progressively worse, there's no question about any of that. That poses very significant problems for us, not just in terms of stress, but also in terms of health and safety, because if you're working twelve or sixteen or seventeen hours a day, you have a lot of accidents, and if you're working in a freelance context you don't have the kind of regulatory health and safety structures which you do in a permanent context. So there's no real risk-assessment out there. It changes that as well. But freelancing doesn't merely change pay and hours and impose pressures which feed back into an absence of job satisfaction, job insecurity, all of those other problems which we've talked about; they feed back, as Judith has said, into very family-unfriendly situations and they also feedback into huge problems about equal opportunities. Theoretically, within a permanent and employed context, as someone has said, you can develop policies to provide opportunity and career development to women and to members of ethnic minorities and to disabled people, and to, as someone said about young fun-loving people, old fun-loving people like me. You can provide those in a permanent context, but in a fragmented, multi-company, cross-sectoral industry, with a mobile workforce, it's very, very difficult to begin to address questions of equal opportunities, very difficult to address health and safety, very difficult to address the question of training as well. Where, as Dinah said, once upon a time people were trained in those great monolithic structures, they aren't now. Most people now come into the industry as freelances and how do they train those?

There was, as Dinah said, a recognition on all sides of the industry that there were going to be problems about training for the future, skill shortages, demographic problems, how do you train youngsters, all of that. We have established in Skillset a model organisation based on social partnerships where all of the employers, all of the unions are represented. It has come up with brilliant and imaginative, still under-funded, but imaginative solutions to training questions inside the industry. I believe that it serves as a model in relation to equal opportunities and health and safety for social partnership, cross-sectoral examples of that kind, between unions and employers in a changing freelance sector. I think it's a very important model, and I think it is a model that will apply to equal opportunities.

Can I now say just a word about one or two things that other people have said? Can I first say we've just finished negotiating with PACT (Producers' Alliance for Cinema & Television) a new equal opportunities policy? It's very, very comprehensive indeed, and addresses precisely the questions that Judith talks about. It lists twenty examples of family-friendly scheduling, concrete examples of actual productions which have changed their working methods in order to adapt to the needs, particularly of women; it lists a whole set of training opportunities, it looks at the other issues you talked about as well. Absolutely crucially, it looks at how work is allocated inside the industry. It is done through black books in the back pocket of the production manager. The way the work is allocated, as it were, through personal contacts is not a good and effective method of allocating work in terms of equal opportunities. People are not aware of the jobs that exist, they are not made aware of those jobs that exist, producers make no attempt really to trawl the available talent because of all those cultural practices. We make whole sets of recommendations about how that might be changed. We also, incidentally, look at every other area, maternity and paternity leave, sexual harassment, equal opportunities across the board in every sense. What we hope to do, and this is a kind of what-are-we-doing-about-equal-opps as it were, we want to go to the Arts Council and say to the Arts Council, 'You're giving away a hundred million quid in terms of funding for film production, we would like you to make sure that this document is adopted as your bottom line in terms of those contracts, your contractors should observe this as a policy.' We want to go to the major commissioners, Channel 4, the ITV companies, the BBC, and say, 'Will you adopt this as the bottom line in terms of the work which you commission from that sector?' We want to adopt a number of pilot projects, working with a number of companies to see whether they can introduce the new scheduling arrangements and introduce effective equal opportunities policies of this kind. I'm really enthusiastic about this and I think it could make an enormous and significant change to the industry, but we need to be clear-eyed. It's only because there's a union that real initiative of this kind is taking place. It would not take place in our absence, and I want to say that democratic, professional, modern and effective unions are indispensable in our society, particularly in an industry now characterised by isolated, vulnerable, freelance individuals. We are indispensable, our role simple in terms of protecting the individual, of enhancing opportunities for the individual, and also of creating initiatives of this kind, is enormously important. And, incidentally, that change in the culture of the industry has changed us as well. We are a very different union now from the three unions which we came from – NATTKE, BETA and the old ACTT. I can recall the days when the main function of those schemes was to keep people out. We used to have long meetings — 'Someone's trying to join again, how can we stop it?' It's true! It's ludicrous! That's changed. Now we actually recruit people and we actually are saying to young graduates, 'You can come into the Union for something like a quarter of the full membership fee with full benefits.' Enormously important, we have a student link-up scheme, and our membership's increased enormously, we are now about 31,000, and probably 13,000 of them are freelances. We are increasing our membership enormously inside that freelance sector. We are one of the few unions in the world that is, but we are doing that very effectively because we are very recruitment-focused.

A few other things I wanted to say. The Working Time Directive will be coming in. It will be coming in under a Labour Government. We hope it will give us the clout to impose effective controls over working hours throughout the industry, or to ensure proper payment in compensation when that's not given. You may not be aware we are the only country in Europe that has no statutory right to annual holiday. It doesn't exist inside this country. Every other country has it. This Directive offers it, initially with three weeks, moving to four weeks inside three years – so, hugely important for us. We've just done an agreement in terms of the exploitation of kids debate with TAC (Teledwyr Annibynnol Cymru – Welsh Independent Producers) which is dealing with £90,000,000 worth of production for the Welsh 4th Channel, the Welsh Language Channel, and part of the agreement we've done with the producers there is no-one will come on a set there now, no kid comes on the set, unless they earn a minimum of £200 per week, an absolute guarantee. Minimum earnings for everybody inside the industry, and everyone who comes into the industry goes on the joint register between the Union and employers, and their training is monitored, everyone's training is monitored. So you can do things, you can act, you can begin significantly to alter things. So I wanted to say those few things there, also to say that the code of practice which PACT has developed for its members is very good in relation to the exploitation of youngsters inside the industry, that's a useful document, it's a voluntary document, but it's one that we would certainly support all the way.

We are changing the world and will continue to do so and if you will join, I shall be very happy. Thank you.

Caroline Millington: Well, there you are, that's part of the picture of broadcasting in the UK with a tiny little window on broadcasting in the States. Over to you, we've got about thirty-five minutes for a discussion involving as many people as possible. Would you mind saying who you are and where you come from?

Steven Kelly (University of Huddersfield): One of the saddest aspects of the whole business is the way young students are becoming totally disillusioned by the industry. Many of my students go off on work placements to large independent companies, small independent companies, and terrestrial companies and they are nearly always exploited. They don't get any money whatsoever. It's an advantage in that they do at least get some experience but they don't get any kind of structured work placement, they either sit in a corner and watch everybody in the office shouting and trying 'to be creative', or they are sent out on their own with a film camera and their own film tools to go and make a film. This contrasts quite sharply with those students of mine who go to various newspapers where there is a much more structured kind of work placement, where the student will shift from department to department and where the workings of that newspaper in that department will be explained to them in a structured way. I frequently find students coming back, particularly those who have gone to work in television, totally disillusioned saying: 'Well, I thought it was going to be an exciting and creative industry, yes it is, but God, I don't think I want to work in that anymore, it's appalling.' The one thing that does really worry and concern them (it's not the money, because they don't at the age of twenty-one or twenty-two expect to be earning a vast amount of money, and most of them are quite happy to take low salaries to begin with) is the lack of career structure. Most young graduates anticipate and hope that in ten years time they'll be earning a reasonable salary, with a company car, living in a three bedroom house which they will be able to pay for. When they look at the industry, they do not see any career structure, any movement, they do not see salaries rising very much and they do not really see where they can go. It's because a whole range of career jobs in the industry has totally disappeared thanks to casualisation. All jobs above producer have gone and it's going to put students off going into the industry. It's not just the money that is the problem, it is the lack of seeing what is going to be available for them in the future in terms of a career structure.

(At this point there is an interruption from the audience which is not clear)

Caroline Millington: Can I ask this question to pick up the previous speaker's comment. What other industries outside broadcasting are there which have a career structure?

Steven Kelly: I accept the point that you're making but I think you are wrong, I think it is significantly different in the television industry. I think there is a far higher rate of casualisation in television than there is in any other industry. Other companies come to my University – banking companies, advertising companies, newspapers, chemical companies – and they all offer a career structure. Maybe the money is not that different to begin with but they do offer a structure where young graduates will be trained in the job and where they can see progression and where they can see in ten years time I will be there. They can not see that in television.

Eleanor Wilson (Institute of Design and Communication): I'd just like to make a point to Roy Lockett about your structuring of pay. I'm wondering if that is the right way to go? The nature of radio and television maybe does not allow for such structures. Perhaps profit sharing would be more appropriate. The fact is that there are no career structures as such, there are very few people can be at the top. Maybe when a programme is successful, the people who created it should have a better share of the profits. There may be phases in their life when they are not working so hard but they have some money put aside for that. Have you any kind of other ways of looking at it other than this Civil Service-type attitude?

Roy Lockett: I love the sort of profit sharing inside the film industry. Our office is situated in Wardour Street where there are a lot of film distributors, and they say therefore it's the only street in Soho that's shady on both sides. The first thing I want to say is that you've got to be a very smart mover to share the profit of anything happening inside the independent production sector. It just doesn't happen. When it was offered to people on deferred payments (i.e. don't take any pay because you'll have a piece of the profits on this deferred payment film) you didn't get any wages and you certainly didn't make anything from the film which was almost invariably not shown. So there's a huge problem in terms of industry profit-sharing in the independent sector which is now £700,000,000 a year. It is not really a very realistic option. However, we have nothing against the possibility of profit-sharing, we would love to share the profits of any of the companies. For example at LWT where they have had a number of enormous deferred share options and things which had gone to Directors, we did a lot of research and we found out that they had in fact paid out in forms other than salary something like £20,000,000. We made that public and, at the end of the day, staff that worked at LWT got very significant payments to them as individuals because we had severely embarrassed the company in terms of their profit sharing systems which had been confined to the Directors and Senior Management. We have no problem with profit sharing, we have no problem with that, we believe it's right that the people who work for a company should share in the profit of that company. They should contribute to the competitiveness, to the effectiveness, to the professionalism of that company. That's what unions are about, about sharing, about assuring that that happens. We believe that they should share therefore in the wealth and the earnings of the company but we do think that you still need a sensible pay structure underpinning that. You need a proper salary structure, proper payment for overtime, a proper safety net of conditions.

Eleanor Wilson: I agree with a basic structure for technicians but over and above that profit sharing.

Roy Lockett: Certainly we are prepared to negotiate with any employer in the industry for a profit sharing scheme as long as it doesn't undermine what we think are proper and correct provisions for pay. We would take that position and it's an open offer. Anyone who wants to come and pay us profits, we will accept it.

Eleanor Wilson: Are you taking that option? Are you actually negotiating on those terms?

Roy Lockett: Well, employers are not coming to us and offering us shares. It's hard enough to get one per cent on the pay, you know what I mean? They are not actually coming to us and offering us shares or offering us payouts, they are not offering us shares as deferred payment systems. If they were, they know that we would be very interested in accepting.

Eleanor Wilson: Are you asking? Is it on your agenda?

Freda Chapman (BECTU): In some cases we are asking for it. There is an independent production company in this region which distributes profits and dividends in the region of one and a half to two million pounds per year and there are only two individual beneficiaries. That company has been asked to institute a pension scheme for its staff and has refused because it's not going to contribute to pensions for its members of staff when they are too knackered to work anymore out of their profits. We do ask, employers turn us down flat, we carry on negotiating.

Eleanor Wilson: When someone works on a particular project they are not necessarily going to be working on the next project, and/or in five or ten years time, why should they contribute to a pension scheme? But if they get enough from the profits they can have their own independent pension scheme, maybe far better than any employer.

Gill Ursell: It's just a caveat which I am sure the Union is very sensitive to. Some employers introduce profit-related pay as an alternative to proper wages, as an alternative to pay increases. Although I recognise that what you're saying describes some of the American arrangements, in this country it does not seem to hold true. You have employers manoeuvring as fast as possible to pay as little as possible. The danger of talking profits is that they will then use that as an argument to say, 'Well, we can diminish pay.'

Roy Lockett: All we can say is, our position is that we want sensible pay structures as the basis on which we negotiate. If we can negotiate and properly negotiate profit sharing on top of that, we are very happy to do so and employers are aware that we are happy to do so. We wish to share in the rewards of the companies where our members work.

Jo Langham (University College, Warrington and University of Manchester): I'm not sure I agree with the gentleman talking about different industry structures. This industry is in the vanguard of the change but it's going to affect other industries too. You are actually looking at flatter structures in the total workforce. Some statistics have indicated that where, about five years ago (and I'm not talking now about just in the media industry workforce, I'm talking about banking or computing and other companies), one person out of fifteen could expect promotion during their working life, by the year 2,000 one person in fifty can expect promotion in their working life. So in other words, there's going to be a vast army of, if you like drones, and only a few people will be promoted up to – was it 'the blameless'? There will be a much more narrow structure at the top. Perhaps the media industry shows us what's going to happen in other industries, rather than being so different from the pattern. It indicates what will develop elsewhere.

Caroline Millington: Thank you. Why don't you tell us from your experience whether you agree that there is a lack of career structure?

Audrey Hall: Yes, is the short answer. I think it's all to do with this whole thing of the casualisation of labour, because the contracts are getting smaller and smaller. I'm encouraged to hear that there is this move towards longer term contracts. I haven't experienced that. My first contract was for three months, and I was appalled. I thought how can anyone work for three months? The shortest contract I've ever had in television was for two weeks. I took that contract because of personal contacts and we've talked about the need for personal contacts and how it's important to be at the right place at the right time, etc, etc.

But I certainly haven't experienced this move towards long term contracts and long term commitments. I think that's why there is this lack of career structure because basically, we're all grappling out there.

Can I go on to make this point? It's just something else I wanted to say and it ties in. This whole subject, everything that we are talking about, ties in together. Going back to Judith's report, and some things that Roy picked up on, this idea of long hours. Judith talks about regularity in working hours as being the main issues. I'm not sure I agree with that. The reason is that when you do undertake work in the media you know before you start that the nature of the work means it's never going to be a nine-to-five job. I'm not saying it's right, but I'm saying that's how it is.

I know, Roy, you talk with great conviction about the things that you're hoping to bring about, for example, this new equal opportunities policy that you're putting forward and you hope that people will implement it. As a freelance – I know this is sounding all gloom and doom and I would pre-empt it by saying I'm in the industry because I do love it and like Ana I'm excited by it and I have a hope for greater and better programmes – however, as a freelance, I don't believe that I've ever had the benefit of any of these equal opportunities policies or any of these Union agreements or whatever. You basically go in there, you do your job, you take your pay and you go home, and that's how it has always been for me. I don't particularly feel as though there's somebody there rooting for me. That is a personal opinion obviously, but it's one that all of the people I know who work in the media share. These are people who are freelances and not people who are employed on staff contracts.

Marie Messenger Davies (London College of Printing): I wonder if I could broaden our discussion a little bit. I'm very much interested in what Peter was saying about the mis-match between the young people who come to us, because I teach students who want to work in the media too. There is a huge explosion of interest in the media among school children and among teenagers and among students in higher education. What does this mean, what is it they are responding to? Why is it so important to them, why is it so exciting? The industry itself needs to take part in that debate. When you use the word 'exciting', when you use the phrase 'I love my job,' what is it that you're loving? Can we have some hard breakdown of what all of this glamour and excitement is? I think we need to respond to that in our students.

I understand it. I've worked as a journalist myself and I kind of agree about the difference in the newspaper industry. It seems to be better organised in telling you what is expected of you, and where you're going. I don't believe it's not possible to do that. I think you can make things nine-to-five or ten-to-six if you really sit down and work at it. You've got to, if this industry is going to become so central in industrial societies around the world. We've simply got to try and get it organised so that it fits in with other aspects of life.

Which brings me onto the other issues which we've been talking about during the conference which is about cultural values. You're describing a world that is completely cut off from the issues that the rest of us are grappling with –

family life, children, community, neighbourhood, and getting involved in your local church, running a scout troop – whatever it is you do, you're describing a world which doesn't play any part in that. I don't think that's right and I don't think that that's good enough. If you're going to be cultural arbiters and you're going to be purveying the values of society or whatever it is, then you do have a duty really to try and get out from this sealed world, spend some time with your kids, get tough with your employers or whatever, and join the rest of us in these debates. I'm not being unsympathetic. As I say I see it from both sides, but I don't except the doctrine of despair. I mean the industry has simply got to recognise that these are very important questions, not just to do with the workers, but to do with all of us in education and in society as a whole.

Caroline Millington: What is it your students want to do?

Maire Messenger Davies: Well, they have this idea that it's very glamorous. I think they see it as a 'starry' industry, there's always this sort of star-struck element to it. But also I think they genuinely, as Peter says, think that it's important. They have a social conscience they have environmental awareness, they do think that it matters and so they want to say things. They have things to say and they want to reach an audience, and that's very idealistic. I think we have to respond to that.

Caroline Millington: Scott made the point about the changing views of people in newsrooms in the States, about whether you're talking about the medium itself or the content within it, but what you seem to be saying is that your students want to use the medium to say something themselves,

Maire Messenger Davies: Well don't you all?

Caroline Millington: I don't know.

Maire Messenger Davies: I mean I'd like to see research about why people go into it. Is that one of the things the BFI tracking study is looking at? I mean what leads people to take this type of work up?

Nick Pettigrew: It is one of the things we are going to ask in the next diary.

Maire Messenger Davies: I think that is one of the things we need to ask students as well. We need to find out more about that.

Kate O'Connor (Skillset): I am loath to give you another mini-speech but the work Skillset has done very recently looking into higher education and the growth of media education is very relevant to your comments. We've just completed our research and circulated it for comment and discussion both within the industry and in higher education. Basically, we're not proposing answers yet, we're raising a whole series of issues for further discussion and debate.

There are 400 courses at undergraduate and postgraduate levels, 32,000 students on them. In our research we found a huge range from the very vocational, very practical higher educational programme to the purely academic and theoretical and deliberately so. Neither employers nor the students seem to know what it is they're buying and where it's going to get them. Our research basically opens the door for Skillset to look at developing policy with the industry in partnership with education to construct a bridge for entry into the industry. The employers have recognised that it is increasingly important for young people to come into the industry with skills. We're not in a situation where the industry can develop people completely once they are in the industry, given everything we've heard today about casualisation, free-lancing and the most normal entry into the industry being through the independent production sector. There is a recognition that vocational training will take place within higher education and the industry has a part to play in informing that. It can't do that on the basis of the huge growth and the large numbers currently in higher education and our research indicates that the majority of those students actively think that they're taking a degree in media or media-related subjects to give themselves an advantage to enter the industry. That is something that our research hasn't borne out, and nor has other research to date. We are now starting the very work which needs desperately to be done to make the career structures and progression, once you're in the industry, clearer and transparent.

Caroline Millington: Thank you. Are there any young people banging on the doors of the media at the moment or about to hammer on the doors, perhaps they would like to tell us why? Meanwhile we've got somebody in the middle of the room.

Martin Harris (Brunel University, Social Science): I would like to concur with the last point about students. It is quite apt in the sense that young students do share a realism about work that was perhaps absent in the past. They really have some very harsh realities to deal with and they soon lose any 'starriness' that they might have about the media.

What I wanted to do was talk a little bit more about the broader industrial comparisons. It's one of the fascinating things about broadcasting that it is a capital-intensive, highly technical industry which is seen to be at the cutting edge of technical advance. It's part of the digital debate. There is a huge European debate about the information society, great uncertainties, strategic uncertainties about how we should plan for skills and training in education in the digital age so I'd just like to make one or two perhaps useful comparisons. I think the parallel with banking was, in fact, more apposite than perhaps would be believed. I mean this tendency towards downsizing and for digitally-led downsizing, for digitally-led de-skilling, for micro electronics to be used to do more with less. This is absolutely across the board. It's nothing to do with specific industries, although broadcasting is specific. So that's the first point.

Technical change in the sense of micro electronics and digitisation confirms the existing tendency within industrial societies to rationalise and to do more with less. There is absolutely no doubt about that, twenty years' research in micro-electronics shows that to be an underlying pattern. On the BECTU point, it is absolutely the case that it is the legislative framework and the strategic choices made at that level which will determine the future of employment. There's a lot of teleology about technology, there's this idea that technology itself will drive the social change but actually it's much more to do with labour law and legislative frameworks and, of course, we don't need to say much more than has already been said about that. I fully concur with that. Finally, underlying all production seems to be the idea of what we call the 'productivity/innovation dilemma'. One has been forced to innovate in all forms of production – services, goods, manufacturing, export, domestic production – but people will innovate cheaply. That is the underlying pattern. With the death of economics, people like Paul Ormerod and Fuka Yama and other clever people are writing about the death of economics, I think it's more than ever the case. I would agree that economics is important but can't actually explain behaviour at the point of production. TV is economically embedded but it's actually deeply culturally embedded as well. That would be the view of somebody who like me studies other kinds of industries as well as broadcasting. Thank you.

Caroline Millington: Do you think we should still talk about the broadcasting industry? I'm interested that somebody's drawing parallels with employment practices in newspapers. Well, of course, a lot of newspapers, in ownership terms, embrace broadcasting and, increasingly, on-line activities are owned by, or are either expanding into a form of broadcasting, or are broadcasting themselves. The media as a whole is converging internationally and actually breaking down a lot of the old structures and barriers that there used to be.

Martin Harris: Well, there was a lunchtime conversation to the effect that perhaps the concern with regulation of broadcasting content from the centre was beginning to become somewhat anachronistic in view of the many-to-many communications allowed by things like the Internet, but I'd like to stop at that point and leave it to the floor again. Thank you.

Mike DiGioia (Pennsylvania State University): My question is based on something Ana Kronschnabl said. You mentioned television as a competitor to the Internet. Everything that I've always heard, and from my own personal experience with it, is about convergence – how TV and the Internet will eventually come together. Do you really think that television is going to have to change to compete with the Internet or are they eventually going to work together as partners, or as one medium? You also mentioned how television programming has become commodified. Do you think that for students who want to be more creative it would be more productive for them to go towards the new media such as the Internet or other multi-media for more creative expression because there aren't as many rules? There aren't as many precedents there so anything you do is new and nobody is going to say: 'Well, you're breaking all the rules, you can't do that because it hasn't been done before.' So my questions are basically: do you think television and the Internet can compete and do you think students and people coming in should focus more on the new areas rather than on an area that's already been pioneered?

Ana Kronschnabl: Yes I do. In terms of the Internet competing with television, one of the things is that it is partly the Internet but it's all sorts of different aspects of new media. People are going to be able to interact in so many different ways and, for the first time ever, people are turning off their televisions. There are so many new forms coming along. Just purely in terms of games, they're getting more and more interactive, more and more challenging. Television is obviously going to become more and more involved in the Internet, people are going to use the Internet more in terms of broadcasting. But I think they also have to take on board what is so exciting about the Internet. It gives you more of what you want as a person sitting there in front of the screen. You can take a lot *more of what you want*, it's more interactive and I think that they have to take on board all the new different strands of what's going on in the world. So that was one question, what was the other?

For people who are interested in broadcasting and are interested in communicating, the Internet offers an area and a chance for people to do that in a way that isn't possible in broadcasting. It is possible on the Internet with very little difficulty and very little money to communicate your ideas, to set up a web site, to join with a group of people who have similar interests, to start off magazine programmes. As multi-media becomes more possible, people can access visuals a lot easier. It's going to be possible for people to actually produce their own material and to communicate with people in different ways that won't necessarily involve going into traditional broadcast media. I really do think this is important for broadcasters to realise. We had a talk yesterday about dance music and the influence of the dance culture and how it's possible for young people, not necessarily just young people but anybody to obtain equipment pretty cheaply and to produce their own product – a product that maybe doesn't have that much status. Some of it's accepted, some of it isn't accepted, some of it becomes changed. But people are doing that now, people are making their own product. That's something that broadcasters have to recognise: that young people can with very little money and effort, (well, not necessarily effort) but with very little money, initially in the music industry, they can do that kind of thing. It's becoming more possible in other forms as well. It is a really exciting industry.

Caroline Millington: I think we've got about four minutes left before we wrap up. So there are four hands in the air. Quick comment there!

Unidentified speaker: I'd just like to nip in the bud this idea about the death of economics. All the problems that we've discussed today are about the onset of free market economics and the belief in them and how we regulate that. That's the problem, how to regulate free market economics, not the fact that it has died.

Caroline Millington: Thank you.

John Gray: Going back to your question Caroline. Should we be talking about broadcasting? No, we should be talking about communications and even more than communications. Even the Internet is only part of general communications. How many people here have Broadsystem? Broadsystem is the place in London which controls your phone-in programmes, whether you're in Birmingham, London or wherever. It's an important place, some of the most important programmes with the biggest audiences, yet we don't regard it as part of the broadcasting industry. This could be repeated: if you take a lot of graphic imagery, it's the software person – the designer of the software, not the operator. We are just the operators. We've got to think completely differently. The danger of Skillset is that by specialising on skills it becomes more difficult to get an holistic impression, that this is all part of a very, very wide general activity. I think you are right in asking us that question because we must never ignore it.

Caroline Millington: Thank you, I always like people who agree with me.

Alexandra Palmer (media student at University College, Warrington): Just a comment really about why so many people want to do media studies. Twenty years ago, for my Dad, university education was not available because he was in the wrong class basically. Why I started to do media studies is that it's something which I know about, I can see it every day and I thought, 'Well, I can't really be a doctor or anything, so I'll do something I know.' Perhaps that explains it. It's something you can really watch, something that you think you know about.

Caroline Millington: Seems a good reason to me. Thank you very much.

Ruth Goldwyn (Salford University): I am very encouraged by the idea of new schedules and new working practices in the industry. For somebody who is a mother with children, having family-friendly production schedules is a great idea but from my experiences within the industry, the people who make decisions, who commission, actually cannot put those family-friendly practices into practice. What happens is, although you may be able to develop programme ideas slowly in a freelance capacity, as soon as you get a commission, it is 'hell for leather' to get it done. Freda talks about feast or famine in work but it's what happens. The same with your ability to organise your life around family. We now actually need to persuade the people above us who are taking the decisions to allow producers to organise their time. We have to get them to allow us to have that freedom and I don't think it's fair really that that backing isn't there.

The second thing is that it's very interesting talking to colleagues about the whole interaction between industry and education. I teach media production and I was in the industry five years ago but my knowledge of the industry, although I keep up with it, is obviously getting slim because I've not been there and things are changing. I'm trying to prepare people to go into the industry with skills and ideas, with questioning minds, not just with a set of skills because I think most people in the industry are probably still recruiting people with politics and economics or history degrees; there is still that mental sense about it rather than media production, media skills, television and radio degrees – there is still resistance there. So what do we do, do we go back to look at old industry practices and what is happening now or do we try, within the educational establishments, to try and do something different, try and create different working skills, practices, that aren't reflected in the industry at the moment but will be in the industry of the future? I think that's a challenge that we have to take on in education. Of course, we've got to deal with the industry and what is going on but within those educational establishments that do production as well as theory we should be trying to do something new. Innovation can't come from the industry it's actually got to come from the educational establishments and I think that's where we have a huge job to take on. Actually we have to try and free ourselves from some of the problems that we've inherited because media production comes from old practitioners who go into teaching, you have to shed some of those shackles at some point.

Caroline Millington: Thank you. Now I'm going to ask each of our formal speakers, if I may so describe them, to do what I asked them to do at the beginning, which is to identify the one thing, the one single thing, of the many on their lists which they would like to see change and who they think will be the driver of that change.

Dinah Caine: Well, as far as I'm concerned and in terms of my particular 'take' on this debate, my one action point would be investment in training so that the skills that are required now and in the future are in place in the industry and that diversity is encouraged and reflected both culturally and in terms of the community which the industry draws from. As far as investment is concerned Skillset has a huge role to play in terms of trying to promote the need to look at training on an across-industry-social-partnership model. We need to make a psychological leap now with our employers, so that they recognise that foundations have to be built on in a meaningful way and in a way that allows the industry to be competitive into the next century. So that would be my main action point and my call to the industry and to all of those involved in training and education? Of course, as somebody said, the legislative framework has a significant effect and the outcome of the next election will affect the seriousness which the industry focuses on training as an issue as well. Can I just make two comments?

Caroline Millington: No! But I'm sure the discussion will go on after.

Judith Jones: Ideally I would like to see employers take on board the responsibility for their employees' welfare through cross-industry co-operation, as Roy mentioned before, and I'd like to see employers being more pro-active rather than reactive in relation to, for example, alternative working arrangements. I would probably like to see some type of legislation which will ensure that not only the main ITV companies and BBC but also the small independent companies have to take some account of equal opportunities. They are not going to do it willingly and it will need legislation to ensure that comes about.

Caroline Millington: So what that boils down to is Government?

Judith Jones: I think it boils down to work across the industry, in terms of BECTU, in terms of PACT, in terms of the BBC, ITV, but ultimately, I suspect it will probably mean some kind of legislation which was lacking in the 1990 Act, which will mean that those small companies have to come under the remit.

Caroline Millington: Employers, Government and Unions ... but not the Church?

Judith Jones: Not the Church, no definitely not the Church.

Peter Lewis: Actually, I was hoping to ask a question which is: what can we share? Perhaps the remaining speakers on the platform can say what they think will happen if a Labour government gets in, because apparently the rewind button will not be pressed. We've heard from Roy that there is an expectation for support in some of the Labour conditions, but I'm left with a big question mark. I've no doubt what I'm going to vote and I think that a huge landslide will allow a lot of pressure groups to bring pressure to bear on this new Government.

Caroline Millington: Fine, I'm going to pass on your question because it would be totally unfair. Time may or may not tell. Thank you Peter.

Ana Kronschnabl: I think all people within the broadcasting area, particularly commissioning editors, should be more adventurous and more risk-taking which means not always employing people that they know, and that's my one thought.

Nick Pettigrew: My one thought would be changing the culture of long hours, we find it really depends on the individual company and department. You can go to work for a company and if you leave at six o'clock people look disgusted by it, it is really not the thing to do. I'd change that culture and that goes right the way up to commissioning editors as well, they are sometimes given such short time spans to do a project, I think that has to be changed.

Roy Lockett: Assuming that the last guy says he wants to see proper and full and effective implementation of the Working Time Directive for freelances, which

I assume he said, I would say one that I want to see all broadcast media, that's cable, satellite, digital, terrestrial and digital terrestrial, showing a minimum obligatory 50 per cent original programme material – that's what I want and it will underpin the industry. That's what I want nationally, can I have some for Europe as well?

Caroline Millington: You want something for Europe?

Roy Lockett: Yes, in Europe what I'd like to see would be public service broadcasting locked in to the European Union Treaty and specifically that public service broadcasting could be exempted from the destructive provisions of article 92 on Competition Policy. I would like to see public broadcasting locked in to Europe and the Treaties so that it is protected effectively inside Europe. So I want one here and one there.

Gill Ursell: If I give as my goal employment then I'm going to endorse everything that's been said already – yes, shorter working hours; yes, opportunities for everybody; yes, original programming, etc., etc. But I'm not going to accept employment as my goal, I'm going to follow John Gray's lead and say that I don't think that the broadcasting industry is an immutable institution, I think its boundaries are changing very, very dramatically, and I think we in education can help that process of change by educating as many people as we can get our hands on, about the processes, the workings and structures of the media. We can enable them, not merely to decode these messages that are being sent to us, but we can enable them to participate and it may mean that they do take their cheap equipment, and they do their own dance routines and they do have their own little clogs, if you like, of media activity and communication and consumption. I won't claim democracy, but we certainly do put these abilities in the hands of as many people as possible such that that institution doesn't have its privileged position for very much longer.

Audrey Hall: As producers our job is to tell people what they want to watch and what they want to hear with all due respect to the listeners and the viewers. I think it's always important for programme-makers to respect our listeners' and viewers' intelligence as well, and so one thing that I would like to see happen, and it's something we can do whether or not we are involved in the industry, is every time we see something that we don't like or hear something that we don't like, switch it off, write to the radio and television authorities and tell them and actually demand quality programmes. What that should do, what that would mean is that employers have to employ skilled people. It means that there would be more emphasis on having quality staff, it would mean that it would be important for the up and coming people to also be trained and that would then allow for the longevity of a quality industry. Janet Street Porter made a comment the other day, and I don't necessarily always agree with the things that Janet Street Porter says, but she was talking about Channel 5 and she was saying that she finds the background behind the news distracting and 'Please, would somebody tell them that less and less is actually more and more.' I don't know why we've reached this position where, as programme makers, we believe that weird and wacky are best. With respect to what you say, Ana, I think that we do need creative programmes but I don't think we should be insulting our listeners and viewers and I think that too often we do.

Caroline Millington: It's a wish list which I don't think that any decent broadcasting employer in this country would, or could, argue with. Let me add one comment myself. About two years ago I was in the audience inside the BBC when Bill Gates came to address about 200 of the BBC most senior people, many of whom had come from a programme-making background and he described them all as 'content providers'. 'You are content providers,' he said, 'and you don't realise what assets you have.' Until then, many people in the organisation had thought of their assets as their archives, the programmes that had been made and were sitting on the shelf. Many broadcasters do still think of it like that, they still want the equivalent of a newspaper cutting, they want a permanence in an impermanent world. I suspect that John is right, what we are talking about is a hugely expanding broadcasting industry, a communications industry with digits which is hugely volatile. What you have seen today are tiny snapshots of perception about it. It's much much bigger than that and it's changing very fast indeed. A speaker from the floor said that skills alone are not enough, the ability to actually use your brain, the ability to contemplate change, to manage change, actually to embrace change and become excited by it. I suspect will lead to better working practices to better managerial practices because those too are creative things, but I'm an idealist really.

I'd like to thank Judith, Scott, Peter, Dinah, Gill, Roy, Nick, Ana, and Audrey very much indeed with the traditional wonderful applause and to introduce Jane Drabble who's got the difficult task of delivering the summation to the last two days.

Jane and I have worked together in the BBC over very many years and at least twenty-five years ago as very junior members of the BBC we were complaining of the fact that there was no career path in the broadcasting industry. There is another member of the BBC over there who reminds me that in 1971 she came into the BBC on a three months' contract because she couldn't get anything longer. I don't know whether to find that despairing or not. I do however know that Jane is one of the most senior women in the BBC, that she has two children and that being a woman and a mother has not stood in her way, Jane.

Summation

Jane Drabble
Director of Education, BBC

Thank you. This is an impossible task, I have decided, but I am going to do my best and try not to delay you too much because this has been a very very long session. I have a T shirt at home which has written on it the provocative words *Theatre is Life, Film is Art, Television is Furniture*, and I thought of wearing it in order to be provocative, but then yesterday Phil Redmond talked about the 'media fridge', this wonderful idea of the fridge that you shout at and it turns into a television, so I thought well, perhaps it wouldn't be that provocative, maybe television really is furniture!

I think we are all here because we fundamentally believe that television is not furniture. This T Shirt came from North America. Perhaps that is predictable. We actually believe that television is life and it's art and it's many other things, it's also an industry like many others, and it's a way of life (I think that's what we've been hearing this afternoon), and of course it's a major cultural force – perhaps I should be saying broadcasting, but I'm stuck with the T shirt, that's the problem. Anyway, whatever our view, I think what we've been discovering in the last couple of days is an industry that's in an amazing state of change. I've been to lots of conferences in the last two or three years which have been predicting change, but we are no longer predicting change, we are actually in it, and I think what I have picked up is a mixture of excitement and confusion and angst. I suppose what we have been tackling during the last couple of days are three realities – the reality of the technology, the reality of the consumers or the viewers and where they're coming from, and lastly, of course, the reality of the workers.

Phil Redmond started this all off with the technology and to remind us he held up in one hand a tiny digital camera which cost less than £1,500, and in the other a tiny digital mobile phone, and pointed out to us that it is not beyond the bounds of possibility to link these two things together and 'off you go'. This is clearly transforming the world, certainly the world that I have been working in all my life, but Phil was remarkably reassuring, he's clearly an enthusiast, he's what's known in the business as an 'early adopter', and he felt very much that we can handle this and he didn't want us to listen to the voices of doom. He thought there were going to be plenty of opportunities – and it's interesting that some people have been making that point this afternoon – and new sources of money too. Remember he reminded us of the date, the 17th of February of this year, when the World Trade Organisation in Geneva passed a protocol which guaranteed common standards and common pricing across the telecoms industry across the world. He exhorted us to remember this, that this would actually be the moment when history changed.

He was also very optimistic about creativity and, again, this point has come up – funny we've come round sort of the full circle really. Phil made the point that the Internet and the new technologies and the convergence of the Internet and television would actually facilitate creativity. He saw a major role for the BBC in acting as the agent of this process, in essentially acting as the exhibitor casting its net as wide as possible, working in conjunction with regional arts organisations and so on, and amongst other things he talked about creating a national Eisteddfod of national culture. I presume he means this as a kind of rolling programme. It's an interesting idea and it's a plea that I've heard elsewhere, it's a plea that the BBC should somehow ensure in this new world the qualities that many people feel the BBC has ensured in the current world, and I think those expectations were echoed in later sessions.

Then yesterday afternoon we were very much back to the realities of today's world, with the schedules and who and what shapes them, the realities of regulation and obligation, and costs of course, the demand of the customers and the demands of the advertisers, and the new world of low cost, high volume, city television. It was useful that we should be reminded of the realities of the market place, and where the advertisers will put their money, and they will put their money where the viewers are, and the viewers increasingly will 'zap'. Choice is all and we ended up in one group yesterday afternoon speculating about what would happen with the arrival of the electronic programme, EPG, whether we would see the end of schedules as we know them. I find it hard to imagine a world in which following the plot of your favourite soap doesn't happen anymore. At the moment so many people rely on the knowledge that when they go into the office or the classroom tomorrow everybody will have seen the same story at the same time. In a world where everything is on demand this is going to disappear, but we will see, I suspect what's going to happen is that many of the aspects of the familiar world of television will co-exist with the new things as they come along and these two things will balance each other out. There's no doubt the lack of certainty about where we're going heightens the awareness of the viewer and, whatever the technology is going to do, all of us need to understand where viewers and listeners are coming from and we need to listen to them.

I found this morning fascinating because we were firmly back in the minds of viewers listening to the research from Leeds. It's not often that television people like me find themselves sharing the same space as philosophers and I, like many others, felt slightly out of my depth, but nevertheless it was extremely stimulating and it clearly provoked a great deal of heat as well, not only in the room but also afterwards over coffee. But I thought it was very interesting that we were, as it were, made to think about the audience as a moral force and not just as an economic one and we listened to the description of the split in the audience, the split which had emerged from asking the audience questions about their ethical value systems which the people who did the research defined as being the difference between the liberal and the Aristotelian value systems: the liberals saying that we all have a right essentially to be immoral, the Aristotelian insisting that the state or the regulator should interfere simply because it's wrong. The interesting thing is that the split is an even one, if you looked at the percentages you could see that on a lot of those questions there was an absolute division and the split was even. I couldn't help thinking who on earth would be a regulator in those circumstances. It was interesting too that the research had established people did not want to make a causal link between the media and anti-social behaviour, but they did want to make a link between the media and unsocial behaviour. On the one hand, I thought it was interesting, the paucity of language and the ability to think about abstract concepts, but at the same time there was this idea that people rely on a kind of scientific rationality. I thought those two things were not quite consistent, that actually what we do is, we try to question and justify so maybe people are thinking more than we think they are. What we picked up was a lack of certainty, a lack of confidence, a lack of any real sense of any moral absolutes anymore, which is perhaps growing from a lack of cohesion in society, and this interesting notion that the conflicts in society are given visibility through television, and therefore, there's a kind of 'in your faceness' about being exposed to people with whom you would not normally mix, or with whose value systems you would not normally agree. This is what is provoking people to feel aggrieved about what they see, and also to feel out of control because the conventions with which they are familiar are being broken down.

Anyway, as you can tell, I think there are profound issues which will certainly encourage me to read the rest of the research, and it's certainly not something that we can ignore. Certainly, from the perspective of being in the business, heaven knows how we resolve this question of the equal split between the two sides of the debate. One person suggested that perhaps the only solution was to leave the judgement to economics, to leave the judgement to money, I would actually rather leave it to high quality leadership, but that's perhaps another story.

Interestingly too, Colin Shaw picked up the point that in the US his experience had been that television broadcasters were traditionally much more puritanical and that was because of commercial pressure, or because of perceived commercial pressure.

Anyway, we then had a very interesting discussion, although one we've had many times before, between the regulators and the broadcasters about where the regulators stop and start and where the broadcaster feel they should be in control. This debate will simply go on and on and on, and it's not unrelated to many of the issues that we have been talking about in the final session. There's a sense that, as the industry changes, as the people within the industry change, then perhaps some of its ability to regulate itself, to train its people to be responsible and to make the right sort of decisions, is diminishing. It's certainly a very subtle and complex business being a regulator and a responsible broadcaster in these circumstances.

We've heard a lot about the fragmentation of society and we've heard a lot about the convergence of the industries, the telecom, computer and television industries, and we've heard a lot about the difficulty, particularly for public service broadcasters of managing diversity, in the competitive environment – almost impossible.

In this afternoon's session we went on to pick up some of the themes that emerged in some of the papers yesterday afternoon where I heard some fascinating insights into how broadcasters and other aspects of the industry are reacting to change in South Africa, in the States and in the BBC, and the political and economic forces they dealing with on top of the technological change. That was from the management perspective but what we heard this afternoon were the consequences of that – of confused and uncertain workers and the two-edged sword of multi-skilling and structural change and so on. I thought it a rather depressing picture of exploitation, uncertainty, stress and all the issues that face women in particular, and the impossible levels of commitment that people are required to make. Just to digress slightly into my own personal view, I think all of the things that people say about the difficulties that women face are true but there are other things too, there is a lot in the fact that the authority systems were created by men for men and it's actually quite difficult for women to inform those processes or affect them, because they just don't quite respond.

Anyway we've heard a lot about casualisation, we've heard a lot about the lowering of skills, but we also heard some positive things. I thought it was very interesting hearing the work that's been done in the States on newsrooms and the changing cultures. We had some evidence that contracts are beginning to lengthen, the pendulum was beginning to swing a little, although Caroline made a very important point that actually there are opportunities, we are moving into a very exciting world and there are skills that young people do possess which will enable them to survive very well. There is a huge, huge range, a pool of talent that we can all draw on, and I suppose if I were going to recommend one thing to try to do something about this, I would say why don't we stop looking for structural solutions and look to the talent that we have got, look to the people who are already here, and many of them we already employ? I liked very much the performance chart of the BBC and I was particularly impressed by the E category on the right hand side saying, 'Can't recognise a bullet when they see them,' or whatever it was. Actually the whole industry ought to make sure that it moves as fast as a bullet, and doesn't sit there thinking, 'Hang on a minute, what's going on around here,' because there is a slight tendency for us to do that. Anyway, I hope I have pulled most of it together, it's not the easiest thing to do, certainly not off-the-cuff in this way.

A couple more things. The first is, this is the first time I've attended the Manchester Symposium and I have found it really very, very interesting and I welcome the opportunity as a senior person in the broadcasting industry to engage with people from academic life and so many young people, too. It's been a very useful and interesting and stimulating experience. Lastly, I must thank not only all of you who are here and who have come and contributed in such an energetic way, but particularly Sue Ralph, the Director, and all the people who have worked with her to put this Symposium together. It has been a very interesting and stimulating couple of days and I am sure we would all like to register our thanks.

Presented papers
(in alphabetical order)

Towards a Political Economy of Children's Media Culture

Quality, Public Service and Cultural Identity in the New Television Environment

David Buckingham and Hannah Davies

Institute of Education, University of London

Over the past two decades, British broadcasting has been steadily dragged into the commercial marketplace. The comparative equilibrium provided by the regulated duopoly has been progressively eroded, and the principle of broadcasting as a public service has been increasingly threatened. These developments can partly be explained in terms of the end of frequency scarcity and the proliferation of new media technologies; but they have also, of course, been driven by the former government's ideological commitment to the so-called 'free market'.

The consequences of these developments are perhaps particularly acute in relation to children's television. Children have always been seen as a 'special' audience in debates about broadcasting – an audience whose particular characteristics and needs require specific codes of practice and regulation. Such assumptions can be traced in successive official reports and government legislation, from the Pilkington and Annan Reports through to the 1990 Broadcasting Act. Indeed, the provision of a distinct service for children could be seen as a defining marker of the public service principle – as the BBC's *Extending Choice* (1992) and its more recent *Statement of Promises* (1996) illustrate.

Much of the debate here rests on an implicit comparison with the fate of children's television in the United States, which is often represented as a salutary lesson in the implications of a wholly market-led system. According to US critics (e.g. Melody, 1973; Kunkel, 1993), the fact that children are not seen as an economically valuable audience by advertisers means that there is no incentive for broadcasters to meet their particular needs. Furthermore, it is argued that in a competitive, market-driven system, there is no room for failure, and therefore for innovation – particularly since it is often assumed that children will watch anything they are given. According to this analysis, the 'logic' of the market dictates that children will be forever consigned to the cultural deprivation of the 'Kidvid ghetto'.

Debates about what kind of provision is appropriate for children thus provide an interesting case study for broader questions about the future of broadcasting in Britain, as we move towards an increasingly market-led system. Indeed, these debates have served as a focal point for discussions of quality, cultural identity and the meaning of 'public service'. In this paper, we offer a brief outline of some of the central issues which have emerged from our ongoing research into the changing nature of children's media culture. We seek to question some of the more pessimistic predictions which have been made in this area; and, more broadly, to ask whether it still makes sense – either theoretically or pragmatically – to conceive of these debates in terms of a straightforward opposition between public service and the market.

The Great Tradition?

The most significant recent analysis of the British situation is contained in Jay Blumler's 1992 report for the Broadcasting Standards Council, *The Future of Children's Television in Britain*. This report was commissioned in the wake of the 1990 Broadcasting Act, amid fears that the new structure of ITV would lead to a decline in the quantity, diversity and quality of children's television. The report was intended to provide a benchmark against which to monitor future developments; and the BSC has in fact recently commissioned an 'update' for purposes of comparison.

Blumler's report promotes a view of British children's television as an internationally-envied 'great tradition'. Children's television, it argues, is a cornerstone of public service, an embodiment of 'quality' and of a distinctively British cultural identity. Blumler identifies several characteristics which, he argues, have guaranteed the health and survival of this tradition. These include: the scheduling of children's programmes at times when children are available to view (for example, after school); the commitment to a 'mixed diet' of programming, including drama, information, animation, news, etc.; the targeting of programmes to meet the needs of specific sub-sections of the audience according to age (for example, pre-schoolers); and the presence of talented and motivated professionals working in the area.

While these characteristics have been protected in some ways through regulation, Blumler argues that they are now under serious threat. Along with the many producers and executives whom he interviews, Blumler fears that the increasing commercialisation of independent television in Britain, and its corrosive effect through competition on the BBC, will lead to an erosion of this 'great tradition' of children's broadcasting. In the early 1990s, when the report was written, these threats were primarily seen to derive from the potential weakening of centralised regulation (the replacement of the IBA by the ITC) and from the changing economic structure of broadcasting (the centralisation of the ITV network, the BBC's introduction of Producer Choice, and so on). More recently, of course, it is the threat of cable and satellite which has attracted more attention – and the potential implications of this development are much more far-reaching.

Public discussions of the future of children's television, encouraged by the lobbying activities of groups such as BACTV (British Action for Children's Television) and more recently VLV (Voice of the Listener and Viewer), have echoed many of these concerns. On the one hand, such groups have been remarkably successful – not least in ensuring that a commitment to children's programming was written into the 1990 Broadcasting Act. Yet, on the other hand, it is hard not to perceive such lobby groups as simply the defensive response of a coalition of cultural elites – as the voice of middle-class, middle-aged, middle England. There is certainly a considerable degree of nostalgia surrounding such discussions; and it is rare to read press reports of such debates which do not hark back (however ironically) to the golden age of *Muffin the Mule* and *Watch with Mother*. There are certainly significant questions that should be raised, for example, about the notions of cultural value and of national identity on which such debates are often premised.

Our primary concern here, however, is to assess whether the more pessimistic predictions about the future of children's television expressed in Blumler's report and in the arguments of such lobby groups are likely to come true in the ever more commercialised environment of the late 1990s. We would argue that they are not – and that some of the reasons for this can partly be traced to the operations of the commercial market itself.

Children's Niche

What is particularly striking about the five years since Blumler's report was published is that, far from being neglected or marginalised, children have emerged as a highly important 'niche market'. While cable/satellite subscription seems to have stabilised at around 25 per cent of the population, this figure is higher in homes with children (approximately 33 per cent); and we now have no fewer than five dedicated children's channels. After sport and movies, children's services are a key subscription driver, as Sky's early marketing of *The Simpsons* clearly indicated. Likewise, new screen technologies such as computer games consoles and PCs, and their associated software, are heavily targeted towards children and parents; while children's video (particularly for pre-schoolers) takes a substantial share of the sell-through market. Partly in response to these developments, the terrestrial channels have also significantly increased their output for children: Channel 4 resumed programming for children in 1993, while the BBC is now repeating its afternoon children's programmes on BBC2 in the early morning, and Channel 5 also has a commitment to this audience. At least in terms of quantity, children now seem to be extraordinarily well-served.

If children do now appear to have become a valuable, sought-after audience, the assumption that they can be bought cheaply still remains. In fact, much of this expansion of provision has been achieved through the increased scheduling of repeats; and most of it can be accounted for by the purchasing of inexpensive imported programming, mainly from the US. Indeed, children's value in the television market is to a large degree based on the cheapness with which a service can be put together out of existing copyrighted material. Most of the new cable providers have significant advantages in this respect, since they own substantial libraries of rights (although the BBC is of course in a similar position). With the exception of TCC – whose imminent demise is frequently predicted – all are US-owned; and they enjoy the additional benefit of the economies of scale of the domestic US market, which means that costs can be amortised before overseas sales even have to be considered. None of the new cable/satellite providers is investing in home-produced programming for children to anywhere near the degree they are investing in sport: it would be fair to guess that the annual expenditure on original programming at Nickelodeon UK is less than

Sky would pay for one premier league football match. Although this is less true of terrestrial television, it is not unduly cynical to point out that Channel 4's increased provision of children's television – most of it imported animation – is likely to generate significant new revenue from toy advertising.

Ultimately, this lack of new product will present significant constraints on future development. Cable channels, particularly Nickelodeon, will have undoubtedly introduced new styles of programming to UK viewers; but in filling a daily service, this material is endlessly repeated and soon loses its freshness. At least some US material is (correctly) judged to be inappropriate for British viewers; yet the lack of investment in home-produced programming may make it make it harder to sustain the presence of new and original material, which will be necessary over the longer term.

Furthermore, given the high penetration of video ownership in this country and the overall increase in expenditure on entertainment services, consumers are likely to be sceptical about whether these new technologies are really offering them anything new. Viewers have limited amounts of time in which they are available to view; and television is now competing with other forms of screen-based entertainment. Children's actual viewing time has not increased in line with provision: indeed, it has actually decreased by 110 minutes a week since 1992. This means that the audience for any single programme is likely to decline as the audience fragments. No one children's programme has been seen by more than 30 per cent of them since 1992. On the other hand, while audiences for terrestrial children's television are declining, two-thirds of children in Britain still live in terrestrial-only homes – a figure that has remained fairly stable since 1995. Even in the United States, the four main networks still enjoy a 60 per cent audience share; and the predicted fragmentation of the mass audience appears to have reached a limit (Neuman, 1991).

Two conclusions might be drawn from this complex and unstable situation. First, the children's television market has very rapidly become overcrowded: at least some of the new operators are unlikely to survive. The market has, in this case at least, been seen to provide; yet there are significant economic reasons why it is unlikely to continue to do so at the present high level. Secondly, however, it is clear that the market has provided for some but not for all. As in the case of children's television in the US, the privatisation of communications may well be leading to a polarisation between the 'information rich 'and the 'information poor', in which those with access to cable and other pay-TV options are significantly better served than those without (Wartella *et al*, 1990).

The Future of 'Quality'

Of course, quantity should not be confused with quality. Yet here too, the picture is complex. On the one hand, it is vital to refuse the easy assumptions that are often made in these kinds of debates – for example, that imported programming is necessarily lacking in quality, or that certain genres are incapable of attaining it. As numerous critics have argued (Brunsdon, 1990), such arguments often reflect the tastes of particular social class groups – and in this case, perhaps one might also add age groups. Many laments for the decline of quality in children's television seem to be based on a preference for historical costume dramas based on 'classic' novels, and on a nostalgia for childhood favourites from the 1950s and 1960s such as *Watch with Mother*, *Jackanory* and *Blue Peter* (as it used to be). Such arguments often appear to rest on a highly protectionist construction of childhood, and an assumption that 'quality' children's television should function as a corrective to children's own instinctive tastes – that it should ultimately be leading them on to 'better things' than just watching television (Wagg, 1992).

Such arguments are also often based on an extraordinary degree of ignorance about the material itself. For example, the fear of 'wall-to-wall American cartoons' is one which is often invoked by lobbyists; yet it is a vision which belies the diversity of the material itself. To be sure, the dominance of animation is partly a consequence of the globalisation of the children's television market: animation is easier to dub into other languages, it is generally less culturally specific than live action, and has a longer shelf life. Nevertheless, it is meaningless to talk about 'quality' in this area without making distinctions, for example between different genres of animation, or between animations which are targeted at different age groups. Arguably, the most innovative and creatively imaginative children's programmes of the last five years have been animated; while series like *Rugrats*, *Doug* and *The Simpsons* have all demonstrated that cartoons can be a vehicle for social commentary in ways that are both entertaining and incisive.

Perhaps even more reassuring for advocates of public service broadcasting is the evidence about what children are actually choosing to watch; although the messages are mixed here too. The fact that the majority of children's viewing is given over to adult programmes is well-established, although it still frequently meets with expressions of horror in certain quarters. Currently, the list of top 20 programmes watched by children includes only one children's show (in 1985 there were eight); although children's programmes still account for 10 of the top 50. At the same time, the children's 'top tens' are consistently occupied by home-grown dramas such as *Grange Hill* and *Byker Grove* and factual programmes such as *Art Attack* and *Blue Peter*. The notion that, given the choice, children will only watch US cartoons seems to reflect an implicit distrust of the child audience which is far from justified. On the other hand, one can point to the growing significance in the ratings of what might be termed 'kidult' programming – such as *Neighbours*, *Gladiators* or *Baywatch* – that still has mass 'family' appeal; although this too is far from being a new development (in earlier decades, for example, we had *Dr Who* and *The Generation Game*).

The debate about quality also has a significant economic dimension. In the global children's television market, genres such as 'quality' drama are extremely marketable commodities; and as such, are often well-placed to attract finance from co-production or video sales. 'Classic' adaptations such as the BBC's *Chronicles of Narnia* or HTV's *The Famous Five* are cases in point. These series reflect a certain construction of 'British' national identity which may well be quite close to the hearts of those who see children's television as being threatened by the encroachment of 'American trash'. What are less easily marketable, however, are more socially realist series which reflect the contemporary experiences of children from other social classes or ethnic groups – and in this respect, the internationalisation of children's media culture may be leading to a narrowing (even a stereotyping) of particular national identities. Interestingly, US representations of minority groups – as in sitcoms such as *Moesha* and *Fresh Prince of Bel Air* – do appear to be more internationally marketable, and are in fact very popular with young black British audiences; although these series could not really be categorised as 'social realism' either.

Ultimately, then, 'quality' does not necessarily equate with a lack of mass popularity, or with material which cannot be marketed. Furthermore, if we define quality in broad terms, it is clear that commercial broadcasters can provide it – and indeed that they have to provide it if they are to retain their audiences. The problem, perhaps, is not so much to do with quality as with diversity. Nickelodeon, for example, provides some animation and situation comedy which (at least in our view) is of very high quality; yet it is singularly lacking in factual programming and in more realist drama – precisely the areas in which the BBC is currently so successful. The extent to which the move towards a more commercial system may result in a narrowing of diversity in children's programmes is one which is being addressed in our current research (cf. Turow, 1981); although, like quality, diversity is exceptionally difficult to measure and define. Despite the discursive centrality of both terms in debates about children's television, and their inscription within legislation (for example, in the remit of the ITC), their meaning seems to be infinitely vague. If notions of quality and diversity are to have any purchase in future attempts to regulate children's broadcasting in the new commercial environment, it is essential that they should be more precisely and rigorously defined.

Public Service Goes to Market

On one level, the demise of British public service broadcasting, so widely anticipated in recent years, has failed to materialise. The ITC has not been content to become a mere 'light-touch' regulator (Goodwin 1992); while the BBC has not yet been privatised, even after 18 years of Conservative government. At least in relation to the child audience, the continuing commitment of terrestrial broadcasters can partly be traced to the constant – if sometimes hysterical – public concern expressed in the press and among lobby groups. Certainly, this is an area in which the BBC remains extremely sensitive to criticism (at least from self-professed 'parents' and lobbyists), as its 1996 Governors' Seminar on Children's Broadcasting demonstrated.

Nevertheless, there have been significant shifts within the BBC, and in the practice of public service broadcasting more broadly. Historically, of course, the BBC has embodied a highly paternalistic attitude towards children (Wagg, 1992; Jones and Kelley, 1997). Childhood has traditionally been sectioned off as a kind of sacred space; and there has been a widespread suspicion of the popular pleasures that television can afford. Nevertheless, the decades of the regulated duopoly saw significant, if very gradual, moves away from this approach. From the late 1960s, a more 'child-centred' conception of children's television began to emerge, which was not solely based on narrow conceptions of what counts as 'educational'. Most obviously through programmes like *Grange Hill*, broadcasters have steadily extended the boundaries of what is seen as acceptable children's culture, and of the kinds of contemporary issues which can be raised with this audience. While there are certainly significant criticisms that might be raised in relation to this approach, it is important to distinguish it from the more conservative account of the 'great tradition' which appears to inform much public debate.

In recent years, however, the BBC has moved more sharply to accommodate commercial pressures. In response to a hostile political climate, and faced with ever-shrinking licence fee revenues, it has become increasingly entrepreneurial. In children's television as in many other areas, programmes are now developed with merchandising and international sales potential centrally in mind. The evolution of its Saturday morning programming, for example, has displayed an increasingly enthusiastic embrace of the commercial dimensions of children's culture: the shows have become increasingly 'media-centric', drawing their primary content from the world of popular music and soap operas. When the new Saturday morning show *Live and Kicking* replaced *Going Live*, the BBC's entrepreneurial division, BBC Worldwide, was involved from the start in developing an accompanying magazine that would promote the new show – a magazine which is now a market leader, reflecting the BBC's hold over its 'captive audience'. Paradoxically, the commercial companies are in some ways more hidebound by ITC regulation and suffer from being part of a federal system. In our research, executives and programme-makers in the commercial sector have tended to talk far more about their special responsibility to children and far less about reaching new markets than those at the BBC. In many ways, the BBC is now perhaps the most commercially advantaged and ruthless player in children's media – not least in the international marketplace, where it is vigorously capitalising on its reputation as a brand leader. In terms of programming, the boundaries between the BBC and the cable/satellite sector have become increasingly blurred: two of the shows screened during the BBC's *Live and Kicking*, for example, are Nickelodeon productions (*Rugrats* and *Clarissa Explains It All*); while Nickelodeon has bought the BBC's pre-school sequence for screening in the UK.

In noting these developments, however, we do not wish to fall back into a simplistic dichotomy between 'culture' and 'commerce' which often characterises debates in this field (Buckingham, 1995). Attacks on commercialism in children's culture often reflect a patrician distaste for 'trade', and a puritanical notion of what is 'good' for children (Seiter, 1993). On one level, it could be argued that marketisation and increased competition have increased the status of the children's audience. In a more competitive environment, broadcasters are forced to take their audiences very seriously, rather than simply giving them what they think they ought to have. The increasingly significant role of audience research is evidence of this shift: both non-terrestrial and terrestrial executives are now spending increasing amounts of money on assessing the tiniest nuance of scheduling and content with the aim of capturing and retaining the audience.

Nevertheless, it would be a mistake to conclude from this that the market necessarily ensures a degree of responsiveness to audience needs (cf. Connell, 1983). There is a significant difference between market research and accountability to the audience: holding a phone-in competition is not the same thing as giving the audience a voice. Indeed, it could be argued that the new commercial logic positions children as 'sovereign consumers': it is only concerned with children's wants and needs insofar as it can discover what will get them to watch or not to watch, to buy or not to buy.

Conclusion

As we have begun to indicate in this paper, the changing political economy of broadcasting has contradictory implications for the child audience. The marketisation of children's television has led to a massive proliferation of services for children; yet it may also result in a narrowing in some areas, and in increasing levels of inequality. Ultimately, as in other areas of broadcasting policy, we must face up to the fact that the stability of the regulated duopoly has gone for good: the question is how we ensure that children are adequately served within a largely market-led, global system. To be sure, we need to sustain the public service commitment to universal provision, and to quality and diversity – and we need to find more effective ways of defining and measuring these. Yet in our view, the response of terrestrial children's broadcasters and the children's television lobby has been backward-looking and conservative. It is inadequate simply to insist on the principle of public service, without also recognising the need for increasing accountability and for democratisation.

Perhaps the greatest paradox in this whole area is that children's needs have been defined and defended, although children themselves have been largely silenced. As in the massive reforms of schooling which have taken place over the past two decades, significant changes have occurred in a social institution whose primary users have been wholly excluded from the debate. If children are indeed a 'special' audience, we need to find ways of ensuring that their needs are more rigorously and systematically understood, and that their voices are heard.

Note

This paper draws on research conducted for an ESRC-funded project 'Children's Media Culture: Education, Entertainment and the Public Sphere' (ref: L126251026). Thanks to our colleagues Ken Jones, Peter Kelley and Gunther Kress for their contributions.

References

Blumler, J. (1992) *The Future of Children's Television in Britain* London: Broadcasting Standards Council.

Brunsdon, C. (1990) 'Problems with quality', Screen 31(1), 67-90.

Buckingham, D. (1995) 'The commercialisation of childhood? The place of the market in children's media culture', *Changing English* 2(2), 17-40.

Connell, I. (1983) 'Commercial broadcasting and the British left', *Screen* 24(6), 70-80.

Goodwin (1992) 'Did the ITC save British public service broadcasting?' *Media, Culture and Society* 14(4), 653-661.

Jones, K. and Kelley, P. (1997) 'Reinventing children's television: lessons from the 1950s', paper presented to the Manchester Broadcasting Symposium.

Kunkel, D. (1993) 'Policy and the future of children's television', in Berry, G. and Asamen, J. (eds.), *Children and Television* London: Sage.

Melody, W. (1973) *Children's Television: The Economics of Exploitation* New Haven, Yale University Press.

Neuman, W.R. (1991) *The Future of the Mass Audience* Cambridge, Cambridge University Press.

Seiter, E. (1993) *Sold Separately: Parents and Children in Consumer Culture* New Brunswick, Rutgers University Press.

Turow, J, (1981) *Education, Entertainment and the Hard Sell* New York, Praeger.

Wagg, S. (1992) 'One I made earlier: Media, popular culture and the politics of childhood' in Dominic Strinati and Stephen Wagg (eds.) *Come On Down? Popular Media Culture in Post-War Britain* London, Routledge.

Wartella, E., Heintz, K.E., Aidman, A.J. and Mazzarella, S.R. (1990) 'Television and beyond: Children's video media in one community', *Communication Research* 17(1), 45-64.

Channels to the Future

Children's views about broadcasting provision

Máire Messenger Davies (with Kate O'Malley & Beth Corbett)

London College of Printing & Distributive Trades

Introduction

This paper describes findings from a BBC-funded study on children and television drama carried out by the authors. The study surveyed over 1300 children in 18 schools in England and Wales. The paper discusses sample responses from children and addresses how children position themselves in current debates about the child audience and the future of public service broadcasting.

Background to the study

The study has taken place in the context of a changing broadcasting environment for children, in which the two main terrestrial broadcasters, BBC1 and ITV (Channel 3), who have traditionally taken the major share of children's viewing, are now having to compete for their audiences with many new channels, including a new terrestrial commercial channel, Channel 5. About a third of all households with children have cable or satellite TV with access to specialist children's channels such as Nickelodeon, The Disney Channel and The Cartoon Network, most of whose programming comes from the United States. Around 43% of our sample had cable and satellite.

The public debate about children and broadcasting, often enmeshed with other issues such as child delinquency, (e.g. Barlow & Hill, 1985; Broadcasting Standards Council, 1996) has coincided with a debate within the academy about the changing 'nature' of childhood (Jencks, 1982; Postman, 1985; Prout & James, 1990). For Postman (1985), mass broadcasting is implicated in what he calls 'the disappearance of childhood': the destruction of the necessary boundaries between childhood and adulthood by a television-based culture which makes no distinctions between the knowledge offered to adults and that offered to children.

Prout and James (1990) similarly define childhood as culturally constructed; they draw an absolute distinction between childhood and the biological state of being a child: 'Childhood as *distinct from* [my italics] biological immaturity, is neither a natural nor universal feature of human groups but appears as a specific structural and cultural component of many societies.' (p. 8) This is not a distinction that children themselves would necessarily make, and it raises the salient question of how much control children have over how childhood is 'constructed.' The children in our study used the terms 'childhood' and 'children'

109

interchangeably. In a discussion about whether it would be possible for a head-master, like 'The Demon Headmaster', (BBC1) to 'get rid of childhood', 10-11 year olds in Co. Durham argued: 'It would be impossible to get rid of child-hood... because you'd have to get rid of every child in the world as well.' Needless to say, they thought this was 'a totally bad idea.'

Children in the market

Some academics (e.g. Patricia Palmer, 1986; Edward Palmer, 1988; Davies, 1989, 1997) argue that there are aspects of childhood that are unchanging, and that still need special services and attention from broadcasting, and other, institu-tions: what Palmer (1988) calls 'legal sanctuary' – a place where children's cul-ture is safeguarded. Other concerns are raised by the increasing commercialisation and globalisation of the media market, one of them being the homogenisation of children's own local cultures. Popular children's genres, such as animation, are particularly vulnerable to this. John Marsden, of Carlton TV, pointed out in an interview with us: 'In the past, Channel 3 (ITV) was almost totally funded by money from ITV stations, we didn't have to look to other countries for income to make cartoon programmes, so we could actually make those programmes for children in the UK... [Now] we can't make programmes solely for the British market – we have to be more politically correct.'

Within this framework of acknowledgement of children as a group with spe-cial needs, but whose needs are becoming more difficult to define in a global, multi-channel communications society, a recognition has been developing among broadcasters and policy-makers world-wide, that these needs include access to media which address them and their concerns directly, and is not mediated through adult, or 'family' material. This is the rationale behind the movement for a Children's Charter in broadcasting, introduced at the World Summit on Children and Television in Melbourne, in March 1995, a meeting to be repeat-ed in London in 1998. The Children's Charter invokes the UN Rights of the Child, specifying children's rights to cultural experience and education of their own.

One of the moving spirits of the Charter is Anna Home, Head of Children's Programmes at the BBC – traditionally providing an international 'gold stan-dard' for children's programming. However, even the BBC is now feeling the pressure of commercial competition: As Anna Home pointed out, in an inter-view with us (Davies & O'Malley, 1996): "The BBC in general is much more aware and concerned about ratings than it used to be... It's more difficult to jus-tify the low ratings minority type programme... We're [also] in a situation where the TV service year on year is required to make efficiency savings, i.e. cuts.'

What is the point of children's programmes?

One issue raised by our study could seem attractive to programme executives trying to keep costs down. Do children really need television programmes made especially for them, when ratings show that the most-watched programmes by children aged 4–15 are adult shows like *The X Files* and *EastEnders*? If children see themselves as well-served by programmes in the adult schedules, what is the need for special, and expensive, drama programmes targeted specifically at them? Our study put these questions to children. While their views varied, and, like those of their elders, were often contradictory, one unequivocal finding was a desire among all age groups for 'more programmes for children my age', with 10–12 year olds (over 70 per cent) perceiving the greatest need. This suggests that being positioned as 'older' or 'younger' than other groups is an important element in the way children construct their own identities.

The methodology of the study: consumers and citizens

Our methodological approaches required children to adopt positions both as consumers (questions about their own tastes and opinions) and as citizens (making judgements on behalf of other people.) Depending on which role they were asked to take, contrasting responses were sometimes produced, as illustrated in the questions below, asking children their opinions about the 'cathartic' function of drama in their personal lives.

Table 1: Proportions (%) of boys, girls and all children combined agreeing with the statements that:

	% answering True			% answering Not True			% answering Not Sure		
	All	Boys	Girls	All	Boys	Girls	All	Boys	Girls
Children's TV helps me with problems in my life	26	26	25	42	45	39	32	29	36
Children's TV helps other children with problems in their lives	39	36	41	22	26	17	39	38	41

The contrast between these two answers illustrates the difference between consumer and citizenship roles. A majority of children agree that television helps other children, but disagree that it helps them. In reality, there is likely to be displacement in claiming that other children are helped, and not oneself.

Role-playing channel controllers

The qualitative tasks probed children's attitudes to these questions in more depth, and enabled them to move spontaneously between consumer and citizenship roles through negotiation with their peers. One exercise, described here, was a 'scheduling task', in which 8–12 year old children were asked to act as controllers of a new children's channel, broadcasting initially for one day a week, between 3 and 6 p.m. Working in groups, each with its own leader, children had to choose six programmes to fill this slot, from a mixed selection of 35 familiar adults' and children's programmes. The six most frequently-mentioned programmes produced by the whole class were selected for the second stage.

The second stage was a tape-recorded discussion between the six group leaders, in which they, as channel 'controllers', were told that their channel was losing money, and hence would have less airtime. They had to get rid of first one programme, then another, until only one of the six was left. These discussions revealed children's priorities in deciding what was, and was not, appropriate material for a specialist children's channel.

Priorities of children as channel controllers

The following analysis comes from two schools: a primary school in Colchester (8–11 year olds) and a Welsh bilingual comprehensive Year 7 class (11–12 year olds). The Colchester school was our pilot school; the task they were given was to select programmes for a non-specialist service, which resulted in a greater choice of adult programmes. In the main study, including the Cardiff school, the service was more precisely specified as 'children's'.[1] The children's priorities for selection, some similar to those of adults, produced the following categories:

1. Diversity (c.f. Blumler, 1992)
2. Age suitability
3. The rights of audiences, including minorities and gender.
4. Public service responsibilities
5. Quality (c.f. Blumler, ibid)

Despite the task specifically mentioning the need to save money, commercial considerations were not invoked, except indirectly.

Diversity

There were two kinds of diversity – first, awareness of diverse audiences, expressed here by one of the groups in the Colchester school (9–10 year olds):

> *999* is very good. It's educational as well. We chose *Songs of Praise* for religious people. *Animal Hospital* is for the people who like animals. We didn't really want *Man O Man* but we thought it wouldn't really be fair on the girls if we didn't have it.

Another Colchester group prioritised diversity of genre, as well as of audience:

> *The X Files* was really popular, there was 4 out of 5, *Man O Man* everybody liked, *Match of the Day* we put on for sport, *Are You Afraid of the Dark*, we put on for comedy and horror as well, *Rugrats* we put on for children, *Animal Hospital* we put on for animal lovers and *Men Behaving Badly* for adults.

Allied to this were considerations of scheduling. A schedule based on 'availability to view', (Barwise & Ehrenberg, 1992) allied to public service considerations, was devised by one of the Cardiff groups, who, like older schedulers, came up with the strategy of 'hammocking' for a potentially less popular information programme:

> We came to a decision that we should put programmes for younger children, e.g. *Fudge*, first and then work up through the ages gradually and finishing with *Top of the Pops*, with *Newsround* in the middle because we think it's important for children to know what's going on in the world.

Age suitability
A major concern for schedulers is the wide age range that children's programming has to reach. Children in the study expressed definite opinions about the
appropriateness of different kinds of programming for different age groups. In
general, their concern was to 'protect' younger children (c.f. adult concerns) –
but they were also able to acknowledge the needs of older members of the audience; for instance, one Colchester group braved the derision of the class to
include *Songs of Praise* in their selection, because 'older people liked it.'

Comprehension was an issue in deciding whether programmes were appropriate for younger children or not:

Llewellyn (Cardiff): *Ren and Stimpy* is a really funny cartoon, but little
children wouldn't find it funny.

And 'suitability' was a major concern:

Briony (Cardiff): *Top of the Pops* sometimes goes a bit over the top. It
doesn't seem like a young children's programme to be watching... A
lot of the songs have got swear words.
Llewellyn: And there's drinking on stage and alcohol and stuff.
Briony: Some of the pop singers take drugs and that might influence
young children.

Adult soaps and series, such as *EastEnders* and *The Bill* too, though popular with
children at the first stage, were often abandoned at the second for this reason,
despite the occasional defence of the needs of 'older people':

Llewellyn (Cardiff): It [*EastEnders*] is not very suitable, it's a bit violent, a lot of aggression.
Briony: It hasn't got very good language in it. My dad hates it.
Martin (Colchester): We could do without *The Bill* though ... because
it is teaching people to sort of like – do things like commit murder.
Someone might watch that and think, oh that looks like a load of fun
and go out and do it.

The rights of audiences
Both in this exercise, and in some of the other exercises, not reported here (for
instance a censorship task), children expressed concern about the injustice of
minorities dictating to majorities about what they should and should not see.
The Welsh-speaking children were sensitive to the importance of preserving their
linguistic inheritance, but also showed awareness of being part of a wider cultural constituency:

Evan: We should get rid of *Slot Meithrin* [a S4C pre-school programme].
Briony: Not everyone speaks Welsh and even the Welsh children, not
a lot of them will watch *Slot Meithrin*. I'm not sure how many of them
watch Welsh television.

Similarly, *EastEnders*, despite being (to some) offensively English, was defended in terms of its appeal to a national audience:

> Briony: A lot of Welsh people don't like a London accent, they don't understand it.
> Ryan: I don't agree with that at all; a lot of my family do live in London now and I think that's a bit prejudiced in a way, just because we're Welsh doesn't mean we don't like the English and just because other people are English, it doesn't mean they don't like Welsh.
> Llewellyn: Yeah I know what you think, I have nothing against London people, but it is a bit too old for people, it should be on later.

Nevertheless, the rights of minorities to be represented in the schedules were also defended:

> Ryan (Cardiff): *Blue Peter* should go.
> Evan: Not *Blue Peter*, because people like it and people who have got problems like leprosy and disability and in a wheelchair.

Again, the Welsh children struggled to reconcile the rights of minorities with the tastes of the majority:

> Briony: I think the same really, you should represent as you said, different countries, but it doesn't really matter if one Welsh programme goes.
> Llewellyn: We've got to have these English programmes; even though I wouldn't watch *Slot Meithrin*, some people would.

The other issue discussed in this context was gender: we were impressed by the generally civilised way in which boys and girls negotiated their differences and conceded points to each other.

> Sarah (Colchester): I think *Man O Man* should be out. It's taking the mickey out of boys.
> Alan: I'd get rid of *Man O Man*.
> Diane: What about the women?
> Martin: So – women can watch *Clarissa, Rugrats, 999, Grange Hill, The Bill* and *The X Files*.
> Jacqueline: I think it [*Man O Man*] should be in, because also it helps women make their decisions for what man they want to go out with.

Clarissa Explains it All, the American programme shown both on Nickelodeon and on BBC1, was seen positively as a girls' programme, and one that fulfilled the valuable function of 'helping (other) people with problems', although it was criticised for what was perceived as typically American narcissim.

> Martin: *Clarissa* is just about herself mainly, not about everybody else.

Jacqueline: They [the audience] might not know about Americans, because she is American.

Diane: She is telling people about her problems so that they can figure out problems for themselves.

Public service responsibilities

Public service priorities like these surfaced in other discussions. An example is the Cardiff group's choice of *Newsround* as part of their balanced schedule because it was 'important for children to know what's going on in the world.' When it came to making decisions between two popular choices, public service considerations were paramount:

> Martin (Colchester): Even though I am a big fan of *The X Files* I think it should go because people with problems should come first.
> Alan: *999* saves people's lives ... *Grange Hill* should go and *999* should stay.

Quality

Quality is a major criterion for evaluating the worth of programmes in the real world of channel controllers, and is a requirement for any commercial channel wanting a licence to broadcast. A number of attempts have been made to define it, for instance Hoggart *et al* for the Broadcasting Research Unit (1982), and producers claim it as an essential ingredient of their products (e.g. BBC People and Programmes, 1995). Academics are more reluctant to proffer definitions, falling back on appeals to cultural relativity, and objections to 'elitism' (see Hartley, 1992 and Davies, 1996, 1997 for discussion of these issues). Nevertheless, for people working in the industry, and in film/arts education, criteria of performance have to be established for creative media workers.

The children in our study rarely invoked aesthetic or cultural value concepts, but when they did, they demonstrated a sensitivity to the importance of style and presentation:

> Ryan (Cardiff): The thing is, on *Top of the Pops* they just show you the music, they don't really tell you the background of the band so you're not learning – not like *Live and Kicking* when the guests come on. On *Live and Kicking* they ask them all about them. On *Top of the Pops* they're just playing.
> Evan: They're more like respectable type bands on *Live and Kicking*, they don't have stuff like Heavy Metal, they have stuff like...
> Briony: Robson and Jerome.
> Laughter...

> Martin (Colchester – talking about *The Bill*): It seems to me that they destroy the middle, they don't finish the story.
> Diane: It's like a two part story, it stops on the exciting part.
> Martin: To find the murderer you have to wait another week.

115

MD: Why do you think they do that?
Martin: To get you to watch it next week. Like a cliff-hanger.

Words like 'good', 'cool', 'bad', 'boring' were used during descriptions of pro-grammes, but these kinds of subjective judgements were rarely used as a rea-son for jettisoning, or keeping, a programme. When children acted as channel controllers, they were far more likely to take a citizenship perspective than a consumerist one. From whatever source (and neither of these schools offered for-mal media education), these children had absorbed the discourses of diversity, responsibility, suitability, audience rights and quality used by their elders in debates about broadasting.

The question is, which perspective would we, as adults, like children to adopt? And what are children's 'rights' in this area? We believe our research demon-strates that children are highly capable of debating these questions for them-selves. The reality of children's lives is that they are almost entirely (and increasingly) shaped and controlled by adult structures and institutions. But the kinds of discussions reported here illustrate children's aptitude both for skilful-ly performing to adult expectations (for instance in fulfilling the different task requirements extremely faithfully); and for negotiating with each other in more characteristically childlike ways. They deserve to be heard in policy debates. These issues will be further discussed in Davies & O'Malley (1997 – forthcom-ing.)

Endnote

1. The programmes elected to be discussed in the second stage were:

Colchester:

> 1. *The X Files*; 2. *Animal Hospital*; 3. *Man O Man*; 4. *Rugrats*; 5. *999*; 6. *The Bill*; 7. *Ren and Stimpy*; 8. *Clarissa Explains it All* (inserted by controller); 9. *Grange Hill* (inserted by controller).

Final choice was between *Grange Hill* and *999* (*999* won).

Cardiff:

> 1. *Top of The Pops*; 2. *Rugrats*; 3. *Home and Away*; 4. *Blue Peter*; 5. *Slot Meithrin*; 6. *EastEnders*; 7. *Live and Kicking*; 8. *Ren and Stimpy*.

Final choice was between *Live and Kicking* and *Rugrats* (*Rugrats* won)

References

Barlow, G. & Hill, A. (1985), *Video Violence* and *Children*, London: Hodder & Stoughton

Barwise, P. & Ehrenberg, A. (1993), *Television and its Audience*. London: Sage

BBC (1995), *People & Programmes: BBC Radio & Television for an age of choice*. London: BBC

Blumler, J. (1992), *The Future of Children's Television in Britain: an enquiry for the Broadcasting Standards Council*, London: BSC

Broadcasting Standards Council (1996), *Young People and the Media, Research Working Paper*, London: BSC

Davies, M. M. (1989), *Television is Good for your Kids*. London: Hilary Shipman

Davies, M. M. (1996), 'Making media literate: Educating future media workers at under-graduate level', in R. Kubey and B. Ruben (Eds.), *Literacy in the Information Age: infor-mation & behavior*, Vol. 6, Transaction, New Brunswick, NJ.

Davies, M. M. (1997), *Fake, Fact and Fantasy: children's interpretation of television reality*, Mahwah, NJ: Lawrence Erlbaum Associates

Davies, M. M. & O'Malley, K. (1996). *Children and Television Drama: a review of the literature*, report for the BBC, London College of Printing.

Davies, M. M. & O'Malley, K. (1997 – forthcoming): *Children and Television Drama: research with British children*, report for the BBC, London College of Printing

Hartley, J. (1992), *Tele-ology*, London: Routledge

Jencks, C. (1982), 'Constituting the child', in Jencks, C. (Ed.), *The Sociology of Childhood: essential readings*, London, Batsford.

Palmer, E. (1988), *Television & America's Children: a crisis of neglect*, Oxford: OUP

Palmer, P. (1986), *The Lively Audience*, Sydney: Allen & Unwin

Postman, N.(1985), *The Disappearance of Childhood*, London: W. H. Allen

Prout, A. & James, A., (1990) *Constructing and Reconstructing Childhood*, London: Falmer Press

What Price Creativity?

Dateline, The X-Files, and Touched by an Angel in a World of Ratings, Shares and Tonnage

Kathryn Smoot Egan
Brigham Young University, USA

When the Salt Lake City, U.S.A., market became metered by the Nielsen Media Research company in November 1996, audience measurements in ratings were supposed to become more accurate. The introduction of metering to a market had been known to change the percentage of the audience reportedly viewing the local television news programmes, and so station news directors were nervous. They consulted with their 'doctors' – advisors paid to help them make their news programmes more attractive to viewers. One consultant gave this advice:

> Find out the zip code of your Nielsen-metered families and park your news truck in that neighborhood.[1]

Is the ratings system antithetical to creativity? William Blake said 'where any view of money exists art cannot be carried on.' In the U.S., a programme that does not generate high ratings (that is, does not 'reach' large audiences) will not attract advertising revenue to pay for production or distribution.

The 'open marketplace' approach to broadcasting to a mass audience presupposes that audience interest, convenience or necessity will determine the financial success of a programme or broadcast entity.[2] To satisfy the requirements of the U.S. marketplace, the programme's creators must somehow be in a dialogue with the viewers. Considering that the 'viewers' are a mass audience rather than one individual, the dialogue must be with representatives of the viewers. This paper analyzes the dialogue.

In U.S. television, creativity is confined by the rules of audience construction for the purposes of the advertiser.[3] The audience is considered coin of exchange in the social and economic context,[4] but this is only one audience image that might influence the writing and production of television news and entertainment programmes. This paper also considers another image, and that is audience as consumer, which assumes audiences have well-formed content preferences to which broadcasters must respond.[5]

Either image, 'coin of exchange' or 'consumer' of programmes, can influence what is produced, successfully, for commercial television. In questioning how much creative autonomy producers and writers have within the organizational, economic and political contexts of their work, Cantor[6] defines 'the negotiated struggle', or the process for getting 'their' content to an audience. Fiske[7] uses 'viewer,' an active participant in the television communication process, as opposed to 'audience', which is passive. The participant brings to television his/her social relations (point of view) and the material situation. 'A viewer is engaged with the screen more variously, actively and selectively than is a spectator.' It would seem, then, that the writer-producer must interact with the programme audience in order to create a successful product. The interaction must take some form of dialogue.

Dialogue has been defined as 'a sustained collective inquiry into the processes, assumptions and certainties that constitute everyday experience.'[8] 'Dialogue is an ongoing conflict of interpretations, involved in the production of meaning.'[9] The assumption here is that 'meaning' of a programme is perceived differently by different people. When the community of people (the viewers) and the programme creator dialogue, they produce a free flow of thought. The programme creator can draw on the shared 'rich store of meaning' to create a programme that will construct an audience from those viewers.

This paper considers three forms of dialogue between creators and viewers. The forms include:

1 *Analysis of ratings*, or *summative evaluations* of a programme by an audience; 'summative' because they are derived after the programme has been produced and aired. Ratings, with a confidence level of about 68 per cent,[10] are toward the 'high reliability' end of a continuum of 'representativeness' of the constructed audience. The primary contribution to the dialogue by the audience is the interpretation of the data by the programme creators in producing the next episode, or group of episodes, for the programme.

2 *Formative research*, which is any scientific or quasi-scientific study of audience reaction to a programme while in the early stages of development or on-going production. They try to predict whether the programme will be successful in garnering an audience; they tend to be semi-reliable.

3 *Informal*, which might include fan mail, critical commentary by published reviewers, and hits on an Internet site by audience members after a programme. Informal dialogues are considered to be of 'low-reliability' in representativeness of the audience, and yet qualitatively they may be given more consideration than more generalized reactions because they come from the desired audience – the 'X-Philers', for example.[11]

Programme creators may choose to attend to, or ignore, any of these forms of dialogue. I propose that programme creators who are successful in terms of generating desired audiences are in some form of dialogue with the programme viewers.

Method

Three sources are examined for evidence of dialogue between producer and audience (viewer).

1. The first is a research study (N=454) of morning television news viewer preferences in the Salt Lake City ADI.

2. The second is my student's masters thesis, *The Analysis of Encoding of a*

Television Message, a research study (N=72) of how the programme Dateline, a quasi-news programme, is encoded for the ideal viewer by the show's creators (writers and producers).

3. The third is an ethnographic study composed of interviews with television programme creators (producers/writers) attending the National Association of Television Programming Executives (NATPE) in New Orleans, January 13–17, 1997.

Analysis

Morning Television News Audience Survey
In the 37th largest ADI in the U.S., news consultants and proprietary research had indicated that a station branded as 'friendly' would appeal to a niche of the news viewing audience. In the Morning Television News Audience Survey (N=454), conducted by telephone by communications research students at Brigham Young University, 68.2 percent of the respondents said that the *friendliness* of the morning news anchor was 'important' to 'very important.' (M=3.84 on a 5-point Likert scale, with 1= not important, 5= very important). A local newscast is predicted to garner higher ratings, because it is more welcome over breakfast, or while preparing children for school, if the news anchors are 'friendly'. On KUTV, that information was interpreted to mean the anchors should chat about their personal lives. The anchors were not particularly friendly off camera, and the female anchor did not like fishing; nevertheless, from 5:30 when the programme went on air, until 7:00, when the national morning news programme came on, they gamely discussed the fishing trip. Their awkwardness was apparent to the researchers – an undergraduate class – who analyzed the videotape of the programme for research variables. Occasionally, seeking to be responsive to research findings regarding 'audience needs and interests' can backfire.[12] The dialogue between programme creators and viewers has been distorted by misapplication or misinterpretation of the message.

The Analysis of Encoding of a Television Message: the Dateline Study
Prime time network programmes are a story different from a local television production. Unlike local news, these network programmes depend on huge audiences to generate the ratings – or audience reach – advertisers want and will pay huge sums of money to garner.

> Tonnage is the industry term for delivery of large, even massive audiences in which the sheer numbers of people reached take on a greater importance than the types of people these are.[13]

Tonnage pays the high costs for prime time programme production for programmes such as *The X-Files, Touched by an Angel,* and *Dateline*. Ratings determine the fates of these prime time shows as they do the news programmes, but even before ratings are generated as summative evaluation, formative research is conducted during programme production. The intent is to increase the probability that if a programme makes it into the network's schedule, it will be a ratings success. Programme writer/producers often claim any kind of research inhibits their creativity, and that they ignore the formative research findings (at their peril, according to network vice presidents).[14] I believe programme creators often do not know how to evaluate research findings for reliability and validity. They do not know how to apply viewer response to their creative thinking to construct an audience of participant viewers. It is possible to use findings as a guide or reference for their creativity, as a book author would use an editor who is in tune with the market to encode a written work of fiction for an 'ideal reader.' Programmes are tested while in production and during the run of the series to ascertain whether they are on track with their target audience.

Natalia Mesheryakova studied the encoding of the television messages by *Dateline*'s producers and writers whose goal was to compete with *60 Minutes* and other news magazine shows. Her research questions were: Who is the ideal viewer' for *Dateline*? How is a specific viewer inscribed in a video message by *Dateline* producers? Is it possible that producers make a television programme for people like themselves? Or for their friends, relatives, bosses, or for an ideal type from research profiles? And, from what bases of information do the producers make an ideal viewer type?

Most of the producers in the study said they do not imagine an ideal viewer. Of the 18 respondents who did, their ideal viewer's amalgamated image was 'a white female, 18–49 years old, college educated, professional, middle class, employed.'[15] From ratings, one concludes the show's producers were successful in garnering their audience, especially Women 18–49. From an interview with Neal Shapiro, executive producer of *Dateline*, Mesheryakova quoted:

> **Q:** Do you watch the stories before broadcasting?
> **Shapiro:** Yes, I watch them many times.
> **Q:** Do you ask producers to make changes?
> **Shapiro:** Yes. Sometimes a little, sometimes a lot. Sometimes they're easy. But the one we did Tuesday night about Kathy Lee Gifford and sweatshops. Poor Americans saying 'I lost my job' a lot. Then Kathy Lee Gifford happened. So that was a much better story. Everybody's watching that. So, we redid the story. We put Kathy Lee Gifford at the top. I like nothing better than a topic everybody is talking about. But there are plenty of 'sensational' stories that I don't do because I think you can't add anything. Most of my decisions I make are based on what I think is a good story.

From this and her survey questionnaire data (N=72) for the programme's writers/producers, Mesheryakova determined that the executive producer and his subordinates were alike in some ways, age (Shapiro was 38), education (all had some college), income (middle), and race (73.6 % are Caucasian). About half the producers at *Dateline* were women (so the subordinates matched the ideal viewer in gender). They, like the producer, said they produced the programme for people like themselves.

The data also suggested the producers were strongly influenced by the executive producer, who said, 'I look at the stories as a white guy, as a Jew guy, as a man, as a thirty-eight-year-old, as a person who lives in New York, all these things I think about.' He worried how to persuade an audience that the message he produced was important.

He wished people who watch *Dateline* were 'Smart people, good thinkers who care about the world, who care about the place they live in, who want to be informed.'

Mesheryakova concluded that in the U.S., news producers have a great deal of freedom in producing news stories and programmes.[16] Perhaps this is true, as long as the show they produce garners ratings, and therefore advertising support for their programmes.[17] In the case of *Dateline*, Shapiro, and the producers selected for the show, dialogue with the audience was facilitated by the degree to which they resembled one another. Speculation exists that the shows that are most successful in terms of garnering the prized audience demographic 18-49 are produced by people that same age.

In-Depth Producer Interviews
In-depth interviews and comments regarding the programme creator's interaction with audience were obtained at the NATPE convention in New Orleans, January 13-17, 1997. The seven interviews provided qualitative information unavailable by any other method. The producers were selected based on variations of success; two of the most successful are reported here as examples of the forms of dialogue that exist between producer/writer and the audience.

Chris Carter
Chris Carter is the creator, writer and executive producer of *The X-Files* and *Millennium*. At a NATPE morning session he told the audience:

> I wanted to make a show that scares people the way *Night Stalker* scared me when I was 12. That's what *The X-Files* and *Millennium* are about. I was a newspaper writer. I wanted the truth about extraterrestrial life. To create new images.
> **Question from the audience:** I know your fan response on the Internet is about 300 messages per day. What is the influence on you and the show of fan feed-back?
> **Carter:** *The X-Files* is of an age with the Internet. I hear from people immediately after a show airs. It's helpful to know how people are perceiving the show. I've never taken a direct suggestion, but it has a cumulative effect for me. I'm a big chicken at heart. The world is a frightening place. We live in peril. I exploit fears.
> **Q:** Do you believe you are pushing limits [of audience taste]?
> **A:** I don't think the programmes are about 'utter darkness.'[18] *Millennium* has a bright, hopeful message. The hero approaches selflessly to make the world a better place. The show has a bright hero, a bright message. *The X-Files* is a quest for truth. The two characters are literally romantic heroes. *Millennium* is grim. I was proud of the pilot. The show is about man who is suffering, which is grim to a lot of people. I wanted the guy to feel weight of world on his shoulders. He has no ego. The goal is the yellow house – the one bright spot in dark world.

Q: The show breaks the television rule to keep it simple, appeal to a wide audience. How do you get away with that?

A: There was pressure early on – there is a term for it – 'closure' – at the end of episodes. You're supposed to tell the audience what happened. Everything turns out o.k. You can't put cuffs on aliens and throw them in the slammer. You have to leave it open ended – you can't explain the unexplainable. You can't keep it simple. I just do what I want to do.

Q: In this imaginative violence, where do you draw line? Do you think about children who might be watching?

A: I don't like violence on screen. Violence is an element of dramatic story telling. It's got to be there ... We want to be accurate. *Millennium* has a TV 14. That rating is fine. The show is too intense for a younger audience. The rating system is a great service. I'm mindful of too graphic violence, but I have stories to tell. People never understood what I wanted to do ... No one bought it, not until it aired for Rupert Murdoch. A room full of people applauded when the lights came up. Ratings for the show [once it was aired on a regular schedule] fluctuated and fell. The best show was lowest rated. Now more people have seen it. Ratings are not a reflection of success. Demographics are a more important indicator as to whether the show has life.

Following the 'Coffee with Chris Carter' session, I interviewed Carter at the NATPE exhibit.

Interviewer: Who would you say is your 'ideal viewer'?

Chris Carter: You're your own ideal viewer. You create what you'd like to see. If you lose original connection you lose connection to show. You must keep your vision of your belief. The demos for the show are 18 to 49. Both shows get demos younger and older than that. These are the indicators – the index of success. *Millennium* has fewer younger viewers.

Interviewer: Have you ever changed anything in the script because of research findings?

Carter: I've never changed anything because of research.[19] I've heard feedback from some episodes, like the one about the three brothers, who are genetic mutants. There were strong hints of incestuous family breeding. We kept it rooted in hard science, made it believable. And there are some images... like in one, people thought they saw a hand chopped of on screen. Not even close. It was slick editing. You listen, you know how far you can go. I get letters, Internet feedback. A few reviewers. When James Wolcott at *The New Yorker* talks, I listen. I liked the Peacock Brothers. He didn't like it. He said I'd gone over board.[20] I liked the episode I understand his concerns. That's as far as we've gone. We've shown we can do these things with good taste. I keep levels of taste and violence in mind. I've always done that. Been diligent.

The dialogue between the programme creator and viewers – the constructed audience – in this case was informal. Carter conceded that hits on the Internet would influence future thought about the programmes, if not specific changes in a script or the way he 'hears the board.'[21] He said he *was* influenced by critical voices, such as James Wolcott, an authoritative voice, representative of a television audience.

Joel Shukovsky

Joel Shukovsky, husband and production partner to Diane English, creators of *Murphy Brown* and executive producers of *Ink*, have endured a longer period of success – and failure – with the creation of prime time programming. He provides an example of ways in which programme creators are in dialogue with the audience, including using research evidence, even when they deny it. In an interview Shukovsky said,

> Typically, the way we come up with ideas is we try and decide what we'd like to see on T.V., that we would like to go home and watch. CBS is mainly into shows that attract female audiences, 18–49. That's appealing to Diane (English) because I think you get your best work from a writer who is writing about what they know – from our life experiences.
> **Interviewer:** Do you ever make changes based on research?
> **Shukovsky:** Research? Yes, we make changes based on research. Research that validates your own opinions. If not you say the research is faulty. We don't write out a character because of research, but if someone doesn't test well or a story line doesn't test well, something we watch – a thread of stories not working – then we make changes. We get specific research, like 30 pages of data. We ask the audience to analyze specifics. But there are no hard – and – fast rules. The research room has 48 chairs. From that, 12 are picked for a focus group. For specific questions. People decide if things should be tweaked. The conversations about how to make shows better are based on ratings. But the writer is writing from their own experience.

Diane English had been contracted to rework *Ink* for initial airing late in the Fall 1996 season. According to David Poltrack, CBS Executive V.P., Research and Planning:

> 34–54 is our target demo. Their lifestyle, their concerns are what interest us, not action adventure. We want 48, 49 watching us. They're in the advertisers' zone. We work closely with writers and producers. Diane English, Martha Williamson, Cosby, David Kelly, all who are producing shows understand what the CBS audience is. We're trying to make shows that are family friendly, with mature, intelligent themes, not action-oriented or glitzy. *Ink* is targeted for the marketplace age 35-54. All the characters in the newsroom are the same age. Diane English is the same age.

For Shukovsky and English, the dialogue with viewers is summative, because ratings are considered in making rules for how new episodes will be shaped; the dialogue also is formative, because representative target audiences are surveyed and studied in focus groups for their reactions to the programmes, their story lines and characters, while the programme is still in production. The dialogue also is informal, considering the suggestions of the vice president of research.

One of the assumptions in hiring Diane English to write and executive produce *Ink* was that programme creators who are in the same demographic as the target audience will share more meaning with the viewers, based on a common, collective background. This assumption presupposes an on-going dialogue with the viewers based, if nothing else, on common life experiences among a cohort.

Summary and Conclusions

Creativity in producing U.S. television news and entertainment programming is influenced by dialogue, formal and informal, with the constructed audience. Viewer/producer dialogue takes the following forms: 1) *Analysis of formal ratings* (summative evaluation); 2) *Formative research* (conducted by commercial researchers with representative target audiences, using dial-response and follow-on focus group discussion; 3) *Informal dialogue* such as viewer response on the Internet, critical comments by credible reviewers representing the audiences of discerning taste, as opposed to the traditional 'lowest common denominator;[22] and interpretations by network programmers of the various messages provided by research and audience – feedback in dialogue with the writer/producers.

Rather than diminishing creativity, dialogue with viewers has the potential to 'transform the mindlessness and massification ... with higher levels of cultural sensitivity, intelligence, and humanity.'[23]

Endnotes

1. Conversation with Dale Cressman, assistant producer, KUTV morning news programme, Dec 9, 1996. KUTV is a CBS Network owned and operated station and had been charged by the Network to produce a local morning news show, according to Cressman, because local shows on other CBS owned-and-operated stations had garnered good ratings. Consultants were hired by the station to help with the transition from diary-kept ratings to the overnight ratings provided by people meters in the market, as of November 1996.

2. Mark S. Fowler and Daniel L. Brenner, 'A Marketplace Approach to Broadcast Regulation,' *Texas Law Review* 60 (1982) pp.207-245.

3. Peter Orlik, 'Business Gratifications,' *Electronic Media Criticism* (Boston: Focal Press, 1994). 'From a business gratifications standpoint, it is essential to realize that radio/television enterprises ultimately are not in operation to select and deliver programmes to audiences. Instead they are in the *audience construction* industry.' Orlik describes the aims of the advertiser: 'to sculpt an audience whose characteristics mirror as closely as possible the type of people the outlet's advertisers are striving to reach.' (p.100)

4. Ettema, James S. and Whitney, Charles D., *Audience Making: How the Media Create the Audience* (Thousand Oaks, California: Sage, 1994). The authors define audience as institutionally effective in that audiences have social meaning and/or economic value within the system. This includes specialized or segmented audiences and hypothesized

audiences whose interest, convenience and necessity are protected by regulators.

5. Ettema and Whitney, *ibid*, p.8.

6. Muriel Goldsman Cantor, 'The Role of the Audience in the Production of Culture: A personal research retrospective,' in Ettema and Whitney, *Audience Making: How the Media Create the Audience* (Thousand Oaks, California: Sage, 1994) p.160.

7. John Fiske, *Television Culture* (London: Methuen, 1987), p.17. Fiske overlaps the terms 'viewer' and 'reader', making it possible to discuss audiences in the way literary critics discuss them, as contributors to the text. The viewer/audiences can then be termed 'ideal' in the way the producer/writer visualises them, just as writers are thought to have an ideal reader. According to Umberto Eco (1984, *Postscript to the Name of the Rose*, New York: Harcourt Brace Jovanovich), he as a writer seeks a new reader, a 'model reader' that his work itself creates, and *in great quantity* (italics are mine). The difference between the text that desires to produce a new reader and the text that tries to fulfil the wishes of the already existing readers, according to Eco, is that, rather than relying on a formula for effective mass-production, the text that seeks a new audience desires to reveal to the reader what it *should* want. I propose that the writer seeking this model audience succeeds when the viewer (audience) agrees with the author. The premise for assigning many producers to programmes is based on their age and 'representativeness' of the target market. Therefore, what the producer thinks an audience should want is more likely to be what the audience feels it should want as well.

8. William N. Isaacs, 'Taking Flight: Dialogue, Collective Thinking and Organizational Learning', *Organizational Dynamics*, a report from the Center for Organizational Learning's Dialogue Project (July-August, 1992), pp.24-39.

9. Patrick de Mare, Robin Piper and Sheila Thompson: *Koinonia: From Hate, through Dialogue, to Culture in the Large Group*, New York: Karnac Books, 1991, p.72.

10. *Nielsen Station Index*, 1987. The explanation for Standard Errors for the four-week audience estimates: 'The standard error for a ten rating on a five day average within the DMA is a 0.7; in other words the rating lies within a 9.3 and a 10.7 68 out of 100 times.' p.6.

11. In the case of *X-Files*, the loyal audience – computer-literate types who christened themselves X-Philes – light up the Internet to discuss each episode, according to Brian Lowry (1995) in *The Truth is Out There: The Official Guide to the X-Files*, New York: Harper Collins, p.4.

12. The research on local television newscasts was conducted as a class project by the author's communication research classes, Fall, 1996. Reports of the research findings by class members, undergraduates in the Brigham Young University Department of Communications, were used as formative research by the assistant producer of the KUTV morning news programme. On January 13, 1997, KUTV (CBS) Morning News received a 4.7 rating/28 share; KSL (NBC), 5.4 rating/32 share; KTVX (ABC) 3.2/19 share.

13. Orlik, *op. cit.*, p.101.

14. Interview with David Poltrack, V.P. CBS, *Research*, January 14, 1997. Poltrack said that when programme producers do not target CBS audience's interests, as indicated by research, the shows are cancelled; *Central Park West*, for example, which failed after attempts to save it by means suggested by audience research.

15. This 'ideal' is also the 'ideal' audience targeted by advertisers.

16. Mesheryakova, thesis defence, December 11, 1996.

17. *Dateline* ratings are indications of the executive programmer's success in reaching the audience. The 11.2 rating/18 share for January 21, 1997, indicates the programme's strength. Of the news magazine shows programmed on the four networks, only *60 Minutes*, the longest running of them, had stronger ratings on Sunday nights compared to *Dateline*; on Tuesdays and Fridays, *Dateline* wins.

18. Carter is alluding to a critical article by James Wolcott, *The New Yorker*, January 6, 1997, pp.76-77. Wolcott refers to the 'doomy milieu of *Millennium*', and the irony that *Millennium* was intended to be an optimistic programme, an antidote to the apocalyptic gloom and jitters collecting around the prospect of the year 2000.

19. ASI, a California-based operation that uses dial response and focus groups to do formative research on television shows, advertising, films and other media, was showing the test video of *X-Files* in their booth at NATPE. The videotape was being shown to potential clients as I spoke with Chris Carter, although it was inconspicuous. ASI's booth was several rows away from where we spoke.

20. James Wolcott, 'Too Much Pulp,' Mixed Media column, *The New Yorker*, January 6, 1997, pp.76-77. Wolcott wrote, 'More and more *The X-Files* exploits gratuitous killing to an unconscionable degree; the nadir was reached this season in an episode where a trio of inbred backwoods mutations savagely beat a black couple to death to the ironic strains of a Johnny Mathis tune. The series is so busy testing our gag reflexes that it has tossed simple logic out the window.'

21. Chris Carter described the story board used to create episodes of programmes – a bulletin board of 3 x 5 cards plot each scene. There are four acts and 40–45 cards on the board representing dramatic progression. 'Until I hear the board and sign off, nothing goes to script. I have to know I can write that board. I re-wrote 20-25 episodes because I understood the board.'

22. Cantor, *op. cit.*, pp.166-7.

23. De Mare, Piper and Thompson *op. cit.*, p.17.

The Coming of the New Media Organisation

Organisational Convergence in Newsrooms in the United States

Scott C. Hammond and William Porter
Department of Communications
Brigham Young University, USA

This paper examines the impact integrated broadcast and print newsrooms have had in several markets and one University in the United States. We show how newsrooms are moving from a competitive orientation, through cooperation to convergence. We examine changes in systems, culture and structure, and argue new news organisations will be integrated in structure, polychronic in cultures and more self-organizing as systems.

In several markets in the United States, news organisations are restructuring to achieve greater competitive advantage. Once-traditional rivals are finding competitive advantage in cooperating or even converging. Some are experiencing a major redefinition from a broadcast or a newspaper publisher to an information organisation. In the first section of this paper, we examine the trend to converged newsrooms. We examine the U.S. trend and show the experiment to create a converged newsroom at the university level. The second section provides an organisational analysis of the converged newsroom. We will discuss the newsroom systems, culture and structure. The final section examines the implications of this experiment for industry.

The Coming of the New Media Organisation

The monolithic structures of American newspaper and broadcast entities are a myth. While print journalism can claim to be the only mass medium in the previous century, modern multi-media news organisations have grown up together. The first broadcast news organisations in the United States were started by newspapers.[1] Many of the early broadcasters worked first as print journalists.[2] But as television emerged in the 1950's and '60's as a significant and then a dominant source of news, newspapers began to see broadcasting as competition. The retrospective sense-making[3] of some scholars suggested broadcast journalism demeans the higher truths found in print journalism.[4] Broadcast journalism was viewed by some print journalists as competitive to the point that the older brother relationship was replaced by the bastard child.

In the 1980's this began to change. Both print and broadcast news operations were faced with increased competition and diminishing revenue. Network television news audiences dropped to almost the same level as newspaper readership.[5] In addition, new technologies were increasing the reach of local newsrooms, creating increased audience expectations and displacing many workers.[6] Owners of news organisations began in the 1980's to look for strategic partnerships.[7] This has led to the emergence of the new media organisation.

Newsroom Convergence
Every media organisation faces the buffeting changes of the new economy and new competition. Three general strategies are evident. The first is retrenchment, which preserves the competition between traditional rivals. A newspaper remains a newspaper and attempts to preserve its reader base. This approach is increasingly rare. Even the conservative local papers have a presence in cyberspace.[8]

The second approach is to become cooperative with, but not dependent upon, other newsgathering organisations. This approach takes on many forms, but generally means that the news organisation identifies the least competitive medium and forms an alliance. These kinds of relationships are characterized by being locally defined and non-dependent. For example, a television station or newspaper starts a home page or develops a relationship and begins some cross-promotion with a once rival. Their traditional organisation forms, audience and distribution remain largely the same. They are not dependent on the new relationship for information or distribution. When there is opportunity for cooperation they gain some advantage.

Cooperative ventures abound in U.S. media organisations. For example, in Florida in 1996, three 24-hour news local cable operations went on the air. Two of the three are owned by newspapers. In Salt Lake City, Utah, U.S.A., the Salt Lake Tribune has experimented with cable news cut-ins read by newspaper reporters.

The third kind of newsroom is identified as a converged newsroom. It is characterized by journalists aligning themselves with content rather than distribution medium and with journalists having an overall sense of the whole. In this environment, there is dependence between the different products to generate the required content.

Figure 1: Three Types of Newsroom Structures

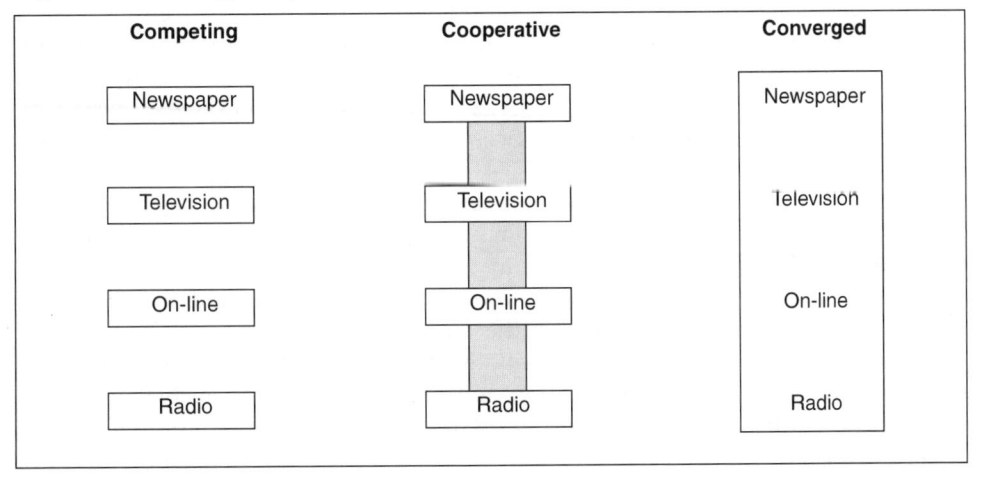

It should be noted that the figure above represents newsroom structure for journalists and those involved directly with editorial content, but production personnel in newspapers and broadcasting are not as directly affected by the convergence. They remain largely identified with the medium.

The BYU Integration

Brigham Young University is working to converge a newspaper with a 33 thousand circulation, a television broadcast PBS affiliated station, FM newscasts on a classical radio station, and an on-line service. Three phases to the convergence are described below:

Figure 2: The Three Phases of Newsroom Convergence

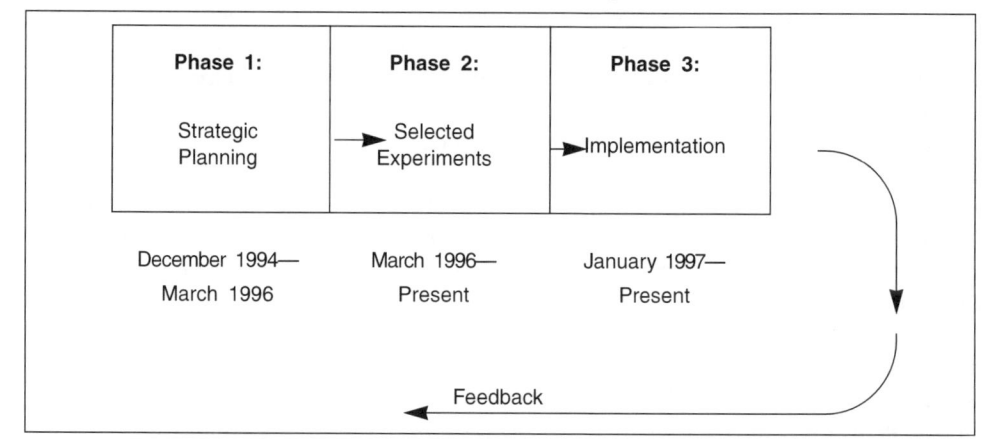

Phase 1: Strategic Planning

Efforts to integrate the BYU newsroom began in Spring of 1994. Four faculty members saw industry trends and could see potential benefits for students who gained a broader vision of news. In November 1994, these four faculty members began weekly meetings to develop a web site on election coverage that would use material from the student newspaper and the daily television news broadcast. By early 1995, the committee agreed that the election web site experiment was successful and that experimentation with web publishing should continue. A design student was hired to redesign the site under its new name 'Newsline.' In 1996, a new editor entered the site in some contests and publicized it through the BYU magazine.

In the winter of 1996, a two-day workshop was planned to help determine whether the faculty and students wanted to keep moving toward a joint newsroom. The workshop involved all stakeholders, from student, to faculty, to industry leaders, and included a careful review of the past, a look at current industry trends and the development of a common ideal future. On the second day, the group had determined that the merger of print and broadcasting was good and should be pursued. Five teams were created to develop various parts of a plan to move forward. Students and faculty spent the next five weeks doing the committee work that led up to a plan for the future.

Phase 2: Experimenting

In the summer of 1996, a series of experiments was launched to understand how student reporters could work together on stories. A remote television camera was placed in the newspaper newsroom and students began short, one minute news cut-ins for cable. Then the assignments editor for the television news operation was given an office at the newspaper site. Finally, management assigned all reporters to a beat. Regardless of their medium proficiency, all reporters were assigned to cover one aspect of the community. When a print journalist found a story interesting for television, other reporters were assigned to the story to help.

While there were some incidents of cooperation, broadcast students resented doing news in the newspaper newsroom when it was more convenient to broadcast from the studio. Newspaper reporters expressed their concern that television reporters might use their story but not give them credit. Newspaper reporters generally kept their distance from the television reporters, and cooperation was sparse.

In November of 1996, KBYU Television produced election coverage. A statewide exit poll surveyed several thousand voters. The results attracted a wide audience to the station. Television reporters had direct access to all of the candidates and were able to secure live interviews with most. Print reporters, who had generally failed to notice the KBYU coverage, got their results from other television stations.

The congressional race was very close, and KBYU pollsters predicted a victory for the challenger. But the newspaper reporters did not have access to the same experts, and at 2 AM they went to press with a picture of the incumbent and a headline implying victory. In the morning, they realized they had gotten the story wrong.

The election coverage and the continuing small successes in coverage led students and faculty to gather for another strategic meeting. In this meeting, the group worked on a concept called News Central, which was an attempt to reconcile differences between a centralized broadcasting newsroom and a print newsroom distributed across half a dozen desks. The group concluded that there should be a central news organisation called News Central. The News Central included the KBYU Assignments editor, the Universe News Editor, Universe desk editors assistant desk editors. The News Central reporting staff included reporters from classes learning basic reporting skills. It was decided advanced reporting classes should specialize in their medium. News Central should direct news coverage during morning hours, hand off to the desk editors during the afternoon – and develop some system for getting late-breaking news.

As News Central operationalized, conflict over the needs of the media became apparent, as described below:

Time vs. Topic – Broadcast coverage is highly time sensitive. The assignments editor needs to get crews into the field early in the day to produce packages for the afternoon show. Newspaper reporters are scattered about on half a dozen desks, and are organized around topics.

Central vs. Distributed – A typical 30-minute newscast contains a small enough number of stories that a single editor or producer can track them. A newspaper reporting staff is dealing, at any one time, with a large enough list of stories that one person cannot accurately track them, so they are distributed over the five or six sub-editors or desk editors.

Individual vs. Team – Broadcast reports, while the product of a team of photographers, editors, reporters, etc., are generally credited to an individual. Newspaper stories are always credited to one writer. Students in the newsroom are trying to build individual files that will lead toward employment. Their sense was that team coverage does not credit them as much as individual work.

Phase 3: Implementation

During the first week of the winter 1997 semester, plans were made to deal with issues that could be anticipated – accountability, copy flow, coordination. But many issues had to be dealt with once the semester had started and the staff was committed to the daily production of a newspaper, a 30-minute television newscast and a daily on-line publication. The content of each of the major products is in some way dependent on the other. Staff members have a greater sense of the whole, and the success of one is seen as the success of the other. In the next section of this paper, we will explain those changes.

Newsroom Conversion and Structure, Culture and Systems

Convergence means significant changes for the newsroom structure, culture and systems. The converged newsroom moves from a differentiated structure to an integrated structure, from a culture which is monochronic to one which is polychronic, and from systems which are externally imposed to ones which are internally generated or self-organizing.

Lawrence and Lorsch describe differentiated organisations as ones reliant on the special, unique skills of each worker. They are characterized by specific job descriptions and organisational charts.[9] The term *differentiated* suggests separate functions, departments and domains for different goals and time spans. The competitive and the cooperative newsroom environment are differentiated. Reporters specialize not only in a particular topic, but in particular functions and medium. In a typical broadcast newsroom a reporter might be assigned the crime beat, expected to work nights, and given live shots in the 6 and 10 pm news show. Other reporters are given day work that allows them to spend more time crafting a feature story or trying to make a political story interesting. They are differentiated based on their abilities to work individually, on certain kinds of stories, using certain kinds of technology.

The newsrooms were extremely differentiated. Because the reporters were associated with a journalism class and coming from a pool of students with limited experience, they were differentiated based on experience. In television, for example, a student might be experienced enough to do a story about a snow storm, but not have the ability to interview the mayor. They might have the ability to conduct an interview, but not the technical skill to edit. This resulted in print and broadcast organisations with clear, systemic processes and differentiated people, who picked up their part of the story and pushed it on to the next person.

The new organisation is integrated. Because there is a topic focus, students/reporters are only differentiated based on their knowledge. If they have information, then the system adapts to get the story out. For example, Kari Wilson, a journalism student focusing in broadcasting, said, 'The first day I arrived with my job description in mind, but as we began to produce a paper and regular newscasts, I realized that the job description wasn't much help. I started focusing on what needed to be done and not what was supposed to happen.'

The most obvious cultural shift in the converged newsroom is in a movement from monochronic to polychronic values. Edward Hall describes monochronic cultures and ones which place items in order and move systematically through their communications. Monochronic cultures are order and agenda driven.[10]

The old newsrooms were polychronic. To get a story out, newspaper reporters would tell their desk editors what they were working on, gather data, write the story and then hand it off to the editing staff. In a monochronic system, there were few ways to bypass the many checks and balances to get a breaking story in the paper.

The new newsroom is polychronic. Each person participates in a variety of activities at the same time.[11] In a polychronic newsroom, a reporter may begin a story for the newspaper, only to find a radio reporter has copied part of it for her or his newscast. Later, television may appropriate part, visualize, rewrite and get the story on the air. While copy editors are working the story for the paper, the same story, in different form, is being used on radio, downloaded to on-line, and being produced for television.

The movement from a differentiated structure to an integrated structure, and from a monochronic culture to a polychronic culture, suggests that the systems in the new news organisations are also moving from externally imposed order to internal self-organisation. Traditional newspaper or broadcast news organisations in the U.S. were all very much alike. The activities of the differentiated positions, such as copy editor, assignments editor, were well understood. All newsrooms adopted basically the same organisation and identities.[12]

In the new news organisation, internally imposed order is more typical. Wheatley[13] describes some of the characteristics of a self-organizing system as:
– The parts are understood only in terms of the whole.
– Change is constant.
– Human motivation is interactive.
– People are multi-skilled and constantly learning.

In the new news organisation, the focus is on the product not the story. The old news organisations were designed so that once reporters broadcast or print the story, their responsibility was over. This differentiated structure has been replaced with a more holistic approach. In the converged newsroom, students preparing stories for broadcast news have been asked to contribute to the newspaper, because the newspaper's need is greater. The old systems did not allow those in leadership positions to change course and organize around a specific editorial need. The new system, however, suggests that each person shares some responsibility for the whole.

For the student reporters, this new integrated, polychronic, self-organizing environment is the ultimate learning organisation.[14] Students are constantly faced with new learning opportunities related not only to the stories that they are generating, but in the technology and the ability to work together.

There is some evidence that the patterns found in the BYU newsroom are similar to other converged newsrooms in the United States. Still we have not identified how advertisers or competition are affected. Preliminary results suggest that the visual content of the paper has improved and the editorial content of the television newscast has been greatly enhanced, but the radio news content and its unique needs have yet to be affected.

References

1. H. Dordick and G. Wang, *The Information Society: A Retrospective View*, Newbury Park CA: Sage, 1993.
2. Barbara Matusow, *The Evening Stars: The Making of the Network News Anchor*, Boston: Houghton Mifflin, 1983.
3. Karl Weick, *The Social Psychology of Organizing*, New York: Random House, 1979.
4. Alf Pratte, 'Micro and Macro Mergers of Print and Broadcast: Looking the Gift Horse in the Mouth,' paper presented at the Western Social Sciences Association, Reno, NV (USA), April 27, 1996.
5. The Pew Report on Television News Viewer Habits, Pew Center for Civic Journalist, August 1995 (unpublished report found on the Internet).
6. John Pavlik, *New Media and Information Superhighway*, Boston: Allyn and Bacon, 1996.
7. Francis Gouillart and James Kelly, *Transforming the Organization*, New York: McGraw Hill, 1995, pp.101-140. Also Gary Hamel and C.K. Prahalad, *Competing for the Future: Breakthrough Strategies for Seizing Control of Your Industry and Creating the Markets of Tomorrow*, Cambridge MA: Harvard Business School Press, 1994.
8. A search of Yahoo in February of 1996 indicated 1,953 newspaper web sites and 193 television news web sites in the United States. The second category is difficult to distinguish because many of the television web sites provide additional services such as programming information.
9. P.R. Lawrence and J.W. Lorsch, *Organisation and Environment: Managing Differentiation and Integration*, Homewood, IL: Irwin, 1969.
10. Edward Hall, *The Silent Language*, New York: Anchor Press, 1974.
11. Hall, *ibid.*, p.7.
12. Kathryn Egan and Scott Hammond, 'What About the Worker? Identity and the Converged Newsroom,' University of Manchester Broadcasting Symposium, April 10th, 1997.
13. Margaret Wheatley, *Leadership and the New Science*, San Francisco: Barrett-Koehler, 1992.
14. Peter Senge, *The Fifth Discipline*, New York: Doubleday, 1992.

BBC Producer Choice and Its Outcomes

An Assessment of the Results of Organisational Change

Dr. Martin Harris and Victoria Wegg-Prosser, M.B.A.
Department of Management Studies, Brunel University

BBC Producer Choice is a trading system based on buyer/seller relationships which now drives the BBC in all its decision-making processes. Producer Choice is a quasi-internal market, ostensibly replacing the old BBC bureaucracy with a more articulated organic structure. It represents a watershed in the history of the BBC as a public sector organisation; it has made people who work there 'think the unthinkable'; it has prepared them for the world of convergence and forced them to abandon a dependency culture; it has shone a torchlight into every area of BBC activity and has produced mountains of paperwork – what has it done for BBC programmes?

This is a vast area of debate, and if we go back to the old days of the command economy, before Producer Choice, we have to scrutinise the ways in which resources were allocated then to programme makers, on command, as it were, and ask ourselves (as many neo-liberal economists then did), were those resources 'fit for purpose'? Was every studio a 'Rolls Royce' outfit? Were there too many 'taxis on the rank' waiting to be used?

We might argue that the BBC needed to be over-resourced in order to transmit programmes consistently of such excellence that the BBC could retain its reputation as 'the least worst broadcaster in the world', but we know that this option was no longer realistic for the BBC, not just because the government would not tolerate such blatant inefficiency in the use of public monies, but because with rising costs and a plateaued licence fee revenue, more had to be made with less. By the summer of 1991 there were new ITV licencees in place, operating on reduced programme budgets, new commercial radio and cable and satellite television entrants, taking increasing share from the terrestrial channels, and on the horizon was convergence, the strengthening interlocking of telecommunications with the information and entertainment media. All the indicators outside of the BBC, and the BBC's audit of resource levels in that summer of 1991, indicated that the BBC's productions were over-resourced by at least 130 per cent.

So, BBC Producer Choice was launched in October 1991 as 'a new way of managing resources'. It was explained at the launch by the Deputy Director General, John Birt. Under Producer Choice, resources would be managed in such a way that producers would have the right to negotiate resource provision themselves, spending money internally or externally of the BBC. Where the money was denied to any internal resource because of the outcome of these negotiations, then the internal resource would fail to break even on its targets of resource utilage. Plant closures and redundancies would follow.

Although John Birt might be described as the architect of Producer Choice, it would be wrong to imply by this description that the then Director General, Michael Checkland, had in any way been out of sympathy with the decision to allocate resources in a different way. He had been the first to say the BBC should behave, in its production paradigm, more like an independent producer, and take advantage of flexible working and new technology, and pass production budgets down to producers with *full* responsibility for how they would be spent, rather than only with responsibility to manage the proportionately small resource element which accounted for cash expenditure outside of the BBC. All other resources used in the making of programmes were available as a resource cost outside of the cash budget, allocated through programme planning in what was termed a 'bulk deal'. This method of resource allocation was the prime characteristic of the old command economy. The prime characteristic of the new quasi-internal market was to be 'working in full costs with full cash budgets'.

The intentions of Producer Choice were to reshape the BBC's strategy and structure so that it would be equipped for *Extending Choice in the Digital Age* (BBC 1996). Most importantly, in the short term, Producer Choice was orchestrated to persuade the government that the BBC was capable of operational change delivering efficiency savings, and therefore worthy of Charter Renewal when its existing ten-year Charter terminated in December 1996. The progress of Producer Choice in the years 1991–1994 ensured that the case for Charter Renewal was advocated by the BBC, and by many of its supporters, on the basis of programme quality rather than on the need for excessive programme cost. Since 1994 the quasi-internal market has been made to work, broadcasting has been separated from production, the Charter has been renewed, the transmitters are being privatised and BBC Resources intends to be a trading subsidiary of the BBC very soon. Cost per hour is falling, and, as far as BBC programming is concerned, more is being made with less. The programme awards still flood in.

The policy implications of Producer Choice are that the Charter has been renewed, and that the BBC is in better shape to survive in a new broadcasting landscape of convergence than would have been the case if Producer Choice had not been implemented.

However, something else happened at the BBC during the implementation of Producer Choice which our research suggests is directly associated with management decisions taken by John Birt, as Director General from January 1993, rather than by his predecessor, Michael Checkland. It was Checkland who had recommended the model of a quasi-internal market after it had been piloted in certain programme areas in 1990, and he had set up the internal audit under Birt's control which began the process of capacity reductions in studios and post-production in the summer of 1991. When Birt became Director General, he introduced new inititiatives and objectives for the BBC which set in train a managerial revolution. Michael Checkland had been happy to describe the BBC as a 'business', but John Birt promised it would be 'the best managed public service in the United Kingdom'.

The relationship between the BBC, the government and the audiences for its programmes is an intricate affair. In designing the strategic programme, *Extending Choice*, to ensure Charter Renewal, and subsequently to take the BBC into the Digital Age, nothing was more important for the BBC than improving the image of this relationship. Everything prepared by the BBC in this regard was designed to show the BBC as being different and better than before. The emphasis laid out in the first *Extending Choice* document published in November 1992 was that the BBC should make quality programmes, *efficiently*, and in an accountable way. When John Birt became Director General some six weeks later, he added the directive that these programmes should be made within an effective organisation. From here was spawned the managerial revolution that still bewilders people today, prompting so many headlines that persist in suggesting that even if the BBC is *different* from before, it is not necessarily *better*. The latest headline that springs to mind is from the *Guardian*, 8 February 1997:

> Veteran Producer Axed after Savaging BBC Chiefs: ... Kenith Trodd who worked closely with Dennis Potter ... said the BBC drama department is a 'total mess' ... decisions are being taken by 'uncreative people whose talent is keeping a shaky grip on stationery supplies.'

Implementing 'effectiveness projects', to achieve an 'effective' organisation, is fraught with unintended consequences, compared with the relative ease of implementing 'efficiency projects'. The Effectiveness Project promised to give BBC workers communication, awareness and training. This was to assist Birt's commitment to make the BBC 'the best managed public service in the United Kingdom'. Delivering these pledges was easier said than done. It has, as John Birt described it, been 'a long haul' to bring about change in the way the BBC views itself, as well as in the way it is managed.

But, for the purposes of this paper, we can put the problems of effectiveness to one side, and concentrate instead on the objectives of quality, efficiency and accountability. Producer Choice, conceived at least two years before the launch of *Extending Choice* in November 1992, was designed to achieve all three. As a means to an end, was it successful? What happened to the concept of Producer Choice along the way – has it become an end in its own right?

The first thing to say is that Producer Choice did not become an end in its own right. In many ways, it was far too unpopular for that. If the end were a quasi-internal market, (which is what the Producer Choice change programme built, over two years, 1992-4), then that has simply become a further means to an end – i.e. the quasi-internal market is used to demonstrate quality, efficiency and accountability. That is what is supposed to happen to means in an ideal world of rational management. Producer Choice was conceived in that ideal world where means do not determine ends and goals are not displaced.

But, the BBC is a complicated organisation in a world which is far from ideal. People who know the BBC well describe it often as a 'labyrinth', 'a sea of treacle', a 'minefield' or 'it's a maddening place, but we love it' – outsiders have offered such advice as: 'don't let the inmates run the prison'. During the course of our research, we wondered if the BBC had changed at all from the days when

Tom Burns conducted research there in 1962 and again in 1972? The research was eventually approved for publication and written up in Burns' book, *The BBC: Public Institution and Private World* (1977). As Mike Reed observed in *The Sociology of Management* (1989:37), Burns uncovered there:

> the complex processes whereby rational control systems are distorted by the long-term impact of substantive conflicts within management over access to resources that will critically affect the future direction of organisational development.

The rationalist concepts of organisational change do not apprehend the ambiguities and unintended consequences inherent in any change process. Our research has scrutinised the ways in which the objectives of the Producer Choice trading system were distorted by the variability in context, process and outcome that always accompanies organisational change. For the purposes of this paper, we can summarise the distortions of the rational control systems as follows:

The BBC has not turned itself into a 'virtual' or 'network' organisation, despite indications in the context of change that flexible working patterns, within a periphery of production units, linked in a network with the BBC, would deliver the most cost effective programming. The notion of accountability can be demonstrated in such measurement tools as the Annual Performance Review, but such tools are always subject to goal displacement during the process of their implementation and subsequent usage. There is still deep-seated cultural resistance to the notion of negotiating by contract in the quasi-internal market, rather than by what were characterised by John Birt and many others as the 'skills of supplicancy' in the days of the command economy.

Furthermore, the internal market is still only 'quasi', and producers' decisions over time have not been allowed (as was their intention) to condition the size of the BBC. There were pre-eminently two reasons for this distortion. The first was that the context of change moved away from the hitherto beguiling concept of flexible autonomous working (utilising devolved budgets) towards a new type of centralised control, emanating from a revitalised corporate centre, where budgets were created in response to a centrally devised programme strategy, and fixed at a level which 'best industry practice' indicated was appropriate. The second main reason for distortion was that the process of change only served to confirm that the BBC was short of cash, and would remain so throughout the period running up to Charter Renewal in December 1996. So, giving producers the right to spend money externally of the BBC was constrained by the lack of available cash. Coupled with what were frequently referred to as 'cash crises', was the inability of the BBC to free itself of certain resource costs when some studios remained in use, but under-utilised, and property disposal yielded less cash than had perhaps been anticipated. And although the headcount did start to reduce in the Resources division of the BBC, it increased in the Production divisions so that the net reduction in staff numbers was by no means as dramatic as many had been led to expect. For example, the latest *BBC Annual Report* (1996) indicates a reduction of 17 per cent in the Home Services' headcount over the years April 1992–6. Even allowing for the BBC's production of news and radio outside of the 25 per cent quota of independently-made programming, the BBC should have reduced its headcount by more than 17 per cent to take account of the quota, the above-inflation rising costs of certain rights, the offer of competitive wage rates, and a reducing price per programming hour.

So what was Producer Choice all about? Was there, in fact, an intended consequence that, regardless of the fashionable rhetoric about becoming 'lean and fit' for the Digital Age, the BBC would remain over-resourced so that it could still be 'the least worst broadcaster in the world'? Or did the powerful bureaucracy of the BBC's traditional processes resist new ways of managing resources and allow the old ways to prevail, providing knowledge only to the elite, whoever that might be, and producing information as a substitute for knowledge to the many, who struggle to find ways of turning the information into knowledge? They struggle because the BBC is still, at its most senior level, pervaded by a culture of closure and confidentiality. The managerial revolution permitted operational change, but it did not take the BBC into a new production paradigm. This may happen now, with the new Resources division trading as a separate subsidiary of the BBC, and with the new Production division making programmes for new BBC digital channels and rival commercial terrestrial channels, but Producer Choice was not the catalyst for these developments – they arose out of that substantive conflict within management over access to resources which Tom Burns noted in 1962 and 1972, and which many commentators have noted more recently is still characteristic of the BBC. The difference between 1977, when Burns' book was published, and today, is that there are now many more outlets for BBC programming, and many more opportunities for BBC resources to operate externally of the BBC. In the words of the July 1994 *White Paper on the Future of the BBC*, the challenge is to 'serve the Nation', and 'compete Worldwide'.

When we consider this challenge as an instruction from the government, we start to come a little closer to understanding what Producer Choice was all about. A rigid bureaucracy allocating resources on demand could neither provide assurance to the government, on behalf of the licence fee payers, that public money was being spent wisely, nor could it offer a cash-based relationship to potential customers, world wide. For the BBC, Producer Choice is a pre-requisite of the global marketplace in the twenty-first century.

If the government is now happier with the BBC's structure and strategy as a result of Producer Choice, can we say the same for licence fee payers – are they being short-changed by these new arrangements? The BBC would argue this is not the case. They expended much effort during *Extending Choice* seeking to persuade their audiences within the United Kingdom of the unique value of BBC programming, and asking them, in the process of the *Programme Strategy Review*, what sort of programmes did they want? The result has been a television and radio schedule which is more reflective of audience wishes – hence, for examples, the emphasis on costume drama, on consumer programming, and on minority interests. If you read the published version of the *Programme Strategy Review* (BBC 1995), you can discern that the BBC has a clear idea of what its audiences want, and is determined to satisfy that, dependent on cash and available talent.

But it has been argued that giving people what they want is the antithesis of public service broadcasting. The economist Martin Cave described public service broadcasting in a 1985 article in *Lloyds Bank Review* (No. 157:25-35) as:

> a form of content regulation which involves the subidisation or cross-subsidisation of certain programme types. Its justifications are ... that viewers have the 'wrong' tastes or tastes ... that certain types of programmes have beneficial external effects ... (and) that viewers have limited knowledge of programmes on offer and would benefit ... from having their choices guided. ... The public service element in BBC output is embodied in the Charter and maintained through the Board of Governors, and perhaps more fundamentally through the whole ethos of the BBC ...

There is greater tension now in that 'whole ethos of the BBC' than ever before. In 1993, the television dramatist Dennis Potter made an empassioned plea at the Edinburgh International Television Festival on behalf of public service broadcasting :

> (It)... is *not* a business trying to distribute dosh to its shareholders, *not* owned by its current administrators,... but something held in trust and in law for every citizen ... of Great Britain and Northern Ireland. (MacTaggart Lecture: 10)

He also commented:

> How much the shifts and turns which seem particular to any one large institution can in themselves be seen as a model for the wider society in which all of us live. ... The glories of privatisation and the brutalities of the unshackled market ... can more or less honestly hold up the battle banners of (their) occasionally healthy, and often vicious indifference to the old class-ridden status-conscious cultures of Great Britain. ... the cry of Yuppie to Yuppie sounded in the land. (MacTaggart Lecture: 3)

Is that what we are left with? A market-driven BBC permanently on a mobile phone whose voice mail takes its messages for it? The command economy of the old BBC protected producers from the rigours of the market, and the new economy of Producer Choice has exposed them to consumer sovereignty. The irony is that it was producers who first advocated Producer Choice as a means of making programme budgets go further, rather than as a means of unleashing market forces. From their perspective, that was an unintended consequence of their intentions. From the BBC's point of view, quality, efficiency and accountability are more easily demonstrated than before the introduction of Producer Choice, and, arguably for that reason, Producer Choice saved the BBC from privatisation. We shall have to see.

The South African Broadcasting Corporation Under Fire

Competition versus Public Service in the New South Africa

Tamela Hultman

Executive Editor, Africa News Service
Co-ordinator, Center for Africa and Media, Duke University

A Microcosm of South African Society

Three years after South Africans massed to the voting boxes in a nation-wide celebration of democracy, actor and arts administrator John Kani captured the spirit of realism that has succeeded the post-polling euphoria. '1994's democratic elections just defined the new challenges,' he told an interviewer. 'It did not end our challenges.'

As the various institutions of South African society, including the police force, the civil service and the schools, negotiate a difficult transition towards transparency and accountability, the struggle to transform the South African Broadcasting Corporation has been among the most tumultuous and the most visible. The success or failure of that attempt will determine the future of public broadcasting in South Africa. But the SABC experience also has broader implications. The corporation's thousands of employees, encompassing all ethnic groups, each political party and every economic stratum, are a microcosm of the nation. Issues of race, gender and power emerge at every point where visions of the future are debated. And because it has aggressively embraced change, the SABC's experiences can be seen as foreshadowing both the opportunities and the obstacles confronting the larger society.

Change and Backlash

Charged with converting a 'state' broadcaster into a 'public' broadcaster, the SABC has launched ambitious reforms that have sparked fierce debate. During one five-day period selected at random, sixteen English-language and six Afrikaans publications monitored by the SABC's media office carried 155 articles, columns, letters and leaders about the corporation.[1]

A July 12, 1996 missive to the *Cape Argus* captured the tone of the majority. 'Judging by the many letters regarding TV licences and the SABC in general,' said the writer, 'it seems obvious that there are almost no people who are actually satisfied, let alone happy, with the current situation.' A letter to the Citizen the following day said that if SABC chief executive Zwelakhe Sisulu is right that the SABC is one of the most transformed organizations in South Africa, 'the national daily prayer should be 'Please, Lord, deliver us from transformation."

Similar complaints have become a recurrent refrain among media reporters. Indeed, regular perusal of major print media, which remain largely white owned, suggests strongly that the SABC has become an institution that South Africans love to hate.

The reaction stems from a highly visible and audible repositioning of the SABC to become a public broadcaster, more nearly reflective of and responsive to the needs of a diverse population. Many critics grouse about what they regard as the mangling of English by presenters from non-Anglophone backgrounds. Complaints abound about multi-lingual productions and the number of both current affairs and dramas in African languages. And Afrikaans-speakers, representing 15 per cent of the population, resent the dethronement of their mother tongue from its preeminent place in the old SABC (although there is still a national Afrikaans radio station and the language accounts for over 20 per cent of prime-time programming on one of the three television channels). In addition, there have been articulate critiques from those of all races who think the corporation is not transformed enough, with a schedule that includes substantial numbers of imported situation comedies as well as live programming that favours sports like cricket and rugby, followed by a minority of South Africans.

Still, there is evidence that substantial portions of the public have welcomed the changes and are tolerant, for now, of the shortcomings. Although white audience figures have remained flat, and for some services have declined, black audiences are growing. The question is whether their approval will bring either the political or fiscal support the SABC needs for survival.

The Challenge

Today the SABC confronts the stark dilemma of how to meet its myriad public service mandates while trying to secure its economic base, overcome persistent organizational inefficiencies, and escape the stigma that continues to cling to it as a legacy of the apartheid era.

Established by Parliament, the SABC began radio broadcasts in 1936 and television forty years later. During the 1980s, advertising came to account for most of the company's revenue, supplemented by television licence fees, although political resistance led to a steady decline in collections – what South Africans call the 'culture of non-payment' that extended to rent and utility charges as well.

In 1993, a transition board, selected by a controversial, political process that was part of the larger South African transition to democracy, assumed control of the corporation. At the time, there was widespread suspicion that the ruling Nationalist party was engineering the appointments to limit the erosion of its influence. In addition, the national priority given to reconciliation, plus the pragmatic consideration that overly hasty staff changes could lead to dead air, has meant that hundreds of employees from the old SABC remained on the job. As a result, disputes among board members and between board and management have hindered coherent policy development, and differing visions and values among staff have often retarded effective implementation.

The other major policy player is the Independent Broadcasting Authority, established by South Africa's Transitional Executive Council in 1993 to regulate broadcasting in South Africa. In August, 1995, the IBA published its 'Triple Inquiry Report,' an investigation into the viability of public broadcasting, local content of programming and cross media ownership of broadcast properties. The report, and subsequent IBA and Parliamentary decisions, have shaped the mandate the SABC must fulfil as a public service broadcaster. Among the IBA-stipulated reforms were:

- the extension of broadcasts in all eleven official languages;
- the provision of 'windows' for regional productions in both television and radio;
- increased local content in programming;
- diversity in religious programmes to reflect the variety of faiths in South Africa;
- expansion of news and information as the core business of public broadcasting;
- the development of a nationwide educational broadcasting service; and
- the sale of regional commercial radio stations owned by the SABC, to open up the airwaves and diversify the options for South African audiences.

The mandates came with a recommendation for triennial government funding to finance their costs. Recognizing that the SABC would continue to depend on commercial revenues, the IBA nevertheless argued that the marketplace could not be expected to underwrite the substantial costs of extending quality broadcasting to the country's under-served majority.

The brief period since the public broadcasting mission emerged has seen substantial mandate-related initiatives. Investments to improve the infrastructure and programmes of the under-funded, regional African-language radio stations have extended both the footprints and the services to listeners, and the stations' advertising revenues grew by 35 per cent in 1996.[2] Increased television transmission in African languages continues to attract new viewers, and surveys show high audience satisfaction with those services, particularly news. In March, 1997, the SABC and the Department of Education launched a collaborative education service for television and radio, catering for audiences from pre-school through adulthood. A fresh line-up of magazine programmes and public affairs features, including coverage of the hearings of the Truth and Reconciliation Commission into human rights abuses during minority rule, has offered riveting insights into volatile current issues. An increase in local productions has provided scope for the creative expression of South African culture in music, drama and dance.

Although it is difficult to find anyone at the SABC who is satisfied with either technical quality or programme content, many staff believe there has been significant progress towards achieving the competence and professionalism that will allow the corporation to fulfil its public service mandate. Jeremy Thorpe, a seventeen-year veteran at SABC television news, argues that improvement in quality and the guarantee of editorial independence are linked. 'We always had a weather eye open for what was acceptable to the government,' he says. 'Most of our bosses were members of the Broederbond. It was 'Big Brother' in a big way; a lot of talent was forced out.'

Where the old style of news was to write hard copy that would win government approval and then cover it with pictures, television journalists are now having to acquire both the reporting and the technical skills to tell a story. Part of that learning process has been the ability to resist inevitable government pressures. The new Constitution guarantees press freedom, but South African officials, like their counterparts elsewhere, naturally seek to influence media coverage. SABC chief executive Zwelakhe Sisulu was watched closely after his appointment for signs of favouritism towards the governing African National Congress, in which both his parents are prominent figures, but he has been rigorous in backing his news teams' independence. 'The integrity and credibility of the SABC cannot be compromised,' he said in 1996, in response to government interest in buying air time to communicate its message to the public.[3] Elaborating that position in a March, 1997, interview, Sisulu said the new SABC will 'celebrate our journalists'. No longer, he said, would there be government – or management – interference in news.

The face of change is further manifest in the faces of staff. Affirmative action programmes, coupled with intensive training and re-training at every level, have led to an increase in African, Indian and Coloured employees from 34 per cent in May, 1994 to 49 per cent two years later. In 1992 the board was all male, all white and all-but-one Afrikaans speaking. The 16-member board that took office in February, 1996, had five women and was 60 per cent black. By mid-1997, SABC top management was 80 per cent black and 20 per cent female. The proportion of African, Indian and Coloured managers and specialists rose from 11 per cent in March, 1993 to 31 per cent two years later, while women in that category increased from 11 to 19 per cent.

Despite these achievements, the reformed SABC faced a mounting fiscal crisis. After a 1994 profit of R106 million, the corporation lost R60 million in 1996, with predicted annual budget shortfalls as high as R500 million for the rest of the decade. The immediate reasons can be identified easily, but a remedy is more elusive. The current national discussion about the way forward is at the heart of decisions about the future of broadcasting in the new South Africa.

Crisis and Questions

As more licences are granted, the South African Broadcasting Corporation faces increased competition: from commercial and community radio, from subscription television entrepreneur M-Net, and from a free-to-air television service that will compete directly with the public broadcaster. The combination of competitive pressures, rising costs and declining revenues is the most urgent problem facing corporate decision makers. Four major factors have eroded the company's income base.

The IBA-mandated sale of six profitable, commercial radio stations has cost the SABC R90 million – a 32 per cent drop in annual advertising revenue. Both the IBA and the SABC assumed that proceeds from the sale would be invested by the broadcaster, producing yearly income of some R80 million. But the government blocked SABC use of the funds, arguing that proceeds from the disposal of state assets should go to the national budget. Loss of station earnings, plus increased costs of upgrading and expanding the regional and African-language services, left the radio division with a deficit of some R40 million for 1966.

146

Also by IBA requirement, Sentech, the signal-distribution division of the SABC, was separated from the corporation to become a commercial, state-owned enterprise whose largest client is the SABC, adding to the public broadcasters' costs and reducing its earnings by R24 million a year.

The declining rate of television licence payments has accelerated in the past two years, with boycotts by newly disaffected audiences, especially Afrikaans speakers. In 1990–91, licence fees provided 29 per cent of revenues; by 1994–95, the figure had fallen to 19 per cent.

Television advertising spending also took a downward slide. According to Adindex, published by Market Research Africa, the industry's market share dropped 2 per cent in 1966. Within the category, however, M-Net's ad revenue increased 18.2 per cent, while the SABC increased just 2.2 per cent – a negative rate of growth when inflation is taken into account. Taken together, the loss of ad and licence income and the rising costs – including local content that can be as much as 25 times more expensive than purchased imports – contributed to an operating loss of more than R6 million per week from January to October, 1966 for the SABC's three channels.

Although many at the SABC fault the IBA for not doing more to protect the viability of the public broadcaster, chief executive Zwelakhe Sisulu is careful to temper complaints against the regulatory agency. 'We're all making mistakes that are easy to see in hindsight,' he says. 'We have to do our best with each decision and learn lessons from those that prove to be flawed.' Other managers argue, however, that if the SABC is expected to be a public broadcaster without significant public funding, then it makes sense to hold on to revenue-generating properties that can subsidize the public service functions. Instead, the corporation has not only lost the profits from its former stations but, in addition, finds itself in competition with them for new ad spending – in a marketplace where the advantage goes to the commercial stations.

Television provides an example of another contested field. The IBA recommended that the SABC sell its third channel, but the corporation successfully argued to Parliament that it could not plausibly fulfil its mandate to broadcast in eleven languages with only two channels. Management of the two bodies continues to disagree on the issue.

SABC financial managers estimate that mandate expenditures by the end of the year will total R639 million: R90 million to upgrade African language stations, R153 million for provincial television broadcasting, R140 for increased local content, primarily in African languages, and R256 million for educational broadcasting. In mid-February, Minister of Posts, Telecommunications and Broadcasting Jay Naidoo said that the government would provide R177 million to defer already-incurred costs, but in an earlier interview, Naidoo insisted that with rare exceptions, the SABC would be expected to fund itself, as it had in the past, through ad revenues and licence fees.[4] Further financial pressure came shortly afterwards with the government announcement that the SABC must integrate more than 200 former employees of broadcasters in the apartheid hinterlands of Transkei, Ciskei, Venda and Bophathatswana.

Road to Recovery?

In February, 1996, the SABC began a resources review process, designed to bring expenditures into line with revenues. Seven months later, the SABC board hired the U.S.-based McKinsey firm of management consultants at a cost of R6 million to assist the restructuring. Three dozen SABC staffers have worked with two McKinsey teams – one to identify immediate cost-saving measures and the other to recommend long-term repositioning of the corporation. The first half of 1997 was marked by an acceleration of transformation efforts. On March 7, the 'turnaround' team reported its findings to management; the 'strategy' team presented its initial report on March 19, and final recommendations in early April.

Following management's acceptance of the bulk of the cost-cutting measures, which included the loss of 1400 of the SABC's 4,700 jobs – a 30 per cent staff reduction – there has been an air of crisis throughout the organization. The three unions that represent some 70 per cent of the corporation's workers rejected the plan, demanding time to produce alternatives to retrenchments, as allowed under South Africa's new Labour Relations Act. Unions also argued that the plan ignored both the public broadcasting mandate and the potential for creative revenue generation while honouring the mandate requirements. The company's decision to offer voluntary retrenchment packages, however, helped to temper union opposition.

Among the McKinsey recommendations were:
- Shutting down the SABC's in-house television production unit;
- Increasing international acquisitions and cutting back on local productions;
- Ending the daily television news and feature programme 'Good Morning South Africa;
- Replacing public affairs with entertainment during prime time to boost earnings;
- Ending subsidies to the National Symphony Orchestra;
- Reducing regional programming in both television and radio;
- Curtailing services on Radio Sonder Grense and SAfm, the national Afrikaans and English-language radio stations; and
- Closing the SABC's London office.

In a March 20 meeting with SABC management, representatives of the IBA raised questions about the mandate implications of the proposed changes, promising to intervene with government to support funding requests. Opinion is split on whether state subsidies are likely in the future and on the critical question of whether it is possible to operate as a public broadcaster on private money. Countering Minister Naidoo's statement that the broadcasting corporation must be commercially viable, SABC radio chief Govin Reddy appealed for 'a rigorous examination and debate into the nature of public broadcasting and realistic measures to finance it.'[5] In a fledgling democracy where over half the population is illiterate, he argued, the existence of 'an informed population that can make wise social, political and economic choices' is dependent on an efficient and effective public broadcaster. But the IBA's potential to assist the process was seriously eroded when five of its seven commissioners resigned in mid-May, following charges of financial mismanagement.

Whatever the resolution of its immediate financial crisis, the SABC, like public broadcasters around the world, faces daunting competitive challenges, with nearly 100 new radio stations competing for advertising, and a new television licensee angling for its share of earnings and audiences.

Some statistics are at least superficially encouraging. Despite the changes that alienated certain audience segments, new black viewers have allowed SABC television to marginally increase its share of the national television audience, from 82 per cent in 1995 to 83 per cent in 1996.[6] Although the white television market is largely saturated, black television ownership has grown at 12 times the pace of white ownership in the last five years. From two to four million people will be added to broadcast audiences over the next decade, according to several estimates.

But advertisers have yet to be persuaded of the value of those new audiences. Unless the SABC can market itself more effectively, adspend will continue to favour subscription services whose viewers are over 95 per cent white. More vigorous enforcement of licence laws will also be necessary. On March 25th, the SABC won a landmark court case against a non-payer, illustrating its intention to press for more effective collection mechanisms.

There remained the dilemma of M-Net, which exploited an administrative loophole to attract advertising in 'open-time' broadcasts to non-subscribers and outbid the SABC for several international sports events. The national broadcaster's Topsport division was already spending 76 per cent of its budget buying sports rights, and was attempting to cut costs by identifying events 'of national interest.' IBA hearings on M-Net's licence conditions began on March 26th, and the possibility of 'anti-siphoning' legislation to reserve certain sports rights for the SABC was being examined, but the process was interrupted by the vacuum at the regulatory body after the commissioners' resignation.

Amid the turmoil and uncertainty, a surprising number of SABC management and staff have clung to a tenacious optimism about the future. There is widespread recognition that the old SABC was bloated, inefficient and corrupt and that major change was necessary. There is also passion about preserving the public service mission in a commercial environment, as well as the beginning of a public debate about how to do so. The stakes are high, according to newspaper columnist and commercial radio personality Jon Qwelane, and not only for the SABC. 'To put it brutally simply,' he wrote, 'if the SABC fails it will be a reliable indicator that transformation of our society has been a failure.'[7]

Genuine transformation is the most difficult of all human enterprise, says Ida Jooste, regional head of television in the SABC's Durban office, who had to lose a third of her staff in the restructuring. 'But in 20 years' time we'll look back on this period and see the miracle that took place here.'

References

1. Unless otherwise noted, the data in this paper are derived from interviews conducted, meetings attended and documents examined by the author during research at the SABC in Johannesburg, Cape Town and Durban between January and April, 1997.
2. *Star Business Report* (Johannesburg), March 1, 1997.

3. *Cape Times* (Cape Town), July 12, 1996.

4. Jay Naidoo interviewed by the author, February 17, 1997, Cape Town.

5. Govin Reddy, 'As the SABC founders, government is conspicuous by its silence,' *Sunday Independent* (Johannesburg), May 18, 1997.

6. *Peoplemeter*, 1995–96 for adults, Johannesburg.

7. *Star* (Johannesburg), April 5, 1997.

The Digital Future – Are we reinventing the wheel?

Keith Jeffrey
Kirklees Media Centre

Marshall McLuhan, in his increasingly unfashionable book *Understanding Media*, stated that we can only really begin to understand how a technology can impact on society once we understand how people use that technology. That holds true for digital technology today – the medium still is the message.

Technological impacts can be quite profound. A simple piece of technology like the stirrup led to the creation of the feudal society, a social revolution derived from the need to support a rider more effectively on a horse. A similar process is under way at the moment with digital technology.

How technology is consumed has profound sociological effects and this is nowhere better seen than in the massive explosion of dance music over the last ten years. If we are looking for parallels, for guidance on the way digital media will develop over the next ten years, then we could do worse than analyse what has happened in the dance music industry.

What these changes are likely to be is the subject of my paper. The questions I want to pose are:

Is there enough work being done to investigate how people will respond to the availability of 150 cable channels, digital TV, the Internet?
– Can we guess how people will respond to this information overload?
– Are there lessons to be learned from other fields of activity?
– What are the characteristics of digital technologies ?
– Can we shape these characteristics to suit people's needs?

These are important questions because those businesses which come up with the best answers will be the ones to reap the biggest rewards.

Some of digital technology's characteristics are becoming self-evident. They include:

Niche markets

Digital technologies have an unparalleled ability to target very small markets and often create new types of audiences by identifying a commonality of interests from previously disparate groups. The numbers of these markets are growing and proliferating to such an extent that even a common understanding of what constitutes a society is being undermined.

Multiplicity of Choice

The increasing numbers of these niche markets, along with reducing costs of production, mean that the consumer is faced with an often bewildering array of choice. The danger of there being so much choice that the consumer tunes out completely is very real.

Interactivity

Digital technologies allow for an increasing degree of communication between the producer and the consumer – this is interactivity. It allows for negotiations to be made about the product being delivered through the cable or satellite.

Nicholas Negroponte says, 'The economic models of media today are based almost exclusively on 'pushing' the information and entertainment out into the public. Tomorrow's will have as much to do with 'pulling', where you and I reach into the network and check out something'.[1]

These developments represent a massive change for broadcasters. In fact they are ceasing to be broadcasters and becoming 'narrowcasters'; no longer are they broadcasting to the nation but to smaller and smaller pockets of people. A fundamental change in the relationship between programme suppliers and the consumer is happening. What programme suppliers have to do is to make sure that this relationship works for the consumer because it is from there that money will flow.

Where on earth do we start? Do we have to invest large quantities of cash in mad experiments to finally find the killer package that sends the viewer wild with desire?

We are not flailing about in the dark – although we are entering an age of broadcasting unlike any other. We have to look to outside broadcasting for role models, for pathfinders, to discover parallels. By using landmarks derived from other experiences we can change the approach to digitally-based broadcasting in a way that is more likely to succeed and serves the public's increasingly individualised needs.

What I am proposing is that an analysis of dance music, its production and consumption, may give some pointers to the way forward. The reason I put this proposition is that digital technology has been available in music production for longer than in any other field. It has had a fundamental impact on the creative and productive processes. Machines like the 303 and 808 Roland drum machines, the sampler, software like Cubase and Koan are changing the way music is being made, creating revolutions in the way the music is being consumed and throwing up brand new types of music that could not exist without this technology.

Broadcasters should be studying the state of dance music and how it has developed. It can give them invaluable clues as to how they should be planning their business and programmes over the next ten years.

Dance music is characterised by 7 attributes:

1. Splintering

There are a myriad of categories of dance music, splintering all the time. Sampling technology allows pieces of music (often of other artists) to be cut and pasted into any sort of setting creating often very jarring slabs of music that fit very particular needs. This technological ability means that dance music has splintered into a myriad of smaller styles each with its own innovations and subgenera, as well as their own particular audiences.

Dance music is constantly changing and mutating so that a glance at the February issue of *Muzik*[2] shows the following categories of music being considered large and separately identifiable enough to merit their own record review sections. These categories include House, Jungle, Hard Core, Trance, Garage, Hardbag, Progressive House, Techno, Breakbeat and Down Tempo. Add to these other styles like Ambient House, Happy House, Industrial Breakcore, and you begin to see what an incredibly fecund state digitally produced music is in these days.

2. Ease of Production

The costs of production have shrunk to an incredible extent and this has proved the main impetus in driving forward these hybridisations. You can produce and release a single for £500. Cost is therefore not a factor and has meant a willingness to experiment. An average track is recorded, pressed, released and forgotten about within a month. DJs find a use for the mountain of vinyl that pours out every week, but most twelve-inch singles rarely make it to into an ordinary punter's hands.

Record companies do not expect vast profits to be derived immediately from releases but a catalogue will be built up over a period of time that can be repackaged in other ways. They live always in the hope that a cross-over hit will emerge from one of their releases but these are rare and projects are costed with small numbers of potential purchasers in mind.

This ease of production has fuelled the splintering of innovative music styles but it devalues the role of the artist. Anybody can release a single now and it will sound, at least on first hearing, very professional and frankly not too dissimilar to stuff they might hear down the club on a Saturday night. As Chris Mann of Emissions recording artists Blue says: 'If I want to hear some techno I just switch on my computer for ten minutes.'[3] For the first time music technology allows anybody to have access to the same sounds and rhythms and be driven by the same sensibilities as so-called professionals. When this happens the role of the artist is diminished. The creator ceases to be special.

3. Remixing

Record companies have come to terms with the splintered nature of dance music and they shape their products to fit as many markets as possible by bringing in remixers. These are usually DJs who have a specific expertise and, more importantly, audience in a particular niche. A typical release may get anything up to 8 remixes in an attempt to hit as many markets as possible. The most successful records are the ones that are able to cross over into the most markets. And this remixing is not necessarily restricted to dance records. More traditional artists such as Tori Amos and Everything But the Girl have seen their careers revitalised through remixing. The dance market is so huge and so influential that to gain a foothold in a target audience you may need to bring an element of dance into the mix.

4. Consumer is King

A side effect of these niche markets is a realisation of the power of the individual. No longer are they just one of millions. A niche market may consist of a few thousand people – they therefore feel nearer the heart of things. This realisation imbues the consumer with a much greater sense of power, a power they will enjoy using more and more.

Because of the rise in the number of records being released the consumer begins to feel that he or she is at the heart of the process. The vast quantity of records being released means inevitably that the product is not valued so highly and in many cases differs very little from any other record so the need to own particular records diminishes. There is no common experience of having to own or like certain records. You buy your own stuff broadly within your normal parameters of taste. The consumer opts out and buys only what he or she wants.

The consumer decides on the style of music he or she is interested in and lets the music come to them. Niche marketing is the key to running a successful record label or club these days. You have to know who your market is, often personally by names, where they drink, which DJs they admire, what pages of what magazines they read to make sure you are hitting your audience.

5. Death of Distance

Dance music is not about consuming material presented by large corporate bodies, decisions are made through recommendations and actual experiences. Dance music culture is now localised in high quality clubs throughout the country, the big name DJs come to the consumer on a regular basis. Quality of service and brand names (often at a premium – a decent club may cost £15 to enter) is the secret of success.

6. DJs as Filters

There has been a vast increase in music releases. The week ending 22/2/97 saw 77 singles released in the techno/house/dance category alone, a staggering 55 per cent of that week's releases.[4] The avalanche of material is so overwhelming you need a filter – hence the rise of the DJ. The DJ is the nearest that you can get to a star in dance music. The DJ is the guide which enables the consumer to make judgements about which records to buy. DJs become identified with particular styles of music; they develop their own audiences, not only within the clubs but also on radio and through record releases. They become the touchstone of quality for consumers.

There is no charismatic aura here. In clubs they stand in the corner of a room and play records. There is a response to the records being played from the audience but the celebrity is based on trust that this person knows quality and that the material s/he is presenting is the best available.

7. The Dance Mix Compilation Album

Dance music has also seen the rise of the dance mix compilation album – often mixed by DJs. They can sell phenomenal amounts of units especially with the right DJ on the cover. It makes economic sense for the consumer; a double CD album giving almost three hours of music for twenty quid is far cheaper than purchasing perhaps 40 twelve-inch singles at a cost of £200.

So what conclusions can be drawn from dance music which have some sort of relevance to programme suppliers?

My conclusions about what needs to happen are as follows:

- Essentially there will be less and less broadcasting and more and more narrowcasting – at least initially. People with more choice will place less importance on the stuff spewing out of the screen and will become more interested in programmes that speak directly to their interests. The sense of unification of an entire nation watching the same programme will disappear. This is obvious, but how broadcasters respond is crucial.
- Suppliers need to think in terms of how the consumer is going to react to the fact that there is more choice than ever before. Suppliers will need to become aware of how their viewers will use the technology, how it will fit into their lifestyles, what other media products like radio, newspapers, books, magazines, cinema will occupy their time.
- People will want to feel more in control of their reception of information and programming. They will want to interact and create their own cocktails of programming but at the same time they will want to be a passive receiver. They will want to pull information towards them and have it pushed at them too.
- They will come to rely on sources of authority whose tastes coincide with their own. These may be visible personalities or impersonal conduits like cable channels. When they want to be passive they will check with these arbiters and follow their recommendations.
- The successful products will be ones that can be tailored to meet the widest number of categories, creating products that can reach the largest number of niche markets.
- Niche markets will splinter and get smaller and smaller, programme makers will have to be much quicker to spot trends and respond to them. Marketing the product will become much more important. Mechanisms will have to be set up to link as many niche markets as possible. Broadcasters will have to know their audiences much better. They may even create, as a result of extensive market research, their own niche markets, putting together unlikely combinations of interest groups to create new entertainment and information packages.
- There will be new aesthetics of programmes developed. Some will appeal to older generations who remember the good old days of the BBC and Channel 4 and some will appeal to new audiences brought up within the digital tv and cable experience. The new narrowcast media already are developing their own types of aesthetics but they still have their feet in traditional broadcasting. To provide a truly potent aesthetic is the challenge of programme makers of the next few years. For example, plays and dramas may become more interactive, emphasis may be placed on developing content which requires long term relationships between the viewer and the characters.

So how can this be translated into a scenario where a consumer has access to a myriad of TV channels being delivered digitally, by satellite or cable? How can anyone make sense of 200 channels pumping out material perhaps 24 hours a day? The experience of dance music would perhaps suggest the following:

The Cocktail Channel: This would be a customised channel where the consumer pays for individual programmes. The consumer and their family are offered on a regular basis or for runs of programmes access to these programmes either when they are broadcast or at a later date. Obviously there are technical problems with delivering this type of on-demand delivery but that is not the issue here. The issue is giving the people the product they want. Nobody wants to purchase the Sci-Fi Channel just for *The X-files* alone and have to put up with the other garbage that surrounds it. Dont waste the consumer's time.

Rise of the Filter: People will always be interested in new programmes but they will not want to spend hours surfing channels in the hope of discovering programmes they unexpectedly find to be entertaining. What they will need are guides, 'experts' who spend their time surfing the channels to find out the good stuff and make recommendations. The viewer will then be able to develop a trusting relationship over a long period of time with this person. This filter may be a journalist writing regularly in a newspaper or specialist magazine. Perhaps this person may even be in charge of a channel picking out and presenting themed or diverse material. *The Barry Norman Movie Channel* or *Richard Baker Presents Classical* could be potential channel ideas. The key is credibility, the filter must not be seen as a lackey of a programme maker, trust is a prerequisite if that imprimatur is to grow and develop.

Remixed Shows: Programme makers will be looking for a break-out hit so we can expect more shows like *The X-Files* or *Star Trek – The Next Generation*, shows which build on a niche market but can be seen as dramas or soaps in their own right. However, another approach may be to create shows which can be viewed from different perspectives. Using the same common plot line but exploring it from different characters' point of view. A soap opera may be available on 5 different channels which appeal to 5 different age groups, in each channel the central characters of the show will be those most easily identified with the age group.

What I've tried to do in this paper is to point out that the consumer has to be at the heart of everything we do and that there are more parallels between TV consumption in all its forms and dance music than perhaps many programme makers are aware. There are lessons to be learnt outside broadcasting. Let's start learning them.

References

1. Nicholas Negroponte (1995) *Being Digital*, p. 170; London: Coronet/Hodder and Stoughton.
2. *Muzik*, February 1997, pp. 105-115; London: IPC Magazines
3. Chris Mann of *Blue* Interviewed 24/1/97
4. *Music Week*, 22/2/97 p. 41; London: Spotlight Publications.

Reinventing Children's Television

Lessons from the 1950s

Ken Jones
University of Keele

This article describes the debates and strategic decisions of a particular group of 'cultural producers' – administrators and programme-makers in the Children's Television Department of the BBC in the late 1950s.[1] The story that it tells is in some ways familiar – other writers have depicted the complexities of the BBC's evolving response to the competitive pressures and cultural shifts of the period. (Wagg 1992, Oswell 1995). But where they tend to find in the statements and practices of producers a considerable degree of coherence, this article discovers uncertainty. Wagg, for instance, has written a stimulating piece contrasting the consumer-centred children's television of the 1980s with an earlier period in which the child-audience was addressed in anti-commercial and educationally-inflected terms. (Wagg p.151) This juxtaposition turns, however, on the suggestion that children's television was motivated in the 1950s by a 'stable and well-defined' understanding of 'childhood' – an understanding which it did not in fact possess. The nature of childhood was not blithely and commandingly assumed by BBC producers; it was, rather, a topic open to continuous, uneasy and ultimately unresolved discussion.

The article aims to draw attention to the main themes of this discussion. In doing so, it both offers an historical interpretation and suggests some points of a more general, theoretical importance. These points have to do with issues of institutional power and popular agency. Over the last 15 years – under the influence, particularly, of Michel Foucault – there has developed a body of work that has established 'childhood' as not only a social construction, but as an institutionally-located discourse which has powerful and limiting effects on those whom it addresses, defines and regulates. (Henriques *et al* 1984) David Oswell's 'genealogy of the child television audience', *Watching with Mother* (1995) extends this approach to television. A characteristic of work within this tradition is its inclination both to over-emphasise the coherence and power of apparently authoritative discourses, and to neglect the ways in which these discourses are qualified, undermined and (to some extent) transformed by their encounter with the attitudes and practices of the social groups which they are attempting to manage. In other words, , they overlook the possibility that 'official' discourses of childhood are shaped, in some ways, by the agency of children.

The history of children's television in the 1950s provides grounds for rethinking this interpretive framework, in a way which places a greater emphasis on reciprocity of the relationship between producers and audiences. The encounter between these groups was never of course direct – how could it be? Children's encounter with producers was mediated through their viewing. Producers met children through the medium of audience statistics. Yet in these statistics was encoded a kind of cultural agency: most children, particularly working-class children, chose not to watch BBC programmes, and viewing figures made this dramatically clear. Their choice was not arbitrary, but culturally grounded. Contemporary research, some of it commissioned by the BBC, made plain the discrepancy between children's everyday cultural experience and the ways in which it was reflected back to them by public service television. (Abrams 1955) Producers, faced with the evidence of their competitive failure, were forced to give some account of the cultural preferences of their desired audience, and to change aspects of their own practice in order to attract it. The ways in which they discussed childhood were thus inflected by the evident workings of popular taste: their deliberations were marked by the agency of their audience.

Of course, the influence of the audience was nothing like complete: as I shall show, the kind of childhood imagined by producers owed something not only to their attempts to capture the nature of contemporary cultural change, but also to the continuing pressures of a Reithian view of broadcasting and a class-limited understanding of children's experiences and tastes. Nevertheless the pressure exerted by the child audience was sufficient to ensure that the versions of 'childhood' that informed the practice of broadcasters were – *pace* Wagg – both unstable and ill-defined. It was the conflict between the demands of the audience and the received ideas of producers which ensured that the crisis of BBC children's television dragged itself out over several years.

Responding to Competition

The first ITV companies began broadcasting in late 1955. At that time, there were television sets in four and a half million homes – about 30 per cent of British households (Abrams 1955; Briggs 1995). By 1960, when ITV broadcasts were able to reach virtually the whole country, the number had increased to ten and a half million. ITV, particularly in the late fifties, was vastly the more popular channel: BBC research estimated that in the first six months of 1957, for instance, ITV programmes enjoyed a 70:30 advantage among viewers who could receive both channels (BBC 1957). ITV companies enjoyed, if anything, an even greater lead among child audiences. 'Children's television,' noted the BBC's General Advisory Council, 'placed the BBC in its greatest competitive dilemma.' (Briggs p.178) A 1960 Granada Television survey of children's viewing estimated that ITV's daily audience share ranged from 66 per cent to 85 per cent (Granada 1960). This imbalance was all the more significant because it did not occur in the context of a duopoly in which competing broadcasters shared roughly the same ideas of quality, purpose and audience need; it was more the case that – particularly in children's television – the two systems occupied sharply contrasting, even hostile, positions. The title of a widely-circulated lecture given by Hugh Greene in 1958 is perhaps the most concise indicator of this tense relationship – *Two Threats to Broadcasting: Political and Commercial Control.* (Greene 1958) For Greene, commercial competition struck a blow at the heart of public service broadcasting: it won audiences, but destroyed standards. Citing children's television as an example, he contrasted the BBC's commitment to causes which ITV, 'by its very nature', could never uphold: a strong educational emphasis, an attention to the needs of the very young, an attentiveness to minority interests, a willingness to 'encourage children to engage in pursuits other than the watching of television'. His speech ended with a defiant but also rather plaintive question. 'Perhaps commercial television gives many, even most, what they want. But is that the full unanswerable argument?'

Producers in the BBC Television Children's Department, who on the whole shared Greene's Reithian assessment, spent a lot of time debating both the reasons for the success of their adversary and the means by which they might redress its advantage. The competitive pressures of ITV thus provided a constant and pressing focus of discussion. But at a very early stage , this immediate worry became entangled with a wider set of departmental preoccupations, concerning the ways in which the BBC should read and respond to post-war cultural change. The initiative in this effort of strategic re-thinking was taken by Owen Reed, Head of Children's Programmes, Television, from 1956 to 1964, whose prolific memoranda provide much of the material for the argument which follows. The deliberations instigated by Reed did not have a particularly successful outcome in terms of a new programming policy – BBC children's ratings remained well below those of ITV, and largely as a result of this Reed was eventually transferred to another post. (Briggs p179 & p346) Nevertheless, they provide both a factual basis on which to reconstruct an institutional history of the period and a 'dramatisation' of the attitudes and dilemmas of the particular group of cultural producers which Reed headed.

Facing the New

In Reed's view, his department faced two problems. First, the BBC since the 1930s had operated with an unhelpfully inclusive definition of the child audience. Second, it failed to understand changes in the nature of childhood. In Reed's presentation, these two failings were linked. The official line of the corporation was that 'children's television is directed towards children between the ages of 5–16 ... While their ages vary from 5–16 and even more, it is believed that they are broadly alike in the pattern of their lives' (BBC Study Group1959). Reed argued that this definition was based on a reading of middle-class social habits and attitudes which were long out-of-date. (Reed 1959) Moreover, it had disabling consequences for programme-makers: it certainly provided a corporate identity – embodied in the fact that children's television had its own listing in the Radio Times and its own continuity announcers – but this identity was repellent to many children. No-one over eleven, said Reed, wanted to be addressed as a child. The 'true' child audience now comprised two groups: the 'kindergartens aged 5-8 who like life to be cosy, believe in fairies, but have growing horizons and are becoming familiar with the rudimentary entertainment conventions' and the 'primaries who like to feel tough, organised and keen, are anti-grown-up, still live in a world of let's pretend but with an increasing appetite for combat adventure and pseudo-men of the world settings' (Reed 1957a). BBC Children's Television, in this respect, wasn't 'tough' enough. It held no appeal for the 'solid, sticky, gang-minded, inky, lolly-sucking and gregarious mob of 5–11s', among whom its failure was 'most conspicuous'. (ibid.)

It is worth pausing at this point to consider what is – and is not – being said. The word Reed uses most often to describe, or to imagine, the new audience is 'tough'. As we shall see, it was a favourite term of BBC producers. At this distance, it appears an odd usage: cultural debate in the late 1950s was customarily organised in terms of distinctions between particular kinds of social or cultural groups – 'popular' and 'elite', 'consumer' and 'citizen' and so on. Reed himself frequently used such terms, arguing that – caught between the requirements of 'prestige and popularity', 'minority interests' and the necessity of 'competing for majorities' – the Childen's Television Department had failed to develop a sustainable unified identity. (Reed 1958). Although not particularly sensitive or complex, these categories at least had the merit of addressing actual cultural processes. Reed's use of 'tough' , however, as the main descriptor of the audience seems an evasion of complexity. It collapses a discussion of cultural processes into a trite psychological shorthand: it has the effect of misrecognising the exact character of change and miscalculating the ways in which the BBC might respond to it. It was not as if the resources for a more perceptive discussion were unavailable. As early as 1955, the BBC had commissioned research from Mark Abrams, one of the most influential interpreters of cultural change in the immediate post-war decades. Abrams had identified a mass turning away from BBC children's programmes, even at a time when it had no competitors. This, Abrams speculated, was 'presumably related to the kind of entertainment offered by the BBC,' about most of whose programmes lingered 'an atmosphere of a kindly middle-class nursery'. (Abrams 1955) Later in the decade, he outlined what could be called the 'proletarianisation' and 'americanisation' of young people's cultural tastes. (Abrams 1959) Arguably, the BBC's achievements of the early 60s involved an approach which recognised the existence – in the general cultural arena – of such preferences. Negotiating with them, it was able to reconcile, in some respects, the demands of quality and popularity. If the Children's Department failed to share in such a success, its failure to think adequately about the audience for children's television may have been a root cause.

Rethinking Children's Television

Nevertheless, the search for popularity and the attempt to reduce ITV's share of the child audience were accepted by the department as central aspects of a necessary, if dangerous, process of change: as Reed put it, the Department had to learn 'how to be popular without being cheap'. (Reed 1958b) The most extensive record we have of its response is a transcript of a meeting held under Reed's chairmanship in November 1960, at which producers discussed the effects of commercial competition upon their work.[2] The impact of competition in the period 1955–60 was concisely summarised. The Department had grown in size, from eight producers to twelve, and its weekly schedule had expanded – from nearly seven hours to eight and a quarter. It now bought in more American material, especially adventures and westerns. It had developed a more coherent identity. It produced more light entertainment programmes. Its production values were higher, with outdoor film sequences being inserted into many programmes. It had dropped the formal, on-screen title of 'Children's Television', and thus enabled itself to develop what one producer called 'a more adult approach'. (BBC 1960)

Beyond establishing these basic facts of change, the meeting attempted to situate them in a wider cultural and aesthetic context. The boldest position was that of the drama producer Shaun Sutton. The advent of ITV, he argued, had been good for the BBC. It had resulted in more money being spent on Children's Television; it had accelerated the development of the Department towards 'semi-adult' programming; it had raised levels of technical competence and professionalism. It was true that ITV still – despite the BBC's advances – gained the best audiences, but this was because their schedules were built around a few 'absolute winners' – *Popeye, Robin Hood,* the *Mickey Mouse Club* (BBC 1960 p.11). To some at the meeting these were scandalous arguments, but Reed tried to develop them further, towards what might be called the aesthetic basis of ITV's success. There was a difference, he suggested, between the BBC's traditional pre-ITV programme-making and its later efforts: once it was 'soft', now it was 'tough'. Others elaborated the metaphor, describing their response to perceived changes in children's culture in terms of the new 'punch' of light entertainment programmes, and of the 'stiffening' of programme content. Reed linked these qualities to a further requirement, that of compulsiveness:

> Since competition has had to be urgently reckoned with, compulsiveness – art of being compulsive – has become one of the standards of good television: that is to say, whether a programme is good or bad is decided not only on whether it is a good or bad programme for children, but whether it is a useful thing for keeping children with you, which is a different thing.' (*op.cit.* p17)

In this reading, the preferences of children operated to transform television output at a deep level: it was not only that they chose to watch one programme rather than another; it was also that they had developed a different kind of television viewing which demanded a reformulating of televisual aesthetics. The issue of compulsion had long been a concern of Reed's. In 1958, he had pointed to the link between what we might call the BBC's traditional 'aesthetic of non-compulsiveness' and the limited means which the Department had at its disposal. Technological poverty combined with traditional aesthetics in a television which could not 'keep children with it'. ITV's strategy of building its daily programme around a 25-minute adventure film compared favourably with the studio-bound, and heritage-centred productions of the Department. Reed summarised the problem like this:

> So far, BBC Children's Television has drawn its strength mainly from the classics ... But the really compelling factors are speed and space and adventure ... Children are conditioned by cinema-going into an intoxicating measure of realism. Studio television is stuck at the point where without more film, it must rely on character rather than incident, and this means going back to the leather-bound family favourites. (Reed 1958)

In some ways here, Reed was restating an old dilemma – the epic versus the novel, the world of action versus the interiority of character. In another way, he was responding to a contemporary problem, though in a form whose effects were markedly unproductive.

Preferring the Old

Reed saw much of the future of children's television in the 'romantic adventure film'. Though sponsoring *Blue Peter* and presiding over the continuation of under-5s programming, the centre of his interests lay with a boyish kind of drama. ITV's success, he thought, was based on importing into television the aesthetics of Hollywood – a move which suited the new 'toughness' of the audience. The 'inescapable' conclusion for the BBC, he thought, was 'to venture into the bear-garden of the world telefilm trade'. (Reed 1958) He regretted 'the BBC's failure to get in first on the dollar-earning co-production of English-made TV films of which ITV's *Robin Hood* is the bitter fruit'. (Reed 1957b) At this point, howev-er, Reed's position began to unravel. In practice, the co-financing of Hollywood-style adventures was ruled out. It would consume the greater share of available resources, narrow the BBC's overall output and 'slant production towards the American market'(BBC 1957). Reed's own attempts at a response to *Robin Hood* – an expensive *Rob Roy*, a mishandled Caribbean drama, *Hurricane* – were unsuc-cessful. What is more, compulsiveness, even for Reed himself, was a problem-atic objective – it was all too close to the 'addiction' which Reed and many of his contemporaries saw as the least desirable of television's effects. (BBC 1960, Himmelweit 1958) Reed's own preferences were at odds with much of children's teleision. He spoke with nostalgia of the days of 'relaxed and civilised thinking' before the arrival of competition. (BBC 1960, p28) He had a distaste for the most successful choices of ITV's programme buyers, especially in the area of anima-tion:

> I would not touch *Popeye* if it was offered to me on a plate for the same reason I would not touch *Huckleberry Hound*, because it is noisy. It harps on a type of violence which, in the aggregate, is far worse than all the duels [in the adventure films]. (BBC 1960, p28)

It was 'agony' to watch this sort of thing; and some of his producers, likewise, fondly remembered the days of 'proper, peaceful entertainment', and regretted the 'thump, thump, thump' of contemporary children's programmes (ibid).

It was at points like these that the deeper preferences of Reed and many of his colleagues emerged. Their introduction into discussion allows us to grasp the *ensemble* of different elements that were involved in producers' responses to com-petition and cultural change. They were willing to respond to evidence of chang-ing tastes in those areas where taste could be accommodated by the familiar, socially sanctioned form of the Hollywood film. But at its other manifestations they drew the line: their own aversions counted for much more, here, than com-petitive advantage. Departmental discourse certainly acknowledged the power of audience preference, but this perception was filtered through psychologistic cate-gories which diluted much of its social force. On top of this, there were tenacious social and aesthetic commitments to conceptions of childhood which were – as the response to animation, quoted above, shows – fairly explicitly prelapsarian.

Roads Not Taken

The 1960 discussion shows the department at an impasse – its efforts unpro-ductively focused on one particular genre (drama), its understandings of its audi-ence still limited. Soon its problems were to be resolved in a drastic manner. The efforts of Stuart Hood – Controller of Programmes, Television from 1961 – were directed towards the break-up of the Department. Rejecting Reed's asser-tion that the Department needed to be seen as a 'sacrosanct minority service', Hood removed children's drama and light entertainment from its control. The result was the making and/or scheduling of programmes like *Dr Who*, *Oliver Twist* and *Bronco*, which deliberately infringed the traditional boundaries of child-hood, and recognised that one of the central facts about the child audience was its liking for adult programmes. Reed was left to protest unsuccessfully at the 'dangerous' and 'frightening' effects of the new programming strategy. (Reed 1961) Later, in 1964, again at Hood's prompting, Children's Television was incor-porated into a 'Family Programmes Department'. Hood noted at this point that the existing schedules were 'tired and repetitive'. 'New thinking' was required, his laconic memorandum continued, with an appeal being made to a 'wide cross-section of children and parents'.

Hood's project is usually regretted (Home 1993), and there are indeed rea-sons for seeing it as mistaken: based on a rejection of the *prevailing* culture of children's television, it culminated in a rejection of children's television in (near) entirety. It was in substance a negative move. It was also unsuccessful. The merg-er which Hood instigated did not revive programming for children – in the internal competition for resources, the 'children's section' of the new department was a consistent loser. Nevertheless, looked at in the longer term, the very neg-ativity of the approach was stimulating. Hood approached BBC television cul-ture as a relative outsider – he was from North-East Scotland, he had not been to Oxford or Cambridge and his political sympathies were on the left. From his perspective, the work of the children's department appeared 'alien' and unat-tractive. Like much of the BBC, it seemed to promote political conservatism and 'west-end' theatrical culture; its lack of 'inventiveness' was in some ways a func-tion of its 'closeness to the establishment' (Hood 1997). Hood, with his Assistant Controller Donald Baverstock, took arms against prevailing assumptions, utilis-ing the results of audience research to argue that children's preferences lay to a great extent with adult programmes, and that the department was failing to address a working-class child audience.

In these ways, though they offered no coherent project for the future of chil-dren's television, Hood and Baverstock at least offered a strong criticism of its present practice – a criticism based on claims about cultural change, children's preferences, and shifts in the relation to each other of 'adult' and 'children's' culture. Whatever the immediate results of the changes they instigated, the gen-eral outlines of reform suggested a way of rethinking children's television, based on a new responsiveness to children's tastes and a redrawing of the boundaries of childhood. When in 1967 its status was restored, the department began to operate with a much broader conception of programme range and audience. In this sense, the negative choices of the child audience and the negative critique of Hood and Baverstock may ultimately have had productive effects.

Endnotes

1 This paper draws on research being conducted for an ESRC-funded project *Children's Media Culture: Education, Entertainment and the Public Sphere,* part of the ESRC's *Media Culture and Media Economics* programme. Thanks to my colleagues David Buckingham, Hannah Davies, Peter Kelley and Gunther Kress for their help and advice.

2 All Departments were asked to discuss the balance-sheet of ITV's emergence, as part of the BBC's prepartion for the 'Pilkington Report' of 1962.

References

Abrams, M. (1955) *Child Audiences for Television,* BBC Written Archives Centre (WAC), Caversham VR55/502.

Abrams, M. (1959) *The Teenage Consumer,* London, London Press Exchange.

BBC (1957) *Programmes for Children,* Report of the General Advisory Council 16/9/1957 WAC T16/45/2.

BBC (1959) Study Group on the Nuffield Report *Television and the Child* WAC T/16/45/2

BBC (1960) *Report of a Meeting held on 22/11/1960. Subject: Children's Television* WAC T/16/45/3.

Briggs, A. (1995) *The History of Broadcasting in the United Kingdom.* Volume V: Competition Oxford, OUP.

Curran, J and Seaton, J (1991) *Power without Responsibility: The Press and Broadcasting in Britain* London, Routledge (Fourth Edition).

Granada Television (1960) *Children's Television Viewing* Manchester, Granada.

Greene, Hugh Carleton (1958) *Two Threats to Broadcasting: Political and Commercial Control* Speech in Bad Boll, West Germany 12/3/1958 (extracts) WAC T/16/45/2.

Himmelweit, H et al (1958) *Television and the Child* Oxford, OUP.

Home, A. (1993) *Into the Box of Delights: A History of Children's Television,* BBC

Hood, S (1964) *Memorandum to Head of Children's Programmes,* Television 9/1/1964 WAC T31/324.

Hood, S (1997) Interview with Children's Media Culture Project.

Oswell, D (1995) *Watching with Mother: A Genealogy of the Child Television Audience,* unpublished PhD thesis, Open University.

Reed, O (1957a) *Memorandum to Controller of Programmes,* Television 5/7/1957 WAC T/16/45/2

Reed, O (1957b) *Memorandum* (to Children's Television Department?) 23/8/57 WAC T/16/45/2

Reed, O (1958) *Memorandum* (to Children's Television Department?) 2/6/1958 WAC T/16/45/2

Reed, O (1959) *Note to Children's Television Department* 27/1/1959 WAC T/16/45/2

Reed, O (1961) *Memorandum to Controller of Programmes,* Television 21/11/1961 WAC T/16/45/3.

Stephens, D (1964?) *Memorandum to Controller of Programmes,* Television, undated WAC T31/324.

Wagg, S (1992) 'One I made earlier: Media, popular culture and the politics of childhood' in D.Strinati and S. Wagg (eds) *Come on Down? Popular Media Culture in Post-war Britain* London, Routledge.

Cable TV as a 'Social and Cultural Project'

The Impact of Public Service and Commercial Perceptions

Yaron Katz

Holon Institute of Technology, Arts and Sciences

N ew media technologies have raised questions about the social and cultural aspects of broadcasting, as technological advancement and policy changes intensify the debate on the role and impact of public service principles within a market-led and multi-channel media. The ability of governments to endorse social and cultural requirements has diminished, since such policy aims tend to clash with the opportunities of commercial distribution. This research aims to examine the notion that early experiences with cable TV can provide important conclusions on the conflict between social and cultural requirements and commercial transmissions. The main argument is that, initially, social and cultural aspects dominated cable TV policy-making, and that the three largest media countries in Europe (Britain, France and Germany) followed the same model in aiming their cable policies as 'a social and cultural project'. These goals included requirements for community transmissions, 'Must Carry' rules, and pilot projects to examine future developments. Despite differences in approach between countries, these social and cultural aspects dominated cable developments, and it was not until the requirements were lifted that cable systems had the chance to develop commercially.

Introduction

Social and cultural aspects dominated the development of cable TV policies until the 1980s, and set the stage for new media policies thereafter. This phase of development is identified foremost with powerful systematic and ideological pressures that changed public policies in the field of cable. The process resulted in the collapse of the social and cultural nature of cable systems and policies and the triumph of commercial perceptions. This article claims that these aspects are common to the three largest media countries of Europe: Britain, France and Germany, despite local variations which can be attributed to social, cultural and political differences. In theoretical terms, it is argued that the social and cultural requirements initiated by governments – although varied among countries – have in large part determined that cable be developed as 'a social and cultural project'. Within this structure, programming was directed to community and public access appeal, development was restricted through 'Must Carry' rules, and the establishment of cable systems was tested through pilot projects. It was not until these experiences proved unsuccessful that commercial competition and market policy for cable was adopted in all the countries examined in this research. The contribution of early experiences of the social and cultural perceptions of cable was decisive to this transition, however, since these were followed by deregulatory policies for the entire broadcast media.

The experience of the social and commercial aspects of cable policy had a profound impact on changes in media policy and the shift in balance between public service and commercial broadcasting in Europe. In the 'old order' of broadcasting, which dominated European broadcasting until the 1980s, broadcasting was a public service system with national monopoly, non-commercial, and had social and cultural goals (McQuail, 1995). This model also had an impact on attitudes to cable developments. Negrine and Papathanassopoulos (1990) say that, if initially television was aimed to encourage a participatory society, in the 1980s European broadcasting and new media policies have shifted their emphasis, from a public service conception of the audience and public needs and services, to a consumer-driven broadcasting and telecommunications market. Consequently, it is argued that cable policy changes can be seen in the light of the overall changes in media policy in Europe.

This article examines the social and cultural impact on cable policy-making as it relates to the relevant experiences of the large media countries in Europe. This focus illustrates the main models of cable policy which existed in the 1970s and early 1980s and provides a context within which the social and cultural impact on the evolution of broadcast and cable policy in these countries in later years can be understood. It is argued that although this period contains lessons about success and failure in public service broadcasting, the experience with cable TV reflects the overall question of public service and commercial aspects of broadcasting, because of the changing role of television broadcasting.

Community Transmissions

A central issue in the development of cable has been the way in which changes in attitudes towards the programming of cable systems have resulted from wider ideological and political shifts in policy-making. In the 1970s, a new orientation towards cable was adopted – paying more attention to its potential in providing community transmissions. Within the rules governing the development of cable systems, a duty was imposed to provide community channels. Although details varied from country to country, the major underlying philosophy was similar: local cable channels were meant to reflect the real desires and needs of local people within the community and foster local means of expression.

Europe had experimented with local and community transmissions in the form of specific projects initiated by national governments. These experiments took place in Britain and France in the 1970s and in France and Germany in the 1980s. Despite local differences between the three largest media countries of Europe, the common result of these experiences was that commercial perceptions have prevailed over community and public service conceptions in cable programming.

In Britain, calls for community and public access television by groups interested in the idea of alternative media matched the strategy of commercial cable operators, who were more than willing to demonstrate the local potential of cable –

if this could open the political door to more profitable forms of programming, such as pay TV channels. In 1972, the Minister of Post and Telecommunications announced the granting of experimental licences allowing local programming services on the condition that no public money would be provided. The transmissions began in Greenwich in August 1972, in Bristol in May 1973, in Sheffield in August 1973, and in Swindon in March 1974. Companies hoped that these initiatives would be the first step towards fully commercial services. However, the return of the Labour Government in 1974 squashed these hopes. The cable companies were forced to reduce services – and most initiatives closed down at the end of the original three-year licences. In programming terms, the British community services produced new and valuable ideas but no new sources of revenue, since neither subscription, sponsorship nor advertising was permitted. It was recognized that, in these circumstances, the projects could not pay their way.

In France and Germany, community projects were also exploited by the national governments, although they provided financial means to support local transmissions. This policy was part of social and cultural policy thinking which supported the establishment of cable systems with the aim of encouraging social participation. But in both these countries, despite the initial financial support, plans have not been realized to their full potential. In France, experiments with community cable systems, which started in 1973, were suspended in 1975 due to lack of government commitment. The plans had been renewed a decade later, when the government encouraged and supported the establishment of local cable systems as part of the Cable Plan, in order to achieve the goal of establishing an advanced interactive network across the country with the capability to offer local and community transmissions and explore social and cultural aspects. But this project failed because of lack of support by the public and by local governments. In Germany, community transmissions were tested during the pilot projects in the 1980s. These projects tested the social and cultural aspects offered by cable, and required local and community transmissions. Despite initial support by the national government and the public, the addition of commercial transmissions in the second half of the 1980s diminished the impact of community transmissions and made it a secondary service to satellite and commercial transmissions.

These unsuccessful and inconclusive experiments with local and community transmissions changed attitudes and cable policies. The idea of public service broadcasting served by cable's ability to offer narrow-cast transmissions did not succeed, and commercial perceptions have prevailed – helped by technological advancement and public demand.

'Must Carry' Rules

In addition to community transmissions, the idea of 'a social and cultural project' had also been identified with the requirement for 'Must Carry' rules, which were imposed on cable systems on behalf of terrestrial broadcasters. These rules were usually the most popular resolution for countries whose broadcast system was founded on public service principles. Although they required cable operators to take all national channels, in order to protect the priority status of broadcast television, they also delayed the development of cable for a considerable time, because the relatively limited technology of cable did not allow systems to provide additional channels much beyond the 'Must Carry' services.

In Britain, the rules had such an impact on the development of cable systems that the cable industry made little progress until the 1980s. The early experience with relay exchange led to the immediate prohibition on signal importation before British cable got under way, with the result that even in the early 1980s expansion was impossible. This had a decisive impact on the development of cable in Britain: since the technology of British systems limited them to only 4 to 6 channels, leaving no room for services beyond the 'Must Carry' package, the new market-led policy adopted later lacked an initial customer base. The 1984 Cable and Broadcasting Bill also required that all national television services would be included as part of the 'Must Carry' package of cable systems, and this was one of the main reasons for the marginal development of cable in Britain in the 1980s. It was not until the 1989 Broadcasting Bill eliminated these rules and initiated a market-led policy for cable and the broadcasting sector, that cable in Britain started to develop.

In France, while the development of cable systems was restricted until the mid 1980s, the Cable Plan initiated in 1984 represented an attempt to reconcile conflicting interests of public service and advanced telecommunications services. According to the 'Must Carry' rules required by the Plan, cable networks had to provide all public broadcasting channels. In addition, foreign channels could occupy up to 30 per cent of a system's capacity, and films could only be shown three years after their release to public broadcasting networks. 60 per cent of the films shown had to come from the EEC and 50 per cent from French speaking countries. Local programming also had to be part of a system's capacity. This plan did not succeed, and by the end of the 1980s cable's development in France was also marginal. It was not until policy changes were enacted and commercial perceptions acquired a dominant influence on broadcasting policy that the requirement for 'Must Carry' channels and programming were eliminated and the commercialization of French cable became evident.

A similar process took place in Germany, but because of the constitutional complexities and the control of the local states over broadcasting, Germany was one of few countries that attempted to go even beyond the 'Must Carry' rules in order to ensure the continuity of the national and states broadcasting systems. According to the agreement made after the Second World War, broadcasting is under the authority of the German states, while all other telecommunications aspects, including broadcasting facilities, are the responsibility of the Bundespost. But the conflict of interests between Socialist and Conservative states over the content of cable programming delayed cable developments until the mid 1980s. Although the Conservative administration wanted cable and satellite to compete with the public broadcasters, because of the shortage of over-the-air frequencies and the control of the states over the transmissions received within their boundaries, the 'Must Carry' rules imposed by Socialist states made the development of cable in Germany impossible. The situation changed after four pilot projects started in 1984 and an agreement between all states was reached in 1987. The agreement established the commercial nature of

German cable by permitting transmissions to be received across the country. This meant the *de facto* elimination of the 'Must Carry' rules imposed by states and the adoption of commercial perceptions in cable policy.

The result of the 'Must Carry' rules was that cable installations were limited. This had an impact on further developments, since cable operators were deprived of initial consumer support. Only in the mid 1980s, with the diminishing impact of the rules and the later elimination of these requirements, did European cable start to develop. The availability of satellite transmissions enforced policy changes. All three of the largest European media countries launched cable plans, which gave subscribers additional channels for the 'Must Carry' transmissions. This diminished the imposition of the rules and allowed for commercial competition throughout the Continent, with the Council of Europe allowing the free flow of movement of television broadcasts within all member states and in whatever way they are provided. This transition in policy meant the adoption of commercial perceptions in all that relates to cable programming and the diminution of the 'Must Carry' policy.

Pilot Projects

Another important aspect that emphasizes the perception of European cable as 'a social and cultural project', relates to cable pilot projects. This perception required prior experimentation with the proposed infrastructure. Accordingly, pilot projects took place in all three of the largest media countries. They aimed to test technologies and assess the social impact of cable on the given environment of their nations, before establishing the new cable infrastructure.

The most elaborate experiment, with certain sophisticated applications of telecommunications, occurred in France. The Biarritz project was the most advanced experiment in Europe, with ventures into areas such as motion video services and video-telephony. This began at the end of 1979, with the construction of a fibre-optic system, as part of the official interest in establishing a multi-service network that would provide two-way capability in the form of images, high-fidelity sound, voice, and data, to users of the public network. The primary motivation behind the development of this technology was to give France a competitive economic advantage via early research and development. The project aimed to enable France to move its industry into the development of a broad-band video-communications network. The policy sought to take advantage of a growing demand for audio-visual services and communication in order to accelerate the installation and interconnection of local video-communications networks. The lessons learned from the experience helped in the development of the Cable Plan initiated in 1982. Following Biarritz many systems asked to join the project. In May 1984, the PTT announced that 133 urban areas, representing four million households, had officially applied to be cabled. But at the end of 1984, it appeared that the cable experiments were stagnating and fading away and non-pilot projects developed rapidly.

Germany also put a high priority on experimenting with cable, although the primary reason was not to build an advanced industry (as in France), but to mediate between the contrasted political policies of the German states. Experiments started after the Federal Government decided on an ambitious

169

programme – to install new technologies and to test the feasibility of a wide range of new telecommunications services. Cable was a primary concern among the advanced projects. Pilot projects started in 1984, in four major German cities: Munich, Ludwigshafen, West Berlin, and Dortmund. These initiatives marked the entry of private industry into the delivery of television programming in Germany. The cable experiments took place under an agreement of German states. They were aimed at testing the various aspects of cable, prior to the full implementation of the industry on a nationwide basis. The experiences gained were very helpful to cabling in Germany. On the basis of the pilot projects the Bundespost formulated an approach which aimed to increase the number of cable subscribers as rapidly as possible, through the expansion of existing systems and the use of a well-tested technology – thereby abandoning the intention to establish interactive networks. The overall impact of the pilot project was noteworthy in Germany. Several cooperative cable projects started after the first cable experiments, with private firms or communities doing the cabling, and the Bundespost tried to standardize these cable systems in order to lay the foundations for an institutionalized national network.

In Britain, one of the important aspects of the industrial strategy towards cable was the government's readiness to license a limited number of pilot projects before the creation of the Cable Authority in order to provide a real indication of its commitment to the future development of cable and to take full advantage of the interest and enthusiasm for cable – with the whole process being erected as a test of the degree of private-sector interest in its development, particularly in view of the financial risks involved. In 1984 the government invited applications for 12 pilot licences to build new systems. 37 were submitted – justifying the government decision – and finally 11 applications were awarded franchises. Another step prior to legislation concerned the existing narrow-band cable systems that served 1.4 million households. Operators were invited to submit applications to provide up to four new channels over the systems. These two initiatives enabled companies to move ahead with cabling; stimulated the design and production of more advanced equipment and new programming; and provided a better view of the market. This was a combination of new systems and new services aimed to build up the audience level required to justify investment in cable.

In all three of the largest media countries, the experiments that preceded the implementation of cable plans successfully indicated the preferred structures, with the results being used to best advantage in Germany, where they contributed to the speed of cabling. But although initially public authorities moved to promote cable development to meet broader public interest objectives, policy changes in the second half of the 1980s – particularly the adoption of commercial perceptions – meant the collapse of the notion of cable pilot projects as part of a government-approved national cabling plan and policy thinking put less stress on social and cultural goals.

Conclusion
The public service culture, which had dominated European broadcast policy until the 1980s, influenced the nature of cable policies, social and cultural perceptions

initially dominating. The impact of these perceptions can be seen as an attempt to meet broader social and cultural goals: requirements for community transmissions, imposition of 'Must Carry' channels and establishment of pilot projects to test the structure of future systems. The research claims that despite differences in approach, the three largest media countries in Europe have followed the same general model of viewing cable as 'a social and cultural project'.

The conclusion of this course of development of cable policies demonstrates the inter-circle of the trajectory of cable's development, and can reflect on the overall transition of the broadcast media in Europe into a market-led industry – where commercial considerations have prevailed over social, cultural and public service perceptions. Whereas in the early phases social and cultural perceptions dominated, the unsuccessful completion of these attempts was the trigger for policy changes, with the result that social and cultural distinctions seem no longer to be as powerful a force as they once did. Consequently, it is argued that the early perceptions of cable, as part of a social and cultural policy thinking agenda, can be seen as indications for later and more comprehensive changes in media policy, with Europe following the American experience of deregulation and market-led policy for cable and satellite. These technologies can now be considered as an economic and technological initiative rather than as 'a social and cultural project' – with the entire media sector following the same trend.

References

Cappe De Baillon, J., The Legal Framework of French Television, in *Journal of the Law and Practice*, January 1987.

Compaine, M. Benjamin, New Competition and New Media, in *Rundfunk and Fernsen*, 1985 Vol.33, Part 3/4.

Dizard, Wilson, *Old Media New Media*, 1994, Longman, New York.

Dutton, Blumler and Kraemer (eds.), *Wired Cities: Shaping the Future of Communications*, 1987, Cassell Educational Ltd. London.

Dyson, Kennet; and Humphreys, Peter, B*roadcasting and New Media Policies in Western Europe*, 1988, Routledge, London and New York.

Ferguson, Marjorie, *New Communication Technologies and the Public Interest*, 1986, Sage Publications Inc., Beverly Hills.

Hollins, Timothy, *Beyond Broadcasting: Into the Cable Age*, 1984, BFI Publishing, London.

Hutchinson, Robert, *Cable, DBS and the Arts*, 1984, Policy Studies Institute, London.

Lewis, M. Peter, *Community Television and Cable in Britain*, 1978, British Film Institute, London.

McQuail, Dennis, and Siune, Karen, *New Media Politics: Comparative Perspectives in Western Europe*, 1986, Sage Communications, London.

McQuail, Dennis, 'Western European Media: The Mixed Model Under Threat' in: Downing, Mohammadi, and Sreberny-Mohammadi (eds.), *Questioning the Media*, 1995, Sage Publications.

McQuail, D; de Mateo, R; and Tapper, H., 'A Framework for Analysis of Media Change in Europe in the 1990s' in: Suine, K; and Truetzschler, W., *Dynamics of Media Politics*, 1993, Euromedia Research Group.

Muller, Jurgen, *Cable Policy in Europe, in Telecommunications Policy*, September 1987.

Negrine, M. Ralph (ed.), *Cable Television and the Future of Broadcasting*, 1985, Croom Helm, London.

Negrine, M. Ralph, and Papathanasspoulos, S., *The Internationalisation of Television*, 1990, Pinter, London.

Suine, K.; and McQuail, Dennis, 'Wake up, Europe!' in: Suine, K; and Truetzschler, W., *Dynamics of Media Politics*, 1993 by the Euromedia Research Group.

Audio News Service Via Telephone

A Service by Kuwait's News Agency (KUNA)

Mohammad Moawad

Abdulbasit Muhammed
Kuwait University

Purpose and Objective

This study investigates the current situation of Kuwait's News Agency (KUNA) personal audio News Service via Telephone two years after its inception in December 1994. The study aims to investigate how residents of Kuwait City, both Kuwaitis as well as expatriates, view a free 24 hours news service which provides a mixture of local, Arab and International events. The audio service broadcasts an average of 145 news items during normal times, and 170 news items during peak times such as when a crisis occurs and on special occasions.[1] The service receives more than 37,000 phone calls each day through its 52 available phone lines.[2]

Method and Type of Study

This current descriptive research study uses a random sample of 200 residents of Kuwait City aged 15 years and over. This sample represents a population of 192,800 residents of Kuwait City equalling 12 per cent of the total population of Kuwait according to the 1995 census.[3] All the sample interviews took place during November and December of 1995, in different areas of the capital, with both men and women, Kuwaitis and expatriates. The questionnaire used in this study was proof-read by scholars in psychology and mass communication at Kuwait University and contains 17 research questions regarding the capital's residents' views of the service. The questionnaire aims to collect data related to the following questions:

- To what degree were respondents interested in following news?
- What sources did respondents depend upon to fulfil their need for news?
- Is the audio news service among respondents' significant sources of news?
- How well is the audio news service known?
- What is the size and type of its users?
- How often do the service users call on a daily basis?
- During what part of the day do users usually call ?
- Why do respondents follow the audio news service ?
- To what extent did the service fulfil respondents' interests?

– What are respondents' opinions and suggestions to improve the service?

A second aim of this study is to content analyze the audio news service itself. Thus, newscasts were tape recorded at various times of the day during four continuous weeks starting from Sunday October 8 to Saturday November 4, 1995. A guide was then designed to analyze the service content using each individual news item as the basis for analysis. Time (second, minute) was also used to investigate differences among news items in terms of geographical location (local, international), subject, source, nature (expected, unexpected), persons involved, repetitiveness, type of language used (slang, standard).[4]

Research Results and Indications

The Current Situation of KONA's News Service
The service starts at 7 a.m. Kuwait's local time, and provides a summary of local, Gulf, Arabian, Islamic and International news. Like cable radio, users dial three numbers (120) over their telephones to receive a free news broadcast. The news service is changed or renewed approximately every three hours or less during peak hours, crisis, and special occasions. The news service average length is two minutes and 34 seconds, and the average number of news items presented is seven and the average time allowed for each news item 22 seconds. The service starts with a special tune and words of welcome to callers which last for not more than 8 seconds. The following is a description of news presented via the personal news service.

Opening News Items:
What is the type of a news item which is usually presented first in the personal news service? Is it local, international or the most important without regard to its geographical location? In examining the content of the first news item of the selected newscasts, it was clearly evident that local news items led most of the newscasts (10 periods) equalling 71.4 per cent, and international news items led fewer of the newscasts (4 periods) equalling 28.6 per cent.

Location of News Events Presented:
The number of local News events presented during the examined period reached 30 equalling 29.4 per cent. Moreover, 10 news items came from the Gulf area equalling 9.8 per cent, 26 news items related to other Arab states equalling 20.6 per cent, and international news items reached 41 equalling 40.2 per cent.

Content of Covered News:
Political news came first in size reaching 51.9 per cent (53 news items) of the personal service content. Military related events came second with 19.6 per cent (20 news items), followed by economic news 8.8 per cent (9 news items), culture 6.9 per cent (7 news items), social 4.9 per cent (5 News items), parliament related news 3.9 per cent (4 news items), and sports 2 per cent (2 news items). Scientific 1 per cent, crime 1 per cent and automobile accidents 1 per cent had one news item for each.

Nature of Events Presented (Sudden vs Expected):
Sudden or unexpected news items represent a great significance to the news-cast, and they are often described as 'Hot News' which raises their value in attracting the audience. Such news items totalled 31 equalling 30.4 per cent while expected news items were 71 equalling 69.6 per cent.

Persons Involved in the News
During the investigated period, a number of main characters were covered by the personal news service as the following:

	News items covered	Percentage %
1. The Amir (Head of State of Kuwait)	5	4.9%
2. Kings and Presidents of other states	18	17.6%
3. Kuwait's Crown Prince and Prime Minister	6	5.9%
4. Deputies of Presidents and Kings	6	5.9%
5. Head of Kuwait's National Assembly	2	1.9%
6. Kuwaiti Ministries	7	6.9%
7. Prime Ministers of other countries	8	7.8%
8. Ministers of other countries	12	11.8%
9. Kuwaities with high ranking positions	8	7.8%
10. Non-Kuwaitis with high ranking positions	3	2.9%
11. Kuwaities not holding high ranking positions	2	1.9%
12. Nominal figures in Kuwait (Ex. National Guards)	7	6.9%
13. International nominal figures (Ex. United Nations)	18	17.6%

Type of News Included (Pure vs Oriented and Hard vs Soft)
The number of pure (straight) news items reached 101 (99 per cent) while only one oriented (commentary) news item appeared during the studied period (1 per cent). In addition, the service included 98 news items (96.8 per cent) of hard (serious) news while only 4 news items (3.9 per cent) could be considered as soft news. Moreover, non of the news items included attempted to explain or analyze events covered.

Sources of the Personal News Service
The personal news service depended upon several news sources, as follows:

	News items	Percentage %
1. International News Agencies	23	22.55%
2. KONA's reporters and correspondents	18	17.65%
3. Other Media (Radio, Television and newspapers)	14	13.73%
4. Unverified sources	47	46.07%

Results indicate that the study shows a great number of unverified news sources (46.07 per cent) which may have a tremendous impact on the credibility of the audio news service.

Projected Influence of the Presented News (Positive vs Negative)
The audio service news items were also categorized according to their possible influence on listeners. For example, news about heavy artillery and fighting is projected to have a negative impact while news relating to completing or starting new public services is projected to have a positive effect. Results show that 63 news items (61.8 per cent) were positive news while 31 news items (30.4 per cent) were negative news. In addition, eight news items (7.8 per cent) were unclear and therefore difficult to classify.

Repetition
Repetition of News could also have a negative impact on listeners as they may feel bored or lose interest in the newscast. However, repeated news items during the analyzed period did not exceed three (2.9 per cent), with slight differences in the way in which they were presented each time.

Gender of Voices Presenting the Newscast
News announcers play a vital role in attracting the audience to the audio news service. With regard to gender, the service utilized female announcers (9 times equalling 64.3 per cent) more than male announcers (5 times equalling 35.7 per cent) during the selected studied period.

Residents of Kuwait City and The Personal News Service
In addition to describing the current situation of KUNA's news service, the following gives an explanation of how residents of Kuwait City view the audio news service.

What sources do residents of Kuwait City depend upon for news?
Results indicate that respondents depended upon several sources for news.
1. Local newspapers were the most selected source (89.5 per cent).
2. Kuwait Television (80.5 per cent).
3. Other Arab satellite television stations (70 per cent).
4. International television stations (52 per cent) such as CNN, CFI, and BBC.
5. Kuwait's local radio (45 per cent).
6. The audio news service (44.5 per cent).
7. The Arabian Gulf television station (27.5 per cent).
8. International radio stations (20.5 per cent).
9. Other Arab states' newspapers (19.5 per cent).
10. International newspapers (13 per cent).
11. Gulf radio stations (7 per cent)
12. Gulf newspapers (5 per cent).
13. Personal communication with relatives and friends (1.5 per cent)
14. International news agencies (1 per cent).
15. 'Internet' (5 per cent).

Do residents of Kuwait City know about the personal news service?
Over half of the study sample (55 per cent) indicated that they knew about the service and a little less than half (45 per cent) of the respondents reported not

knowing that KUNA's audio news service existed. In addition, most of those who knew about the service (80.9 per cent) indicated that they dial the phone to listen to its newscasts. Among the service listeners 12.7 per cent listen to it regularly and 68.2 per cent call the service sometimes. Moreover, about 19 per cent of those who knew about the service do not call or listen to the service newscast. When asked why 85.7 per cent indicated that they are satisfied with reading local newspapers, 90.5 per cent reported that they relied on watching television for news, and 46 per cent listened to news on radio.

What is the best time to call?
After dinner until midnight was the time most used by respondents to call the service (23.6 per cent). After sunset until dinner time was the second most report-ed time to call (22.4 per cent), followed by mid day (19.1 per cent), morning (15.7 per cent) and afternoon (10.1 per cent). In addition, several respondents (9.1 per cent) indicated that they call the service whenever they chose to do so without regard to a specific time.

Why do listeners listen to the service?
When asked about the reasons which motivated them to call the audio news service, most respondents (80.9 per cent) reported needing to know 'international news' and (79.8 per cent) 'local news'. Moreover, about 67.4 per cent dialled the service for news of other arab nations, 60.7 per cent for news of the gulf area, and 33.7 per cent for news in general.

Although previous research indicates audiences' preference for local news, one interesting result of this study is respondents' great interest in international news. A possible explanation could be related to the circumstances surrounding the Kuwaiti people after liberation. Relations between Iraq and the International community, including Kuwait, has not been normalized yet, and Iraq remains a regional threat after six years since a US led coalition forced the Iraqi forces out of Kuwait.

What do listeners suggest in order to improve the service?
Of the sample used, 38.2 per cent of respondents provided suggestions to improve the service. They are summarised in the following table.

1. A greater variety without extensive emphasis on political news	70.6%
2. Increase time allowed for the newscast	52.9%
3. Increase quantity of local news	61.8%
4. Continue to inform citizens and expatriates about the service	79.4%
5. Increase the service number of phone lines to match increase in users	26.5%
6. A greater effort in explaining and analysing the presented news	79.4%
7. Increase the percentage of Arab and Gulf States news	17.6%
8. A greater effort in presenting the news order according to its significance	52.9%
9. Authority figures announcements should be in their original voice	29.4%
10. Make use of KONA's correspondents reports	35.3%
11. Add new services such as sport and economic news	44.1%
12. Contain rumours through the audio news service	8.8%
13. Developing the service in the future into a sound and picture service	2.9%

Conclusion

Based on the description of KUNA's audio news service and the manner in which residents of Kuwait City view it, we can make the following recommendations:

1. In order to satisfy the audiences' different needs some effort should be made to present a greater variety of news without concentration only on political news. Results from the study show that political news overwhelms the newscast.

2. The quantity of news items (7) and their length of time (2 minutes and 34 seconds) needs to be increased. This is especially significant with regard to events occurring in Kuwait in order to inform audiences of what is happening around them. The service should also make an effort to relate local news to audiences' interests in different fields and matters of daily life.

3. The service should increase the quantity of news related to Kuwait's development plans and projects.

4. More use could be made of government officials' original sound announcements and correspondents' reports in order to increase interest in the service. In addition the service should use standard and simplified language and a variety of voices during the news presentation.

5. Start new services to serve public interests such as economy, sports or weather conditions.

6. Encourage research regarding public opinion feed back and evaluation of the audio service to strengthen positive elements and avoid negative aspects of the service in order better to fulfil audiences' needs and interests.

7. Continue to advertise in newspapers, on radio and television and in other media about the audio news service for more enlightenment among citizens as well as expatriates.

References

1. The following sources have been consulted:

   Information and Research Administration, KUNA, *News Agencies Guide*, Second Edition, Kuwait, Taleaa Publishing, 1989, p. 27.

   Alsomait, Yousef, Chairman of KUNA's Administration Council, Opening Statement of 'Kuwait News Agency Third Correspondents Conference', Sheraton Hotel, Kuwait, March 26, 1994.

   Ministry of Information, Kuwait, Twenty Seventh Yearly Book, Government Publishing, p. 700.

2. Alyagoot, Yousef, A Meeting with Dept. of Mass Communication Students, College of Arts, Kuwait University, November 1995.

3. Alameem, Mosaad, Assistant Deputy For Calculation Affairs, A published announcement in Kuwait's local newspapers, Dec 18, 1995, see p.4 in Al-Qabas Newspaper.

4. The following sources have been consulted:

   Abuzaed, Farooq, The Art of Reporting Journalistic News, second edition, Book World, Cairo, p.157-169.

   Shalabi, Karam, Broadcast News, Alsherooq Publishing and Distribution, Cairo, 1985, p.19-21.

Moawad, Mohammad, News in Mass Media, Arabian Thought House, Cairo, 1994, p.13-14.

Wahbi, Ibrahem, Radio News, Arabian Thought House, Cairo, p.96

Imam, Ibrahem, Radio and Television Media, second edition, Arabian Thought House, Cairo, p.46.

Alyagoot, Yousef, *op. cit.*

Dominick, R. Joseph, The Dynamics of Mass Communication, Fourth Edition, McGraw-Hill Inc., 1993, p.339.

Channel 6 and TexTV and the Introduction of the New TV RSLs

(Restricted Service Licences)

Dave Rushton

Institute of Local Television & Queen Margaret College

Introduction

This paper reports on the introduction of Channel 6 TexTV and the arrival of restricted service licences for television, or TV RSL's. It was first presented at Opening Channels, a conference organised by the Scottish Association of Small-scale Broadcasters, in Edinburgh on 6 December 96 and revised for presentation during the workshop at the April 97 University of Manchester Broadcasting Symposium.

But by the time of its presentation at the Symposium in Manchester, the Department of National Heritage had advised the Radiocommunications Agency to withhold the WT Act licence from Edinburgh's Channel 6 TexTV service because of possible VCR interference resulting from Channel 5's use of the channel 34 frequency. The potential impact upon VCRs was exaggerated by Channel 5 and the ITC, as Channel 6's local household survey in May 97 eventually confirmed.

With the Channel 6 service grounded for review by the DNH from 11 March, the ITC intervened to extend the scope of the guidelines for the new restricted service licence for television (the TV RSL) to incorporate the text and audio only services – which the ITC had hitherto decried.

Given the separation of the ITC from formal influence by the DNH and RA the government has since pleaded it has had no choice but to accept (subject to litigation) the revised ITC view that TexTV is licensable by the RSL. The revised view is not at all bad by any means (give or take the odd sacrificial lamb required to achieve it).

So the future of TexTV as a separate service has still to be resolved but it looks uncertain; with the ITC finding the means (and willingness) to regulate local terrestrial TV, its job has been done.

But the story takes another twist – and a twist which exposes to ridicule the original reason for withholding the licence for TexTV. For when digital television is switched on in Scotland in six months or so, up to one million homes will suffer VCR interference as a result of Channel 5's use of the channel 34 frequency for VCR retuning – compared to the 5,000 estimated for TexTV (which in turn would be overtaken by digital interference).

Clearly, the efforts to push TexTV outside legitimate transmission collapsed into Whitehall farce – as the Radiocommunications Agency described the recent twist.

The upshot is that for Edinburgh 400,000 viewers have been deprived of a long-awaited and much wanted local TV service because the remaining frequency available for a local RSL service will require viewers to purchase aerials to receive a decent signal. The difficulties for the local Channel 6 TexTV service can be imagined without a pen-portrait of a collapsed and haemorrhaging business plan.

Nonetheless, putting the little local difficulties to one side, the new RSL guidelines are immeasurably better than expected and were generally well received at the ITC's launch organised by the Community Radio Association in Sheffield on 7 June – they do now include most of the recommendations that have been made during the consultation and with text no longer being frowned upon as an inferior species should enable viable services to be introduced.

The major criticism that occupied minds in Sheffield was the ITC's unwillingness/incapacity to ensure that the larger media players did not acquire a controlling stake in any of the local and community services either to benefit themselves or simply to reduce the commercial impact of the new local broadcasting venture on their existing less than local services.

Delegates agreed that this prospect remained a fundamental weakness in the ITC proposals – a weakness which required urgent attention. Many community radio broadcasters present in Sheffield testified to the interruption and abandonment of their own local and community radio plans once small-scale applications were intercepted by the major players, sometimes openly and sometimes bearing false gifts of cooperation.

The ITC's guidelines for TV RSLs are available from: Information Office ITC, 33 Foley Street, London WIP 7LB.

Channel 6 TexTV and the TV RSLs

TextTV is a new terrestrial television phenomenon which has grown from attempts to develop small-scale television over a number of years in this country. In my case, I started to look at local TV in 1988 and organised a conference titled 'Edinburgh Television' at the first Edinburgh Science Festival in 1989. At this conference representatives from the Cable Authority (now a department within the Independent Television Commission), the Radiocommunications Agency and the Department of National Heritage – or Home Office as then was – came to Edinburgh to talk about the potential of microwave to deliver specifically local TV services. But microwave came and went as a technology favoured by the government and it didn't emerge for use in its own right. Cable investment in the UK had stalled and the majority of investment being encouraged into cable was North American, and these investors wanted – and were given – local cable (or local delivery) monopolies, absorbing microwave instead of facing it as a completing platform. Many of the cable companies took the opportunity offered in the 1990 Act to overlook the local channel opportunities and essentially elected to provide a delivery platform for satellite.

Meanwhile Channel 5 came along with some local potential and, with Philip Reevell from Mersey Television and Graham Moles from Southampton, we lobbied for a local Channel 5 service to take the form of a federation of local options across the country. But once again we found ourselves frustrated, on this occasion by the ITC and the Department of National Heritage, who continued to insist (without legal merit as they later admitted) that Channel 5 had to be an essentially national service.

Channel 5 was to be awarded as a single licence to a national broadcaster which left us in August 1995 looking at the possibility of running a local television service in Edinburgh without a frequency on which to broadcast. We convinced the Radiocommunications Agency that we should borrow Channel 5's local frequency – channel 48 – which was not being used while the bids were being sifted by the ITC. But, some fifteen minutes before broadcasting across north Edinburgh, the Department of National Heritage stepped in and refused to allow the Radiocommunications Agency to issue us with the W.T. Act licence. In our effort to broadcast legally we had uncovered a loophole in the 1990 Broadcasting Act that permits a mainly nonrepresentational television service to be transmitted without need of an ITC licence.

To get round the fact that our service as proposed was not nonrepresentational but an all-singing, all-dancing, festival-oriented full-scale video service, we proposed to push the programmes through a digital video effects machine to reduce the size of the image on screen to a postcard which would be surrounded with scrolling text. Our view – and that of legal opinion – was that we had a mainly nonrepresentational service which did not require an ITC licence.

The extent to which this proposed new service – TexTV as we dubbed it – was mainly nonrepresentational came to occupy the minds of lawyers in London and Edinburgh, and the proposal went backwards and forwards for about a week, or a week and a half, before the DNH finally decided to prevent us from broadcasting fifteen minutes before the transmission.

The proposal had become pretty wacky by the time that negative decision was made. We were going to broadcast nonrepresentational programming featuring a visual history of tartans with the TV screen flooded with tartan washes from twelve o'clock at night to eight o' clock in the morning.

We held a competition for the best finger paintings by three year old kids – again screening abstract nonrepresentational material to which the kids would provide voice overs to describe their finger paintings on air. Is that really Mummy? No (they would have to say), it is just a smudge of paint (silly billy).

Another programme featured wallpaper patterns favoured by Edinburgh householders. For these our film crew visited various homes around the city, council houses, Georgian houses, to video families talking about their favourite wallpapers. Nonrepresentational papers only – of course.

We had plans for sixteen hours of nonrepresentational television a day at one stage, and since this was Edinburgh at festival time, these were the slightly loony things we thought should be done with TV to push at the boundaries a bit.

It was a disappointment not to go on air in August 1995 and we spent a year arguing that we were legally right and the ITC, and Department of National Heritage, were fundamentally wrong in their interpretation of the legislation. That legal fight was won.

Today I can announce that we did get our Wireless Telegraphy Act licence and that six weeks ago we got our radio licence, and we are going to go on air, sometime early in 1997. We now have the paperwork to permit us to broadcast across the city of Edinburgh, and we will be broadcasting from what would be my living room if it wasn't probably the smallest television station in the UK. We will have three staff, possibly four if we are lucky, and we are going to broadcast a text service and initially take an audio feed from a radio station.

The transmitter is going to be sited on Corstorphine Hill in Edinburgh. Siting TV transmitters presents a problem that many of the new RSL's will face across the country. In Edinburgh, as in some other cities, the television signals come into the city from two different directions. One from Craigkelly, to the north of the city, and the other from Black Hill to the west of the city. So half of Edinburgh gets television coverage from the west and the other half from the north. In our proposal for Corstorphine we are splitting the difference between the two trying to provide a television service for all the city.

We expect to reach between one hundred and one hundred and forty thousand people when we turn on in March rising to about three hundred and twenty to three hundred and fifty thousand people when we have gone through the process of encouraging people to take a new aerial or put a set top aerial in place.

Basically what we are offering is an over the air television service free to the viewer providing them with a number of things they don't have at the moment.

I don't want to be too ambitious, this is a text-based nonrepresentational service after all, the screen will carry text and graphic information and a local teletext service running underneath, offering 800 pages of fast teletext plus roll-over pages, carrying local public service information, community information as well as commercials and advertising.

Viewers will be reminded of what is available on their teletext pages by menus and advertisements on the TV screen of what we've called Channel 6. By comparison, teletext normally appears like a hidden newspaper without a front page. With Channel 6 we will provide that front cover, revealing what is inside the newspaper. The front screen will continually headline the information that is available on text.

The audio service may be produced in conjunction with Radio Forth. The synergy is that an audio advertisement on radio or on audio on Channel 6, say for Joe Boggins' cars, can finish 'and see page 750 of Channel 6 TexTV for details of our current range.' Another service will provide theatre and event booking information, ticket sales in the festival period, science festival, arts festival, jazz festival, up to date information on seats right up to the very minute of the performance. Over time we will install remote terminals which will permit festival organisers to key in the ticket information to their own TexTV magazine pages.

We propose that our service will largely be run by those who want to be information providers, in terms of the city for example council pages, minutes of meetings, dates of meetings, closures of swimming baths for repair, all of this information that has restricted circulation now can be available on the local television set. So long as the viewer has a teletext television, they will be able to receive it.

So Channel 6 TexTV is basically an information service. But in conjunction with the RSL amendments in the Broadcasting Act (guidelines introduced June '97) there is a possible marriage of convenience between the two services.

An RSL in a particular city, it could be Bradford, it could be anywhere a suitable frequency can be found, might not be able to run for fifty-six days let alone two years. What they might do is put a full television service out at peak time for an hour or two while another group might wish to provide a service for an hour at three o' clock in the afternoon.

Should these two organisations receive a two year RSL licence, they can then fall back on the text service in between the individual programmes. Alan Stewart (presenting the ITC's consultation on the RSL's) suggests there should be a gap in between each RSL, but with a TexTV service the audience can be retained, fixed on the TV dial with their local information, which periodically can open up and blossom into full scale local TV, before winding down again for another few months until somebody else decides to do an RSL. The value of TexTV is that it can retain the audience and effectively maintain the infrastructure, the transmitters and the links with the audience.

The reason for adopting the text approach while RSLs are in their infancy is that we believe that for RSLs to be successful they will need to have the infrastructure we suggest: in fact, RSLs will need support.

Fifty Years of Prime-Time Network Television Programming

Spinoffs + Ripoffs + Recombinants = Creative Exhaustion?

Garry Wade

School of Journalism and Mass Communication, Drake University, Iowa, USA

Originality is imitation that has not yet been detected
(author unidentified)

The distinct dichotomy set up by this paper's title and its opening quote sets out the problem inherent in any evaluation of the fifty-plus year history of American television which has presented great moments of popular culture but which critics have also assailed for being overrated and uncreative. **Problem:** This paper attempts to measure the overall creative aspect of television programming over its fifty-plus year history. Hand-in-hand with creativity goes a measurement of *success* in creating programmes. After all, the American world of entertainment broadcasting is built around a commercial model – programming has to sustain itself.

Throughout the history of American broadcast programming, there have been two very obvious, practical measures of success. First, if a show survives its initial season and is renewed into a second year, it has generally been classified as a success. However, broadcast executives prefer a second measurement – generally, if a programme makes it through three seasons, it has created enough programme stock to be a success in syndication. Selling programmes off to local stations to fill access slots (after successful network runs) is where the real money is made in broadcasting. The level marking real success in broadcast programming is a run of three seasons. Therefore, this research will evaluate programming at the two levels of success.

In its measurement of success, this paper will utilize a combination of the two definitions of *creative* in the dictionary. The first relates to being successful in *production* and the second has to do with being *original/imaginative*. This study will consider a key network strategy which is *imitation* and work backwards on this measure, exploring the effectiveness of programme *copies* (called *Spinoffs*, *Ripoffs* and *Recombinants*) versus the original programmes.

This study will further examine whether a prolific number of copies of three specific programme formats (Standup comics in sitcoms; the 'Buddies' genre built around *Friends*; and the Supernatural copies of *The X-Files*) stretches beyond acceptable limits and is a sign of programming executives reaching 'creative exhaustion'.

Definitions: The study defines *Spinoff* as a television programme that directly spins off a character or major theme element from one show into a new show in hopes that it will prove as successful as the first. A *Ripoff* is defined as copying a major theme or composite character of a given show directly into a new show, again in hopes of capitalizing on the success of the original. Finally, this study coins the term *Recombinant* as a unique combination of elements (plot/theme/character) drawn from a single show or genre of shows in hopes that it will also take advantage of the initial success. All of the given definitions have in common the element of taking someone else's work and using it in a manner that is not entirely unique or innovative – the antithesis of being creative.

Methodology
The researcher has chronicled 52 years (1944-1996) of nearly every, single 'new' programme offered by the various commercial television networks throughout the time period studied (ABC, CBS, NBC, DuMont, Fox).

From the Start
This study should point out that from the very beginning of television programming, industry members quietly adopted the art of the Ripoff. From the very first broadcast programme, copying has been an accepted strategy. This practice was commonly referred to as 'formula' programming. The minute one network hit on a successful programme combination, the others soon followed. In fact the first longest-lasting network programme *Gillette Cavalcade of Sports* made its debut in 1944 and was a highly-successful boxing show that lasted 16 years on NBC. In 1945, CBS followed with *AAU Boxing*. In 1946, DuMont aired *Boxing from the Jamaica Arena* and CBS added *Sports from Madison Square Garden*. The very first copycat frenzy culminated in 1949 with DuMont's popular *Roller Derby*, a violent, 'cheesecake' athletic contest on roller skates. All these shows enjoyed highly successful network runs. From the very first day of network television, imitation was an accepted strategy.

Most of the television shows established during the industry's infancy were borrowed straight from network radio programming. In the very early years before complete network lineups were established, a number of television programmes were simulcast on local, network-affiliated radio stations. From its infancy, the television world accepted and encouraged copying. Why? Simply because in the early days, radio paid the bills. Television was still an experiment and television network executives chose to take the easy way out. That has been a consistent problem for creativity – network television executives have always taken the easy way out and, rather than encourage and reward original and innovative programming, it has been easier to schedule 'formula' programming.

Results
Table One displays the data collected from the research to help analyze the first research question: *Are copycat shows successful?*

In summary, of the 52 years of television programming,12 per cent of all new shows were deemed successful and 25 per cent were considered highly successful. In combination, the final success rate for all shows was 37 per cent.

Shows defined as original rated very near the overall success rate with an equal 12 per cent successful and 24 per cent highly successful. In combination, the final success rate for original shows was 36 per cent, just below the all shows average. Shows defined as Ripoffs, Spinoffs or Recombinants rated higher than both all shows and original shows in all three categories. Copies resulted in 15 per cent being successful; 29 per cent highly successful and a final combination rating of 44 per cent.

In addition this study examined four further, visually-similar forms of copies – movie, comic book and comic strip copies and British imports.

Movie copies rated average in success (12 per cent), but were lower in the highly successful category (17 per cent) and thus lower in the overall combined success score (29 per cent). *Lassie* has been history's most successful television movie copy with 20 years of airtime. *Alice* (*Alice Doesn't Live Here Anymore*) is second with eight years of success. *The Dukes of Hazzard* (a copy of *Smokey & the Bandit*) is third with a longevity of six years. (See Table Two for a listing of movie copies.)

There have been five newspaper comic strip copies on television – *Dick Tracy*, *Superman*, *Dennis the Menace*, *Hazel* and *The Flash*. Three of the five shows were highly successful (60 per cent). *Superman* lasted the longest – six seasons, *Hazel* ran for five years on network television and *Dennis the Menace* survived four years.

Comic books had insignificant numbers for comparison. *Wonder Woman* and *The Incredible Hulk* lasted three years and thus just met the 100 per cent highly successful rating criteria.

British imports rated 7 per cent on the success scale and 53 per cent on the highly successful rating for a combined overall success rate of 60 per cent. *Masterpiece Theatre's* 25 years of drama anthologies tops the British import list. *All in the Family* (a Spinoff from BBC's *Till Death Do Us Part*) ranks second with 12 years of airtime on American television. *Monty Python's Flying Circus, Sanford & Son* (Spinoff of *Steptoe & Son*) and *The Saint* are successful British copies on American television – each survived five years on the network schedule.

Analysis

What do these figures tell us? Quite simply, the overall numbers show that just over one-third of all television shows produced in the last 52 years were successful (at any level). That means that two out of three of the industry's efforts end in failure. What other industry accepts such dismal failure rates? Original shows (given the higher desirability standard at the outset of this paper) fall just below the success rating of all shows – just over one-third successful. Surprisingly, the less desirable alternatives (Ripoffs, Spinoffs and Recombinants) outscore both all shows and original programmes and at a significantly higher level in the combined success rating. Clearly, the programmes are being copied for a reason – they are more likely to succeed. Apparently, programme executives have learned that audiences accept familiar television programmes. The statistics do not lend a great deal of support or hope for creativity in the future of television programming.

Problem
Tables Three to Five lay out the data to answer the second research question – *Does the proliferation of three specific genre copies in recent years indicate that the industry has reached the point of creative exhaustion?*

All three analyses exhibit highly significant differences in the number of copies produced within a short timespan. Table Three deals with the historical development of the 'Buddies' genre. There have been sixteen copies or Recombinants of the very popular sitcom, *Friends*, since it began in 1994. The copies range from a plot line where young friends simply hang out (in San Francisco or New York or a New England harbour town) to a group of friends running the New York City Mayor's office, to the unbelievable juvenile, young, single guys in *Men Behaving Badly*. Table Four indicates that there have also been a significantly higher number of copies of shows starring stand-up comedians in their own sitcoms in recent years. While providing comedians with their own sitcoms has been a long-standing television tradition (since *Burns & Allen* in 1950), nearly half of the total have been developed since Home Improvement with Tim Allen hit the airwaves in 1991. Table Five indicates that the numbers of copies of *The X-Files* are also significantly higher with a record ten copies recorded in the genre in a single season (1996). The progressive development of the supernatural genre also provides the backdrop for a section on creativity.

Analysis
Again, the higher numbers of copies of the three formats in the last few years indicate a trend to even more imitation in a television world already overrun by copies. Does this threaten the industry with 'creative exhaustion'?

In addition to formula programming, this study discovered a second, more unsettling pattern of programming over the historical development of network television which is related directly to problem two. It is tied to the efforts to be creative in television programme origination.

```
  •    •    •

  •    •    •

  •    •    •
```

Be creative: With a pencil, use four straight lines and connect all nine dots without picking up the pencil or retracing lines.

This simple, yet critical exercise serves as the introduction to a *Brainstorming Unit* which the researcher teaches to senior-level broadcast management class. It serves as an attention-getting introduction to a critical endeavour. The first half of the unit concentrates solely on mind-releasing exercises. The second half blends in problem-solving and students are given a common broadcast station problem to solve using the techniques presented.

The key to the exercise above is getting students to 'go outside the lines' to solve the puzzle. It frees up the mind because it escapes the traditional 'boxes' that formal education and life construct for us. 'Boxes' impede creativity.

Unfortunately, the research indicates that too many programming executives and decision-makers have encountered such an exercise somewhere in their education or training. The second 'pattern' of programming detected in the historical analysis shows that in copying programmes, producers are, in addition, compelled to come up with an 'angle' that is a 'little bit different'. Just as most media marketers are seeking their own niche in today's world, production executives are looking for an 'angle'. Research presented in this paper suggests that the 'angle' has been bent around the corner and back with too many lines retraced too many times!

The historical analysis shows that the Supernatural genre began in 1953 with *Topper*, a staid banker occupying a house with a ghost. *The Ghost & Mrs. Muir* added a new 'angle' – a New England house with a sea-faring captain for a ghost. *Jennifer Slept Here* included a family with a ghost.

The Lloyd Bridges Show (1959) began the strange circumstances genre when a writer began turning up in his own stories. In 1996 two copies of this idea emerged with *Strange Luck* (a photographer who miraculously always shows up at news hot spots just in time) and *Early Edition* (a man who gets the newspaper a day early and does his best to change and rearrange the future positively) – again, simple updated versions of older shows.

The real fun and creativity began with the introduction of extra-terrestrial beings in *My Favorite Martian* (1963). The Recombinants from this programme bordered on the outrageous. The show began with a Martian crash-landing on earth and portrayed the comic situations which resulted from this. Soon, television produced shows about a family lost in space (*Lost in Space*), and astronauts and scientists lost in space and travelling back in time (*It's About Time* and *Time Tunnel*). *The Voyagers* featured a not-too-bright fellow assisted by an orphan travelling back in time to correct history. Today, *Sliders* features travel between dimensions rather than in time. *Starman* was a space traveller who returned to earth to locate the earthling son he had fathered. Beginning to stretch the limits of the genre, *Land of the Giants* featured an aircraft crash in a land overrun by giants. That was topped by *Planet of the Apes* (another airplane crash in a futuristic world run by apes). The theme grew wilder with *Mork & Mindy* where a wise-cracking alien crashlands in Boulder, Colorado. From there it moved into silliness with the cult-popular *V* where lizard-like aliens invaded the earth. Today, *Dark Skies* features college graduates battling aliens trying to change history. Who can forget *Alf* – the furry, cat-eating, wise-cracking animal alien visiting earth? Perhaps the genre reached its outer limits of creativity with the raucous *Third Rock From the Sun*, another sitcom with truly nutty aliens stopping on earth in 1996.

Bewitched (1964) presented a winsome witch married to a mortal. Her daughter *Tabitha* provided a natural Spinoff while *Tucker's Witch* combined a detective with a crime-fighting witch. Today, *Sabrina, the Teenage Witch* entertains teen audiences.

Recombinants of these shows stretch the imagination a little further includ-ing – *My Living Doll*, a psychologist who lived with a female robot, *I Dream of Jeannie*, featuring an Air Force Officer with a female genie and *Nanny and the Professor* focused on a nanny with mysterious powers.

Another series of imaginative Recombinants began with the *Six Million Dollar Man* where an injured astronaut was rebuilt as a part robot. The Spinoff fea-tured *The Bionic Woman*, who was also a rebuilt operative and *The Girl With Something Extra* had ESP to help her. *The Invisible Man* was an invisible scien-tist; *Gemini Man* was a think tank expert who could become invisible for up to 15 minutes at a time; *M.A.N.T.I.S.* was the first black superhero, who developed an exo-skeleton that provided him with super strength; the *Man from Atlantis* had underwater superhero skills; *The Flash* was a police scientist hit by light-ning and given super speed and strength as a result; and *The Incredible Hulk* featured a scientist who turned green and grew immensely large when angered by evil. *Something is Out There* included a mind-reading alien assisting the police and *Alien Nation* presented another polite, but rather stiff and dense alien coop-erating with a big city police department. Today, *The Profiler* presents a psychic woman profiling serial killers. *The Manimal* moved further from reality with a detective who could turn himself into whatever animal he desired to fight the 'bad guys'. *The Pretenders* featured a human chameleon; *Nightstalker* investigat-ed murders by aliens, monsters and werewolves; *Werewolf* was a search for were-wolves set in the 1600s.

Then there are the angels: in *Out of the Blue* (1979) a probationary angel helped five orphans; in *Highway to Heaven* an angel helps earthlings to over-come trouble, in *Second Chance* an angel who has failed on his first chance to get to heaven keeps on trying. The latest version of the genre is *Touched By An Angel* where a new team of angels help earthlings overcome problems.

In *Mr. Merlin*, King Arthur's magician emerged from the Middle Ages and resurfaced in 1981 in an auto mechanic's garage in San Francisco and in 1987 there was an updated version of *The Beauty & the Beast* staged in modern New York City.

In 1964 *The Addams Family* and *The Munsters* made their debut. These shows featured bizarre, ghoulish families of motley misfits and one of the familes includ-ed a 'normal' girl!

We must include the traditional superheroes – *Superman* and his spinoff (*Lois & Clark*), *Flash Gordon*, *The Green Hornet* and 'campy' *Batman* with its childish video tricks).

Prominent science-fiction vessels have also played a creative role in the super-natural genre. In *Voyage to the Bottom of the Sea* shipmates on a submarine battled monsters and aliens. This theme was recently copied by *Seaquest DSV*, in which a futuristic submarine battleship fought off monsters with the aid of a talking dol-phin. In futuristic space (*Star Trek*; *Star Trek: The Next Generation*; *Star Trek: Deep Space Nine*; and *Battlestar Gallactica*) the travellers have remained fairly 'normal'.

The most popular science fiction programmes have been the many copies of *The Twilight Zone* (1959). These have included *Night Gallery*, *One Step Beyond* (and its *Spinoff*, *Next Step Beyond*), *The Outer Limits*, *Journey to the Unknown*, *Ghost Story*, *Darkroom* and *X-Files*. Most of these had reasonable imaginative plots and made good television. Perhaps the most symbolic of all was *The Greatest American Hero*, a tongue-in-cheek look at the average guy who found a 'super-hero suit' and had fun with it.

Comment

Statistical analysis shows that the programming segment of the television industry over its 52-year history has not been highly successful – less than one-third of the offerings lasted more than a single season. Historical analysis shows that TV industry executives have consistently taken the easy route at critical junctures and initially copied radio show formats and, from then on, successful ideas. Copies have proven to be more successful than originals on average but have stretched the imagination to the breaking point in certain genres. This paper has analyzed the creative stretching of the supernatural genre but analyses of the crime and western genres show even more bizarre examples.

Do the results mean that the television industry is overly concerned with imitation and not interested in encouraging imagination and innovation in programming? Probably! The industry does not appear to be interested in totally new, creative and imaginative ideas. All producers hope to discover the one truly creative (and successful) new 'formula', however, they are mostly content to stick with proven winners and copy their competitors' successes (with slightly different 'angles'). On balance, they hope to make money and stay in business.

A major part of the problem is the system. There is an inordinate amount of pressure on producers to fill prime-time schedules, especially in comparison to the demand on writers of movies, books and plays. Somewhere between 2,400 and 3,000 hours of television programming are needed annually for the networks.

Secondly, the American audience is so diverse, it is nearly impossible to guess the next successful programme idea. More and more, advertisers (the bottom-line sponsors of television programmes) demand to know exactly who they are reaching. They want guaranteed success. Niche marketing is critical to advertisers. The narrower the focus on a specific group the less likely it is for a programme to attract a large mass audience. The two viewpoints are incompatible in today's intense, media-saturated, technologically-advancing market. Fifteen years ago in the introduction to their book, *Watching TV*, Harry Castleman and Walter J. Podrazik (p. vi) set out the dilemma very effectively:

> American television must be viewed as the embodiment of contradiction – a miracle of spectacular technological achievement imprisoned by the demands of its mundane day-to-day operation. So-called 'high class' programming almost always competes with mass appeal presentation because, with 365 days a year to fill, programmes cannot possibly stock each moment with uplifting culture.

Suggestions

What might industry executives do to end the emphasis on copying and control the imagination within acceptable bounds while still encouraging creative and successful television programming?

First of all, although American television is about making money, industry experts have to learn to operate and be imaginative and innovative within that context. They have to learn from the marketing industry how to market highly creative shows that appeal to smaller audiences with highly saleable demographics.

Second, for too long industry executives have overextended and overworked production houses and producers with enviable track records. The workloads and rewards should be spread out among more people. The industry has built an insulating wall around itself; agents and other mid-level executives frustrate the efforts of young writers who lack industry connections. Yet one of them might prove to be the young phenomenon, given the opportunity. Executives have to provide opportunities for young unknowns at the grassroots level through, for example, workshops in creative writing. They should create workshops and reward the development of new formats and new ideas. They should lecture on college campuses and interact with bright, young writers and producers to re-energize the industry with fresh faces and ideas. The strategy may not be successful right away but two thirds of the highly-developed, professional programming ideas have not worked for 52 years either. Find out what's new and creative with the next generation of writers. Use it! Use them!

Table 1: Overall Television Programming Success Rates – General Programming, 1944-1996

Programme Type	Successful (%)		Highly Successful (%)		Combined (%)	
All Shows (1,421)	174	12%	359	25%	533	37%
Original Shows (999)	112	12%	238	24%	350	35%
Copies (424)	62	15%	121	29%	183	44%
Movies (90)	11	12%	15	17%	26	29%
Comic Strips (5)	0	0%	3	60%	3	60%
Comic books (2)	0	0%	2	100%	2	100%
British imports (15)	1	7%	8	53%	9	60%

Table 2: Movie Spinoffs

Year	TV Show	Original Movie
1949	The Front Page	The Front Page
1954	Lassie	Lassie
1954	Rin Tin Tin	Rin Tin Tin
1954	Mickey Hooney	Babes in Toyland
1955	It's Always Jan	How to Marry a Millionaire
1955	Robin Hood	Robin Hood
1956	Sir Lancelot	Sir Lancelot
1957	Zorro	Zorro
1959	Wichita Town	Wichita
1960	National Velvet	National Velvet
	My Sister Eileen	My Sister Eileen
1961	Bus Stop	Bus Stop

	Dr. Kildare	Dr. Kildare
	Father of the Bride	Father of the Bride
1962	Mr. Smith Goes to Washington	Mr. Smith Goes to Washington
	Going My Way	Going My Way
1963	Greatest Show on Earth	Greatest Show on Earth
	The Farmer's Daughter	The Farmer's Daughter
1964	Voyage to the Bottom of the Sea	Voyage to the Bottom of the Sea
	No Time for Sargeants	No Time for Sargeants
	The Man From U.N.C.L.E.	The Man From U.N.C.L.E.
	Peyton Place	Peyton Place
	Twelve O'Clock High	Twelve O'Clock High
1965	Legend of Jesse James	Jesse James
	Gidget	Gidget
	Please Don't Eat the Dasies	Please Don't Eat the Daisies
	Tammy	Tammy
	Mr. Roberts	Mr. Roberts
1966	The Monkees	The Beatles Films
	Tarzan	Tarzan
	Shane	Shane
1967	Garrison's Guerillas	The Dirty Dozen
	Hondo	Hondo
1968	Here Come the Brides	Seven Brides for Seven Brothers
	The Ghost & Mrs. Muir	The Ghost & Mrs. Muir
1969	Mr. Deeds Goes to Town	Mr. Deeds
1970	Barefoot in the Park	Barefoot in the Park
	The Interns	The Interns
1972	Anna & The King of Siam	Anna & The King of Siam
	M*A*S*H	M*A*S*H
1973	Adam's Rib	Adam's Rib
	Bob & Carol & Ted & Alice	Bob & Carol & Ted & Alice
	Shaft	Shaft
1974	Born Free	Born Free
	Planet of the Apes	Planet of the Apes
	Paper Moon	Paper Moon
	Sons & Daughters	American Grafitti
1975	Swiss Family Robinson	Swiss Family Robinson
1976	Alice	Alice Doesn't Live Here Anymore
	Serpico	Serpico
1977	Logan's Run	Logan's Run
	(Star Wars, Close Encounters)	
1978	W.E.B.	Network
	Battlestar Gallactica	Star Wars
1979	Buck Rogers in the 25th Century	Buck Rogers
	The Bad News Bears	The Bad News Bears
	Brothers and Sisters	Animal House

	Dukes of Hazard	Smokey and the Bandit
1980	Bosom Buddies	Some Like It Hot
	Harper Valley, P.T.A.	Harper Valley, P.T.A.
	Breaking Away	Breaking Away
	Freebie & The Bean	Freebie & The Bean
1981	Private Benjamin	Private Benjamin
	Flamingo Road	Flamingo Road
	Walking Tall	Walking Tall
1982	9 to 5	9 to 5
	Bring 'em Back Alive	Raiders of the Lost Ark
	Tales of the Gold Monkey	Raiders of the Lost Ark
	The Quest	Raiders of the Lost Ark
	Seven Brides for Seven Brothers	Seven Brides for Seven Brothers (musical)
	Fame	Fame
1983	For Love and Honor	Officer and a Gentleman
	Webster	Woman of the Year
1985	Stir Crazy	Stir Crazy
1986	Starman	Starman
1987	Beauty & The Beast	Beauty & The Beast
1988	Dirty Dancing	Dirty Dancing
	Baby Boom	Baby Boom
1989	Alien Nation	Alien Nation
1990	Ferris Bueller	Ferris Bueller
	Parenthood	Parenthood
	Uncle Buck	Uncle Buck
1991	Teech	Dead Poet's Society
1992	Young Indiana Jones	Indiana Jones Series
1993	Lois and Clark	Superman
1994	Hardball	The Major Leagues
1995	The Client	The Client
1996	Clueless	Clueless
	Dangerous Minds	Dangerous Minds
	J.A.G.	Top Gun

Table 3: 'Friends' Recombinants, Copies & Spinoffs

Year	Show Success	Description
1951	Young Mr. Bobbin (1)	young singles sitcom with 2 spinster aunts
	Actors Hotel (1)	boardinghouse sitcom
1952	My Hero (1)	single guy & 'friends' in real estate sales sitcom
	Meet Millie (4)	single New York secretary and 'friends'
	Mr. Peepers (3)	high school science teacher and 'friends'
1953	Private Secretary (4)	private secretary with 'friends' sitcom
1954	Dear Phoebe (1)	professor turns romance writer with 'friends'
	Willy (1)	young, single female New Hampshire lawyer

	It's a Great Life (2)	two G.I. bachelors to a California apartment
	It's Always Jan (1)	How to Marry a Millionaire—single girl sitcom
1956	The Brothers (1)	bachelor brother photographers in San Francisco
	Oh, Susanna (3)	young single woman as a cruise ship director
	Hey, Jeannie (1)	young Scottish emigree as a doughnut shop waitress
1958	The Ann Sothern Show (3)	young hotel secretary—copy of Private Secretary
1959	Dobie Gillis (4)	girl crazy teen sitcom....into junior college
1960	Bringing Up Buddy (1)	bachelor with two spinster aunts—spin Mr. Bobbin
1962	It's a Man's World (1)	3 male college students & 'friends' on houseboat
1964	Many Happy Returns (1)	young singles work in an L.A. department store
	90 Bristol Court (1)/ Tom, Dick & Mary	1 of 3 alternating sitcoms—young singles in apt.
	Valentine's Day (1)	swinging New York publishing executive
1965	Tammy (1)	young girl secretary on a southern plantation
1966	Hey, Landlord (1)	two bachelors own an apartment building
	That Girl (5)	aspiring young actress and 'friends'
1968	The Good Guys (2)	childhood single friends buy a diner
1970	Mary Tyler Moore (7)	young, associate TV new producer & 'friends'
1971	Funny Face (1)	young student teacher also does 'commercials'
	Getting Together (1)	young, single male singers
1972	Sandy Duncan (1)	student, secretary also does 'commercials'
1973	Diana (1)	young Londonite moves to New York in fashion
	Calucci's Department (1)	singles sitcom with unemployed goof-offs
	Needles & Pins (1)	young, singles sitcom in New York garment district
1974	Friends and Lovers (1)	young, single violinist/friends in Boston symphony
1977	On Our Own (1)	two single, female ad. exectives in Manhattan apt.
	The San Pedro Beach Bums (1)	five single guys live on a houseboat
	Three's Company (7)	young male shares apt with two females—all single
1978	Mork & Mindy (4)	odd, young singles & 'friends' sitcom with alien
1979	The Last Resort (1)	college kids work at a summer resort
	Working Stiffs (1)	brothers as janitors in a Chicago building & 'friends'
1981	Making a Living (1)	waitresses at a plush Los Angeles restaurant
1982	9 to 5 (3)	working single women
	Cheers (9)	sitcom with 'friends' in a Boston bar
1983	We Got It Made (1)	bachelors with a maid & jealous girlfriends
1984	Three's a Crowd (1)	young single moves in with his girlfriend—spin
1987	Hooperman (2)	offbeat single San Francisco cop & 'friends'
1988	Dear John (3)	singles group sitcom
1989	Baywatch (8+)	young, singles with bare bodies at the beach
1990	Going Places (1)	four young, single TV staffers share a house
1991	Princesses (1)	three young, single females share an apartment
1992	Hearts Afire (2)	sitcom of young, single Senator's staffers
	Hangin' with Mr. Cooper (4)	substitute teacher with female roomies
	Going to Extremes (1)	young, single medical students on an island
	Melrose Place (4+)	young, singles & 'friends' in an apartment complex

1993	Living Single (3+)	four black career women in an apartment
1994	Friends (2+)	New York 'friends'
	Models, Inc. (1)	sophisticated, young single L.A. models &'friends'
1995	Too Something (1)	a 'buddy' sitcom
	Misery Loves Company (1)	four young single guys hang out
	Can't Hurry Love (1)	single, New York girl & 'friends'
	If Not for You (1)	couple dump dates & find each other with 'friends'
	Partners (2+)	young, single San Francisco architects
	The Drew Carey Show (2+)	young personnel director & 'friends'
	Naked Truth (2+)	divorced tabloid photographer & 'friends'
	Single Guy (2+)	single guy with four pals
	Caroline in the City (2+)	young, female cartoonist with friends in the city
1996	Men Behaving Badly	stupid, young singles
	Suddenly Susan	innept, young female executive
	Spin City	friends run New York City Mayor's office
	Townies	young, single friends in New England harbour town
	Party Girl	young singles coming of age in New York
	Lush Life	struggling, young artist and friends

Table 4: Stand-Up Comics Recombinants, Copies & Spinoffs

Year	Show	Spinoff of	Og Yrs	Og Rtgs Spin Yrs Spin Rtgs
1950	Burns & Allen	(8)	George Burns & Gracie Allen
1951	I Love Lucy	(6)	Lucille Ball
1952	The Jackie Gleason Show	(15)	Jackie Gleason
	Mr. Peepers	(3)	Wally Cox
1953	Make Room for Daddy	(11)	Danny Thomas
1954	The Mickey Rooney Show	(1)	Mickey Rooney
1955	Sgt. Bilko	(4)	Phil Silvers
1956	Stanley	(1)	Buddy Hackett
1958	The GeorgeBurns Show	(1)	George Burns
	The Ed Wynn Show	(1)	Ed Wynn
1959	Fibber McGee & Molly	(1)	Bob Sweeney and Cathy Lewis
1961	The Dick Van Dyke Show	(5)	Dick Van Dyke
	The Joey Bishop Show	(3)	Joey Bishop—spinoff (Make Room for Daddy)
1963	The New Phil Silvers Show	(1)	Phil Silvers—recombinant
1964	Mickey	(1)	Mickey Rooney
1969	The Bill Cosby Show	(2)	Bill Cosby
1970	Make Room for Grandaddy	(11)	Danny Thomas—updated copy
1972	Sanford & Son	(5)	Red Foxx
	Paul Lynde Show	(1)	Paul Lynde
	The Bob Newhart Show	(6)	Bob Newhart—Chicago psychologist
1974	Chico & The Man	(4)	Freddie Prinze—white garage owner & Mexican-American helper
1976?	The Tony Randall Show	(2)	Tony Randall—widowed superior court judge

1977	Sanford Arms	(1)	attempt to rescue Sanford & Sons
1980	Bosom Buddies	(2)	Tom Hanks and Peter Scolari—men in drag
	The Tim Conway Show	(1)	Tim Conway—charter airline owners
1982	Newhart	(8)	Bob Newhart—recombinant—New England writer & country lodge owner
1988	Roseanne	(8+)	Roseanne Barr (Arnold)—average American sitcom
	The Van Dyke Show	(1)	Dick Van Dyke—recombinant-small regional theatre
1989	Chicken Soup	(1)	Jackie Mason—eastern urban ethnic love sitcom
1990	Lenny	(1)	Lenny Clark—blue collar Irish Catholic sitcom
1991	Home Improvement	(5+)	Tim Allen—TV handyman show
1992	Hangin' with Mr. Cooper	(4)	Mark Curry—substitute teacher
	Mad About You	(4+)	Paul Reiser—young Manhatten couple
	Martin	(4+)	Martin Lawrence—radio talk show host
1993	Daddy Dearest	(1)	2 comics: Don Rickles and Richard Lewis – single guy whose father moves in
	Dave's World?	(3+)	Harry Anderson—magician/entertainer
	Thea	(1)	Thea Vidale—mother of 4
	Grace Under Fire	(3+)	Brett Butler—single mom of 3; works in oil factory
	Sinbad	(1)	Sinbad—computer graphics owner with foster kids
	Mommies	(1)	2 housewive comics—Marilyn Kentz & Caryl Kristensen
1994	MartinShort	(1)	Martin Short—a TV sitcom star
	All-American Girl	(1)	Margaret Cho—westernized Korean-American battles parents
1995	The Drew Carey Show	(2+)	Drew Carey—department store director & friends
	Bless This House	(1)	Andrew Dice Clay in a Honeymooners copy
1996	Mr. Rhodes		
	Life's Work		
	Common Law		Greg Giraldo—Hispanic Harvard-educated attorney
	Everybody Loves Raymond		Ray Romano—sportswriter & father
	Bill Cosby	(1+)	Bill Cosby—downsized professional

Table 5: Supernatural Recombinants, Copies & Spinoffs

Year	Show Success	Status	Description
1951	Superman (6)	1st	alien youth sent to earth by parents to avoid destruction; becomes superhero
1953	Flash Gordon (1)	copy	superhero
	Topper (2)	1st	staid banker buys haunted house
1959	Men Into Space (1)	1st	1st post-Sputnik space show – straightforward

	Twilight Zone (5)	1st	1st popular sci-fi anthology
1960	One Step Beyond (2)	recombinant	occult & supernatural anthology
1962	The Lloyd Bridges Show (1)	recombinant	writer actually ends up in his stories
1963	The Outer Limits (2)	recombinant	extra-terrestrials
	My Favorite Martian (3)	1st	first alien crashes and lives on earth
1964	Bewitched (8)		winsome witch married to a mere mortal
	My Living Doll (1)	recombinant	psychologist and live-in female robot
	Voyage to the Bottom of the Sea (1)	recombinant	battling aliens, monsters from a submarine
	The Addams Family (2)	1st	sitcom based on a motley, bizarre 'nuclear' family
	The Munsters (2)	1st	sitcom of a motley family of misfits—one normal girl
1965	Lost in Space (3)	recombinant	family lost in space
	I Dream of Jeannie (5)	recombinant	astronaut and life with a genie
1966	Star Trek (3)	1st	23rd century, aboard the starship Enterprise
	It's About Time (1)	recombinant	astronauts travel back in time
	Time Tunnel (1)	recombinant	scientists able to travel back in time
	Green Hornet (1)	copy	masked crimefighter
	Batman (2)	1st	comic superhero—'campy' on TV
1968	Ghost & Mrs. Muir (2)	recombinant	writer buys a house with a sea-captain ghost
	Journey to the Unknown (1)	copy	undistinguished British sci fi anthology import
	Land of the Giants (2)	recombinant	aircraft crashes in strange land of giants
1970	Night Gallery (3)	copy	Rod Sterling hosts sci-fi anthology series
	Planet of the Apes (1)	copy	astronauts travel ahead in time & land in ape land
1971	Nanny & the Professor (1)	recombinant	nanny with mysterious powers
1972	Ghost Story (1)	copy	supernatural tales anthology
1973	Six Million Dollar Man (5)		injured astronaut rebuilt as a Cyborg
	Girl with Something Extra (1)	recombinant	girl with e.s.p.
1974	Nightstalker (1)	recombinant	reporter investigates mysterious murders – by aliens, werewolves, etc.
1975	The Invisible Man (1)	recombinant	invisible scientist
1976	Wonder Woman (3)	copy	powerful woman crimefighter
	Bionic Woman (1.5)	spinoff	rebuilt female as a Cyborg
	Gemini Man (1)	copy	invisible man works for a 'think tank'
1977	Tabitha (3)	spinoff	teenage witch's daughter
	Man from Atlantis (1)	copy	underwater superhero
	Logan's Run (1)	recombinant	young man tries to escape futuristic society
1978	Battlestar Gallactica (1)	copy	more spacecraft travel adventures
	Next Step Beyond (1)	copy	of the occult & supernatural anthology
	Mork & Mindy (4)	copy	comic young alien visits earth

200

	The Incredible Hulk	copy	scientist who grows immensely when angered
1979	Out of the Blue (1)	recombinant	probationary angel helps five orphans
1981	Darkroom (1)	copy	supernatural anthology series
	Greatest American Hero (2)	recombinant	tongue-in-cheek, average guy with a 'hero suit'
	Mr. Merlin (1)	recombinant	King Arthur's magician turns up in S.F. garage
1982	Voyagers (1)	recombinant	goofy guy & orphan time travel to change history
	Tucker's Witch (1)	recombinant	two detectives, one is a witch
1983	Jennifer Slept Here (1)	copy	family buys a house with a ghost
	Manimal (2)	recombinant	detective can turn into any animal he desires
1984	V (1)	recombinant	lizard-like aliens invade the earth
	Alf (3)	recombinant	furry wise-cracking alien animal stops on earth
	Starman (1)	recombinant	space traveller returns for son he fathered on earth
	Highway to Heaven (4+)	recombinant	angel helps needy earthlings
1985	Twilight Zone (2)	copy	more tales from the dark side
1987	Werewolf (2)	recombinant	1600's werewolf hunts
	Max Headroom (1)	recombinant	character-generated futuristic TV sci-fi world
	Second Chance (1)	copy	angel tries to get to heaven
	Star Trek:		
	The Next Generation (7)	spinoff	80 years later and larger
	Beauty & The Beast	recombinant	modern New York update of the fairy tale
1988	Something is Out There (1)	recombinant	mind-reading alien & cop
1989	Alien Nation (1)	copy	another alien & cop
1990	The Munsters Today (2)	copy	updated version of the spooky family
1991	The Flash (1)	copy	police scientist high by lightning – fast & strong
1993	X-Files (3+)	recomb	FBI agents study paranormal phenomenon
	Star Trek: Deep Space Nine (3+)	spinoff	different space location
	Lois & Clark (3)	recombinant	superhero & 'love!'
	Seaquest D.S.V.	recombinant	futuristic research submarine-with a talking dolphin
1994	M.A.N.T.I.S. (1+)	recombinant	black superhero with exo-skeleton superstrength
	Touched by an Angel (2+)	recombinant	team of angels help earthlings
1995	American Gothic (1)	copy	sci-fi anthology
1996	Strange Luck	recombinant	news photographer—always at the right news spot
	Early Edition	recombinant	guy gets newspaper a day early & trys to change
	Third Rock from the Sun	copy	comic aliens stop on earth

Dark Skies	recombinant	aliens help revise history with college graduates
Sabrina, Teenage Witch	recombinant	young teenage witch
The Pretenders	recombinant	human chameleon
Sliders	recombinant	genius travels between dimensions
The Profiler	recombinant	psychic woman profiles serial killers
Millenium	copy	tormented FBI agent with the occult & supernatural
The Burning Zone	recombinant	the plague is the thing

A Penny for Your Thoughts?

Keith Yeomans
Electronic Communications Strategy

Broadcasters, publishers and telecommunications, as their industries converge around the world, are peering anxiously into the black hole which is the developing information economy, wondering how it can make them rich. While most agree that content is the key, and some have invested heavily in it, few seem to have a clear idea of the winning formula. This paper reviews some of the factors which may shape it.

The interplay between technology and content has long been apparent. The British government was reluctant to allow radio, initially a point-to-point medium for communication between warships, to go public.[1] Budapest telephone subscribers in the early years of the century dialled in to hear the latest news while their counterparts in London were treated to live relays of concerts from the Queen's Hall. John Berger discusses in *Ways of Seeing* the influence of oil painting, and later the camera, on the representation of objects in a changing world view.[2]

Audio books, CD ROM encyclopaedias and hypertext novels are all current instances of technology-driven genre bending. The first two examples are simply adaptations from one medium to another. It is only in the third where the technology has 'retro engineered' the original conception.

Some genres, like news and feature films, seem comparatively robust in surviving the media passage from, in the first, newspaper to radio to television and, in the second, fairground stall to Granada, Tooting Bec to television to video and cable. Others, like the single broadcast drama and the current affairs documentary seem more dependent on a particular regulatory, financial and technological context. Their durability is due in part to their status as goods in the information market place.

A Strange Economic Good

In an early (1982) attempt to map the contours of the information economy Gordon Thompson explored the relationship between tangible and intangible goods in what he termed 'a theory of ethereal economics.'[3] In an article entitled *How to Sell Nothing and Get Rich*, he acknowledged the peculiar characteristics of information as an economic good:

> If someone should offer to sell me a joke for two dollars I'd want to know all about the joke before agreeing to purchase it. Once I knew all this, my desire would probably evaporate. Economists tell us that if a market is to work really well, then buyers must have perfect information. In an information market, if the buyer has perfect information, the market is destroyed, not perfected. Clearly, information is a strange economic good.[4]

He goes on to argue that information has had to be trapped into a physical form to be exploited:

> Our past economic experience has done little to prepare us for the task of identifying exactly how a society can generate real worth by simply shuffling information around. Because we have had to imprint our information on physical carriers, like the paper in a book, or the vinyl in a phonograph record, we have avoided the most difficult aspects of forcing information to act as a conventional economic good. We sold books and records, not information.[5]

Broadcasting and publishing are attempts to embody this principle in organisational form. There are cases in both of information being packaged as a public or a private good. In the West the book is known better as a private good, though the concept of government publishing blurs even this definition. The case of broadcasting is more problematic. Europeans, those in many of the former European colonies, and some totalitarian states have become used to broadcasting as a public good, financed either from the public purse or a version of the licence fee, in which there may be some scope for the exercise of individual intellectual property rights through, for example, the sale of scripts or music.

But this public good, however produced, exists in a wider commercial context. Some of the tensions in this environment are reflected in the status of a broadcast programme. In the simple public good scenario a programme is the end product of the enterprise. This was the case even in the pre 1990 days of strongly regulated commercial television in the UK. The 1990 Broadcasting Act marked a change summarised neatly at the time by one senior television executive, as being 'from making money to make programmes to making programmes to make money'. Programmes as public goods can be sold, as the BBC's programmes have long successfully been, in the international 'private' market place. They are now, via UK Gold and similar ventures, bought again by a licence fee paying public through cable and satellite subscriptions.

The Value of a Programme
A programme's status is more complex in a commercial regime in which the audience may be defined as the product sold to advertisers. In this case, according to one authority on accounting, it may be treated as a sales cost.[6] In the event of the production company or broadcasting organisation being sold the same programme could also be regarded, according to this source, as an asset or as part of the organisation's brand value. These distinctions permeate production values and reflect the prevailing role of such cultural forms in a society at a particular time.

A New Form of Conviviality?
The organisational forms that have grown up around broadcasting and publishing contrast with that characterising contemporary telecommunications. Nicholas Garnham observes:

There is a huge gulf between the industries concerned with publishing, video and audio-visual technologies and telecommunications companies. They have little conception of how each other operate. ...[7]

Telecoms' development as a global network for point-to-point communication has apparently yielded a different form of information economics from that applying in the other two communications industries. Jean Voge, in another early 1980s vision of the information society, saw broadcasting challenged by interactive networks like telephony because it is a pyramidal structure acting, he claimed, as a bottleneck to communication.[8] By contrast, the decentralised structure of the telephone network hierarchy is, he argued, more economic in terms of its contacts.

This distributed network model has created an organisational and commercial culture in the telecommunications industry whose mission has not been revenue generation from the sale of cultural products but rather from the sale of connections and line charges. Telecommunications companies' incomes have hitherto derived primarily not from information packages themselves but from their carriage. Voge argued an evolutionary trend towards a decentralised, cellular model of communications and economic growth:

By providing a new form of conviviality on a human scale among members of local groups or work communities, local networks will revive the concept of the forum.[9]

The Platform Debate

This vision of global collegiality is, however, in conflict with the commercial interests of the content industries, shaped as they are around the exploitation and protection of copyright. Those who live by the sale of rights on tangible information goods see their transformation into intangible digits in cyberspace as commercial suicide.

The idea of a distributed network does not, however, accurately reflect patterns of use across the system. In a study of the relation of business telecommunications to urban development in New Jersey and New York Moss concludes, 'New telecommunications technologies reinforce existing economic forces'.[10]

Jussawalia notes a similar process in Fiji where: 'Supply of telecommunications equipment is generating its own demand.'[11]

There is a difference, it seems, between potential and practice. A further consideration is the route map of the information superhighway now being built and the traffic flows it allows. Revenue will be generated differently by point-to-point traffic than by radial commuting in and out of the 'information capitals.'

Promulgation of the Internet as a model for the global information infrastructure has encouraged the Voge vision, whereas the reality is already turning out to be different. The dynamics of infrastructure development became apparent in what was known in the United States as the 'platform debate'.[12] Argument raged between communications industry giants on where the intelligence (and, therefore, the value) lay – with the user (computer industry), at the centre (cable and satellite companies), or in the network (telecommunications companies).

The dilemma for the cable industry has long been whether the investment needed to deliver intelligent, two way broadband to every subscriber's door would ever be repaid by the demand for value-added services. The rate of growth in these services continues to be slow. Telebanking and teleshopping were being vaunted in the early 80s in the UK and still have yet to realise their potential. Now digital satellite and mobile communications are fragmenting the market for interactive services of all kinds making investment even riskier.

Threats to the Net
The Internet paradigm is itself under threat. Price is being used to regulate demand in several ways. Internet service providers are floating the idea of tiered subscriptions as frustrated users tire of long down load times. This 'executive lane' approach is being made all the more likely by the shift in responsibility for Internet infrastructure development from US federal funds to the communications industry. This private sector involvement is accelerating the need to find a return on investment by making the Net secure to encourage higher revenue streams from business. The call for greater security is also coming from the multimedia content industry to enable them to safeguard their intellectual property rights in this new environment.

How will the ordinary surfer fare in this process? One view is that they will be able to sit back and let 'push technology' do the work. Heralded as a solution to long waiting times, this new application will let users receive information 'broadcast' to their computers on a Web 'channel'. According to Louise Kehoe:

> The TV terminology is no coincidence. It is widely believed that push will bring Web content to an audience of people who would not take the time or trouble to search out information on the Web. It also creates an attractive vehicle for advertisers who can be sure that their materials will be delivered to viewers – just like a TV channel.[13]

This scenario follows the pattern of history. American radio started as point to point communication between amateurs and survived an early bid by AT&T to canalise it down nationwide cable channels[14] only to be saved from 'chaos' by a gradual process of legislative intervention through licensing designed to allocate the spectrum as scarce resource. This, combined with a growing recognition of radio's commercial value, culminated in the network system.

It is tempting to see *Netties* as the radio hams of the future, banished to their attics and to the margins of a commercial Internet largely configured asymmetrically downstream for mass audiences and only fully interactive for high ticket corporate and public services.

Attention
In these circumstances the simple advice to would-be Web entrepreneurs would be 'digitise your product and sit tight' as the factors shaping global trade in knowledge products will be much the same as those for books, films and television programming, just at a more competitive level. Certainly, the corporate

rights owners and managers, in concert with the other sectors of the communications industry, are working hard to make that happen. But is this view of the future information economy as *the present with digits* a fair prediction? There are some indications which suggest not.

Using the example of popular music Thompson argues that:

> ... the value of an ethereal good is not in the good alone, but is also rooted in the creation of a consensus of value creation in a very large number of people, which is, in turn, a function of the underlying or supporting technology.[15]

He concludes:

> Attention may be the rare good in an information economy and recording the way that attention is spent is likely to be the principal role of an information economy.[16]

Just in Time Content

This view may help to explain the rapid rise in popularity of Web advertising where, not only is the user profile commercially attractive, but the number and distribution of 'hits' can be cheaply and quickly recorded. It is even more true of full scale Internet trading which of any electronic medium brings customer and supplier closest to the market place ideal in which they can intercommunicate their individual wants and products and conclude the deal through a secure financial transaction. This relationship is the strongest counter to the view that cyberspace will be the commercial television of the 21st century. In the dominant commercial environment a clear marketing advantage is likely to have more impact than more altruistic ideas of equitable information flow.

Thompson's distinction between tangible and intangible goods may be contested on the basis that they are similar in respect of the value accrued to them by the market. It has lain largely in the 'marketing technology.' *Just in Time* manufacturing is one instance of this technology being used to reverse the traditional relationship between producer, customer and value. In this respect, the manufacturing industry is ahead of broadcasting and publishing which are still in the state Thompson describes in his account of the demise of broadcast programming as 'a public good':

> When a good that behaves in this public fashion is forced into market-place conditions, choice becomes limited, and externalities like copyright are required to assure a degree of fairness. As the most efficient marginal price for information behaving as a public good is zero, there is no use proportional reward available to the creator. Hence the important marketplace messages that convey the individual preferences of consumers to the producers are denied. The creation and development of content is left to 'experts', guided at best by blunt statistical instruments. The essential stimulating economic messages are just not

present. The content stagnates, and is under-produced and of low quality.[17]

The Half Life of the Information Entity

How, then, should 'expert' content creators in broadcasting and publishing respond to the challenge of a *just in time* communications environment? The first step is to abandon any preconceptions of the value of their products, services and skills and then re-evaluate them in the context of the new environment. The third is to refocus all of these on exploiting the opportunities it offers.

These processes are currently being undertaken more or less painfully by most media companies of all sizes. Revaluation can only take place in the light of a critical understanding of the nature of information products and their behaviour in the new environment. Expertise in this area exists to some extent in the computing and telecoms industries which are having to adapt traditional content to fit the parameters of their technology. Research in these industries has gone into what one Microsoft executive described as 'the half life of the information entity'.[18] This research should be more widely accessible to the content industry, especially to the core of small companies who now dominate audio-visual content creation.

Learning as a Model

Some of the more obvious interrelated factors shaping the value of information products have become apparent through the author's work in developing electronic learning strategies. They include:
- system capacity, accessibility and reach
- production and distribution cost
- content redundancy/durability
- user-perceived content utility
- affordability
- immersions (the extent to which the user is engaged by the product)
- availability of alternatives

No claim is made for the exhaustiveness or analytical acuity of this list. Most of it also applies to conventional information products. Much of the difference lies in the degree to which it is consciously applied to product development and in the changing relationships between these factors.

Further work is being developed on an examination of the structural and dynamic principles underlying these relationships. New theoretical approaches are needed to help understand how the transactional nature of information and knowledge products is influenced by interactivity in the network and how this affects their cultural and economic status. Evidence is beginning to emerge of parallels between multimedia cultural forms (computer games, for example) and those of oral societies where storytelling, for example, is more interactive.[19] Work in these areas should have a direct bearing on product development and distribution in both the public and commercial domains.

Education offers a fruitful field of investigation not only because of the existence within the education community of conscious models of information knowledge commerce (though not as developed as they could be) but also because of the existing interchangeability of producer/user roles, especially in higher education where academics are usually both. As a result some of the issues and problems relating to the technology's role in facilitating distributed knowledge networks are being identified, though not as yet solved.

Knowledge Assets

One model extendable not only to the wider learning community but also to the information society as a whole is that of exploiting knowledge assets. The management science literature in this field is growing apace around core concepts such as Nonaka's 'tacit knowledge' (personal, unmodified knowledge) and the 'hypertext organisation.'[20] Companies are beginning to identify and codify their human intellectual capital as a first stage in realising its value.

Some of this thinking is beginning to transfer to the education community through ideas like the national learning grid but there is a need for systematic investigation of the knowledge assets of, for example, a local education authority or a city using yardsticks adapted from industry before clear indications can be given of this area's impact on the industry.

The knowledge asset model adds credibility to Voge's view of a hierarchical system as a bottleneck to communication. It is not hard to imagine how the technology can help generate value from the inputs of teachers, students, libraries and museums. The challenge for the communications industry is to find ways of profitably refocussing their activities to facilitate this change.

The knowledge asset model can be applied more broadly to the electronics communications market place and to the domain of public information goods (local authority planning regulation and the output of the BBC, for example) in anticipation of a version of Warhol's vision in which everyone is an author for 15 minutes. In this way the traditional communications industries may be able to identify and develop new, broader based mechanisms of wealth creation and distribution in the information society rather than drawing the blanket of copyright more tightly around themselves as the cold winds of technology change blow harder.

References

1. Briggs, A., *The History of Broadcasting in the United Kingdom*, Vol. I, OUP.
2. Berger, J., *Ways of Seeing*, Penguin 1972, p. 3.
3. Thompson, G. B., *Intermedia*, November 1982, Vol 10, No 6.
4. *Intermedia* 1982.
5. *Intermedia* 1982.
6. Prof Brian Rutherford, Professor of Accounting, University of Kent in an interview with the author (1993).
7. Garnham, N. et al., *The Information Superhighway. Britain's Response*, ESRC Policy Research Paper, No 29, 1994
8. Voge, J., 'From the Information Society to the Communication Society' *Intermedia*, November 1982, Vol I., No 6.
9. Voge, *Intermedia*.
10. Moss, M.L., 'New York isn't just New York anymore' *Intermedia*, July/September 1984, Vol 12, No. 4/5.

11. Jussawalla, M et al., (eds) *The Cost of Thinking: Information Economies of Ten Pacific Countries*, Ablex Publishing Corp, New Jersey.

12. Yeomans, K *Learners on the Superhighway?*, National Institute of Adult Education, 1996.

13. Kehoe, L., 'Nature of the Beast', *Financial Times*, 26th March 1997.

14. Sumilyan, S., *Selling Radio*, Smithsonian, 1994.

15. Sumilyan, S., *Selling Radio*

16. Sumilyan, S., *Selling Radio*

17. Sumilyan, S., *Selling Radio*

18. Corddry, T., Creative Director, Consumer Division, Microsoft, interview with the author (1994).

19. For example: Summersby, P., current doctoral research, Canterbury Christ Church College, University of Kent.

20. Nonaku, I., *The Knowledge Creating Company/Intellectualizing Capability*, OUP, 1995.

Papers presented in the session
What About the Workers?
(in alphabetical order)

The Search for Identity in the Converged Newsroom

Kathryn S. Egan and Scott C. Hammond
Brigham Young University, USA

Instruction in news reporting on converged technology began at Brigham Young University, in Provo, Utah, with two desks pushed together in the same news room, at the *Daily Universe*, the university's newspaper. This was in 1996, when the academic view of traditional news media was that they would eventually converge, and that audiences (readers) would not care which 'pipe' brought them the news, only that they had access to it. The goal of BYU's attempt at 'integration' was, first, to teach students to learn to report the news, using any one of four media: print, television or radio, and the Internet. They were to cooperate in gathering, sharing and reporting information.

The project in cooperative news gathering and reporting on various media would be student – driven, with the oversight of two professors of journalism, an experienced broadcast news producer, and the *Universe* editor and staff.

One BYU professor of journalism claimed the focus on teaching students to learn how to use technology would make them too entrepreneurial.[1] A local television news director said a newsroom that combined television and radio reporting, indicated that the reporters could not work co-operatively. Television could provide sound for radio, but radio had nothing to contribute to television.[2] None could conceive of how a 'convergence' of television, radio – and *print* – could possibly function.

Background

Prior to the newsroom integration, Communications students at Brigham Young University were told by professors and communications practitioners that the converged newsroom would better prepare them for journalism careers of the future. Technology would become their tools, not their masters. Indeed, what they would learn, according to one cable entrepreneur, a graduate of the BYU communications programme, would 'create a map of the world you will enter. Your experience here will prepare you for careers in communications for which content is king.'[3]

It seemed, from such an entrepreneurial – point – of – view, that 'news' or 'content' was to be thought of as a commodity. Information was to be packaged and sold, according to consumer demand, on the market. It was predicted that those individuals who have the resources: money, time and interest, would become the 'information haves' in the Information Society.[4] They would support the news-gathering businesses. The question then became: would commercial interests also drive news gathering? Would journalists become only entrepreneurs, out to sell their information for profit?

According to the entrepreneur of news and entertainment on cable:

213

Opportunities will be great if you have the aptitude and the education. Everyone wants stuff live, local, exclusive, that they alone can
own. People who can't adapt to change are being shuffled aside. Some
people I thought were very capable are being replaced by young people
who can adapt to change and exploit the opportunities presented by
technology.[5]

Entrepreneurism is encouraged by journalists who have become salespersons
or managers. Matthew Winkler, a former Wall Street Journal reporter, now editor
– in – chief of *Bloomberg Business News*, tells young would – be journalists, to
'go to the heart of the matter.' The goal is to be 'different' from the average
person with a home page on the Internet by having judgement, knowledge and
the ability to speak. 'If we become slaves of the technology that is in front of
us we will forget the original purpose of being in the news business.'[6]

Pratte listed the shortcomings of radio and television in reporting news: their
primary purpose is to entertain and advertise. The purchase of networks by huge
conglomerates to form oligopolies has created pressure on network news operations to become more efficient and profitable, which has led to the downsizing of
network news and a decline of 'enterprise journalism,' which is time – consuming and expensive because it requires extensive backgrounding of stories, cross –
checking of sources, and an increased reliance on the packaged press release –
including the ubiquitous video news release and/or packaged satellite feed.

Neil Postman's charge was included: that TV has conditioned the public to
tolerate entertainment in place of news and in place of rational public discourse
and reasoned public affairs.[7] And, since deregulation, the broadcast editorial has
nearly disappeared, a sign of the rejection of controversy in favour of commercialism, which in turn creates a need for immediacy, which, in the college newsroom, produces a 'frenetic pusher of nonstop jolts to the nervous system,' rather
than the 'quiet disseminator of facts and truth.'[8]

In the final analysis, the converged newsroom experience will produce students who 'want to become managers, who think like the boss,' according to
Pratte.[9]

Therefore, the students prepared for careers by their experience in the converged news room, co-operating to report for The Daily Universe, KBYU and
the KBYUniverse web site, were destined to lose their identities as journalists
and become, instead, commercial, conservative entrepreneurs.

Identity

Identity is more than what you call yourself. It is who you are. Identity is an
important issue in newsroom convergence, because it forces strong identities,
built over time, to come together at once in one organization. Newspapers, broadcast organizations and on-line services all have strong histories of building 'corporate we's.' The traditional corporate 'we' built by newspaper and broadcast
organizations are converging in ways that are problematic.[10]

The notion of corporate 'we' begins to define what we mean by identity.
Kenneth Burke says, 'Identification arises as a communicative, cooperative
response.' The result of this response is the identification of the individual with

a group and the adopting of symbols, values and hierarchy, and the individual acting in turn as the guardian of group ideas. Individuals become distinguished, gain prestige and status, because of their identities.

Burke and Cheney's[11] notion that identity comes when we share hierarchy values and symbols, and become guardian of each other's ideas, is important in this study. And, according to Burke, as this identification becomes stronger, the organization defends the status quo and blocks, or regulates, change. A new invention or creation that changes what already is ritualized faces the probability of alienation from others (such as entrenched professors). This alienation persists until others in the group have experienced the same invention (or idea) and now call it their own—a transcendent act. In the next section we will discuss how convergence generally results in a change in hierarchy, values and symbols, and how the journalists in a converged newsroom have yet to become the guardians of one another's ideas and are struggling to maintain rituals, all toward the transcendence of calling the newsroom 'their own.'

Case Study

To strengthen broadcast journalism, the KBYU broadcast news director, who came into the programme summer 1996, said that the broadcast students needed more training to improve their reporting skills. 'Our students need more exhaustive experience in basic reporting and writing that is associated with print – the *Universe*,' he said. He supported the integrated newsroom, and one, centralized, news desk. The initial strategic planning sessions, March 1996, with faculty and students, which resulted in the converged newsroom at BYU, began with discussion of the Communication Department's core values and strengths. The summation of this strategic planning was a presentation by a group of students representing print, broadcasting and Internet journalism to demonstrate what the programme should look like in ten years. The vision of newsroom cooperation was created.

News Central was established in the *Daily Universe* newspaper offices as a clearing house for news flow to meet deadlines for the daily KBYU television, cable and KBYU-FM news broadcasts, The *Daily Universe*, and Newline. It is staffed from 8:00 a.m. until 5:00 p.m. by a KBYU Newscentral editor and by a *Daily Universe* editor from 11:00 a.m. until 3:00 p.m., making co-operation between print and broadcast students difficult. 'If anything breaks when there's no NewsCentral editor, no one knows whom to call after 5:00,' one Newscentral editor said. The initial student efforts to integrate print journalists into the television broadcast news programme, *KBYU News 11*, demonstrated the strengths of students trained in each medium – also the disadvantages of having learned to report on one medium.

In the 1996 fall semester, the KBYU news director reported: there was no technical integration between the Universe and the broadcast newsrooms. Just a desk with a computer and a police scanner squirrelled away in the back corner of the *Daily Universe*. The broadcast student said the only thing that had changed from the way they worked previously was that she was now located in the print news offices instead of at the broadcast news desk, so the television assignment desk was in a far – away place for no good reason.

The broadcasters thought the print people were late starters.[12] With a 4:30 live broadcast to produce, they arrived at Newscentral and found the place 'virtually empty' at 8:00 a.m. The print people arrived about 10:00 a.m. and stayed later than the broadcasters. They discovered the newspaper had no computer data base detailing daily and future assignments. The print reporters, assigned to beats, worked off hard files – clipping here, a press release there, all gathered at five separate desk editors, producing five separate papers-in-one, so that 'no one person has a grasp of the whole picture.'[13] What was needed was a computer data base 'for some central editorial observation,' according to the KBYU news director. The TV assignments editor had to check with five different print editors to coordinate stories; that is, 'to find out what they were doing and offer what we had.' The 'front-page news' meeting for the newspaper was at 1:30 p.m., which was an hour and a half past the KBYU TV news meeting, 'too late for us to do anything of substance.'[14]

'Besides the meeting focused on what was already done or being done. And, as a matter of pride and practicality, we were not anxious to simply let the DU set our agenda,' the KBYU news director said.

True attempts at integration took place in early 1997 when two students, one from the newspaper, one from broadcast news, sat side-by-side at Newscentral and at daily meetings to select stories for the newspaper's front page and the KBYU news broadcast.

Indifference seemed to be the biggest hurdle: most students lacked a vision of the integrated newsroom and themselves in it. The students who did have a grasp of the co-operation required to gather and report the news in the integrated news room became its leaders. Their job then became to both train reporters and coordinate the news coverage.

One news event, the results of which were reported differently by the newspaper and the broadcasters, changed that. Election results in Utah are traditionally reported live on KBYU, with a BYU political science professor and pollster predicting the outcome. In the November 3rd Congressional Race, the professor called the election results correctly on KBYU. The *Daily Universe*, relying on the raw vote tally until deadline, announced incorrect results on the front page the next morning.[15] The professor in charge of the integrated newsroom called a meeting and urged the students and faculty to prevent the 'scuttling' of the convergence project based on petty contention.[16] The student newspaper editor, 'was very much a part of the discussion and seemed anxious to make something work.'[17]

From the start, success of the convergence project was seen as dependent upon its being student – driven. Until students in key, leadership positions saw themselves in roles in the integrated newsroom, and news gathering and reporting as a team project, they functioned side-by-side but oblivious to one another, with the theme: things will carry on as usual. More recently, the students have recognized value of integration. A story that broke February 14, 1997, illustrates how student – vision has helped individuals define their identities in the converged-media newsroom:

Editor (*Daily Universe*): We, my fiancee and I, were having pictures taken in Aspen Grove. We came down the canyon and there was a cop car in the middle of the road. The cop told me there was an armed suspect in the Grove, in one of the cottages. The were not letting anyone come down the canyon until they searched car trunks for the suspect. The photographer with us scrambled to cover what was happening in the cottages. I went to a pay phone and made one call to News Central. They sent two more still photographers. Our photographer shot a roll of cops, the SWAT team going in. She got the information. We came down the mountain, borrowed a cell phone and called the news room. KBYU sent a cameraman. It could be KBYU will be the only station to get a cameraman up there. It's kind of frustrating. It will be late news by the time the Universe prints it We won't get the story in until next Tuesday [this was a Friday; Monday a holiday], and KBYU will have it on air at 4:30 today. But we're getting the news out. We'll get it on Newsline, on the Internet. We'll come in at 9:00 and get it on. We'll get a still frame or video clip from KBYU and post a photo. I got to three news organizations out of one [Newscentral desk] with one call.

KBYU news reporter/anchor, a student in the programme prior to the 'integrated news room,' now with a perspective based on 'how print journalists used to see broadcast news people'[18] said,

I guess we're doing this so we can get jobs in the future. That's what they tell us. The hard part for broadcasters is, we go over there [to the *Universe* offices]. The cool part is, we do live shots from the *Daily Universe*. We toss three times a week for the campus news, with a camera set up over there.

The most positive aspect of the integrated newsroom is sharing sources and information. When Dan Quayle [U.S. Vice President during last administration] came to Provo, it was a big deal that the Utah Republican Party got someone of his stature to come here. A *Daily Universe* reporter came, and I came with a camera from KBYU, so we could share the information. The problem is just getting people to realize the benefits of working together. Information is everything. Access to information, that is. I wouldn't have known about Dan Quayle coming if NewsCentral hadn't coordinated the story. My story can be better because of integrated information. I can work with broadcast constraints – like thirty seconds to tell a story – but still tell the story in-depth, which some professors think is not possible for a broadcast reporter.

Traditionally, broadcasters are supposed to be TV people first, and print students are only concerned with the newspaper. Now, with the integrated newsroom, we're all journalists first. We get the information, and it doesn't matter for which media.

The KBYU news director said the purpose of the television news student for being in the integrated news room is foremost to be a journalist:

The greatest challenge for the broadcast journalism students is not whether they can find their way around a converged newsroom. It's not whether they can hold a microphone in one hand and bang out a print story in the other, or whether they will dumb down the integrated news operation, spreading the evil of style – over – substance. The biggest challenge is for each student to forge a passion for gathering and telling the truth, and to articulate why it all matters.

The traditional drive to get the scoop, be first to report the story, is evident in this editor, as it is among the TV news student reporters. They are beginning to recognize that by getting the story on any one or all of the distribution media available to them, they are still getting their scoops. Initiative and enterprise in getting 'the story' is rewarded as it has always been in that the stories are disseminated in a timely manner.

Although the page editors of the *Universe* initially created and updated their own homepages, they no longer put stories on the Internet. 'Reporters are not technologists,' according to the Internet Newsline editor, who is an engineering student ('I have no training in journalism; I don't need it.') Two students were hired to update Newsline with print stories, photos, and video from KBYU. Currently, a two-minute video requires an hour to download and view. This semester new software and computers will be added to allow video to be downloaded and viewed simultaneously.

The 'rough spot' in the system, according to the Newsline editor, is the daybook. Reporters use slugs to file all materials. Currently, the NewsLine editors must get the slugs from the news editor.

> Often we don't know what the slug is. We have to search for what goes with what, and the Newscentral editor has to figure it out for us. The future daybook will be a data base with both KBYU and the *Universe* combined. We'll be able to look at a list of current day's slugs and put them on line. We're working to make the daybook easier to use. Each reporter e-mails their story to Newscentral editors who have to enter the slug by hand into the daybook. In the future, reporters will make entries directly into the daybook, into a form on the Internet page. All access will be controlled by pass words.

Another challenge to the integrated newsroom a year after its inception is to provide students more classroom teaching in basic journalism, especially reporter training and skills. A student KBYU reporter/anchor said:

> We have to figure out for ourselves how to report. The programme is not focused enough on reporting skills. We learn theory of reporting, especially how to be politically correct, but not basic reporting skills. The key to making this integration work is knowing how to report, which means we need to strengthen the curriculum. If you know how to get the story, you can get it on any medium. I have not yet had a class where the teacher is a working reporter, practising reporting skills and analysis. I

intend to go into investigative reporting, and I've found that the integrated newsroom makes it possible for a broadcaster to do that. The programme is going well; but the way it's managed now, we're relying completely on experience to learn how to report. The main problem is the missing connection with everyday practice. We need feedback about our reporting. It's been better since Dean (KBYU news director) took over, but he can't give feedback to everyone and direct a daily news cast. We need a reporter teaching us practical application. There's no connection between our reporting class and what goes on in the newsroom.

Crowding is yet another challenge for the newsroom. There were too many reporters in one room, not enough computers, telephones, desk space or pagers. By spring 1997, plans were underway to add 'found' computers (from other areas) to the newsroom, provide key editors with pagers and messaging capability, and replace large desks with new modular furniture for more efficient use of limited space.

Good journalism practices, not technology, is the goal of the integrated newsroom. 'Everyone in television news is a reporter first,' according to the news director, who evaluates students for reporting/anchoring positions by testing their ability to gather news stories, write, edit and 'look at things substantively – don't just ask for a handout [news release] from the desk.' For the journalist who gets the story, the integrated newsroom makes technology transparent, the channel for news dissemination, not the controller of it.

The allegiance of the individual reporter will be self – determined. Some of the student journalists do have an allegiance to the university and the ownership of their enterprise. When they are in news careers, the entrepreneurial motivation will drive some of them. They may have inclinations to move into management, or to 'sell' their information. Their goals may include 'editor' or 'media owners' and so business success will motivate them.

Others will be driven by social goals: a desire to contribute to an informed society, for example. Educating the journalist at BYU is not intended to inculcate one goal over another in the minds of our students. As professors of journalism, we strive to instil autonomous ethical decision making by our students when they become journalism practitioners. We attempt to provide the training and practical experience to prepare students for their roles as communicators. The goal of the BYU Communications department, with its integrated newsroom, is to provide students with opportunities to make their own career choices.

Endnotes

1. Alf Pratte, 'Micro and Macro Mergers of Print and Broadcast: Looking the Gift horse in the Mouth', paper presented at the western Social Sciences Association, Reno Nevada, April 1996.

2. Conversation with Ray Carter, News Director, KSL-TV, Salt Lake City, Utah, February 17, 1997.

3. Steve Rizley, G.M. Cox Communications' CableRep, Phoenix, Arizona, in a Brigham Young University, Department of Communications, Symposium speech, February 13, 1997.

4. Pratte, *op. cit.*

5. Rizley, *op. cit.*

6. Matthew Winkler, 'The 21st Century Media Worker,' in *Looking Over the Edge: The Impact of Technology on Communication Education*, publication adn videotape: a Roundtable hosted by the Manship School of Mass Communication, Louisiana State University, May 1996.

7. Neil Postman, *Amusing Ourselves to Death: Public Discourse in the Age of Show Business*, New York: Penguin Books, 1985.

8. Karl Fleming, Los Angeles Daily News, 'Another verdict is reached – and the media are found guilty,' in the *Deseret News*, October 15, 1995, v.2.

9. Conversation with Alf Pratte, Brigham Young University, February 13, 1997.

10. Kenneth Burke, *The Philosophy of Literary Form*, Berkeley, CA: University of California Press, 1993, p.306.

11. George Cheney, 'The Rhetoric of Identification and the Study of Organizational Communication', *Quarterly Journal of Speech*, 1987, 69, 143-158.

12. Dean Paynter, KBYU-TV news director, unedited report, February 13, 1997.

13. Paynter, *ibid.*

14. Paynter, *ibid.*

15. Hart, Katy, *Universe Staff Writer*, 'Orton Edges Ahead of Cannon,' *Daily Universe*, November 6, 1996, p.3.

16. Students attending this meeting were confused; they hadn't sensed 'contention', but rather lack of communication due to the distance between the two, separate newsrooms, one located at the Universe, the other in another building at KBYU.

17. Paynter, *op. cit.*

18. William C. Porter, Associate Professor of Communications, Sequence Leader: Journalism; memorandum to the chair, January 24, 1997.

Passion and Commitment:

The Difficulties Faced By Working Mothers In The British Television Industry

Judith Jones
Media, Critical and Creative Arts Department
John Moores University, Liverpool

This paper is based on research into whether the television industry in Britain is a sympathetic working environment for women with children. It was conducted through a series of interviews with women currently working in the industry, both employers and employees, to provide a personal insight into their working and personal lives. The strategies for change, proposed by various organisations to improve the working conditions of women programme makers, are also considered.

Because of its obvious limitations, this paper cannot hope to provide a definitive picture of what is currently taking place in the British television industry. However it does highlight some of the particular difficulties faced by female workers with children.

Industry Changes

The dramatic changes within the British television industry over the past 15 years have affected not only its structure but also its workforce. The media has long been a popular environment in which to work and has never been short of new recruits. Indeed, it is estimated that by the year 2000 some 20 per cent of the European workforce could be working in the broad communications industry.[1] But how welcome is this growth, particularly to those women who make up an increasing percentage of the workforce?

Two specific features of the industry create difficulties for women generally, but especially those with children. The first is the culture which exists within television. The industry continues to be male-dominated and is a prime example of gendered job segregation. Research by Skillset (the Industry Training Organisation for Broadcast, Film and Video) in 1994 showed that 'there are still substantial gender imbalances in specific areas' and in those occupational areas where women dominate such as wardrobe, production support and research, the report concludes that 'they are also the lowest paid'.[2]

This 'male culture' has bred an environment where the general expectation is of 100 per cent commitment to the job. One manifestation of this is the hours worked which have traditionally been long and often unsociable. Because television is a highly competitive industry, demanding a high level of commitment, little attention has been paid to the needs of employees with care responsibilities.

Movement between different programmes, and indeed different companies, is usually based on personal contact rather than responding directly to an advertisement. Consequently, it is particularly important not to be labelled as lacking commitment. This work culture causes particular difficulties for those attempting to juggle motherhood and a career. Furthermore, job sharing, part-time working, or a career break may be considered to show divided loyalty.

The inequality which exists in broadcasting is not peculiar to British television, nor is the concentration of women in administrative rather than managerial or technical posts. The European Union in its Third Action Programme on Equal Opportunities for Women, is targeting the media as one of its key sectors. Initiatives have been launched to improve equality in broadcasting. The BBC, for example, aims to increase the percentage of women in senior positions to between 30 per cent and 40 per cent by 1996.[3]

The second feature which has caused difficulties for women in television has been the trend towards cutting permanent staff jobs and casualising the workforce. This in turn has threatened the implementation of policies on equal opportunities. Freelance workers are employed on varying lengths of contracts and varying conditions. Under the terms of the 1990 Broadcasting Act, ITV licence holders and Channel Four are required to make practical arrangements for promoting equality of opportunity. However, independent production companies, of which there are now approximately 1000, which predominantly employ freelances, are outside the scope of the equal opportunities clause of the Act.

Related Research
In December 1994 the British Film Institute published some early results from its television industry tracking survey which is conducting intensive research over five years into the lives of 391 people in creative television jobs.[4] Although only in its first year, the BFI found initial results so significant that they were made public. The *Independent* reported:

> Women working in television are under such strain from a combination of long, erratic hours and short-term contracts that they avoid having children, delay until it is so late that they have only one, or sacrifice family life for the job.[5]

The following year, 1995, at the Edinburgh Television Festival a session entitled *Life After Birth?* tackled the question of combining motherhood and a TV career. In a lively debate women (and indeed men) programme-makers looked at the problems working mothers face in such a pressurised and competitive industry which now has the added difficulty of being staffed by an increasing number of freelances. One of the most controversial statements was made by Channel Four Commissioning Editor, Sara Ramsden, who said:

> I do not know how it is possible to be 100 per cent committed to the project and have children at the same time.[6]

The question of whether it is possible to be a good mother and a good programme-maker seemed central to the future employment of women within the television industry. This research set out to analyse the real situation faced

222

by ordinary women working in television production, both employees and employers.

Core Research and Findings

The eleven women I chose to interview could be separated into three groups which to some extent overlapped. Firstly I wanted to interview Sara Ramsden whose remarks had provoked such a strong reaction at the Edinburgh International Television Festival. I also thought it important to contact Claudia Milne, a programme-maker with many years' experience who set up the independent production company Twenty-Twenty. Although not at the Edinburgh International Television Festival Claudia responded publicly in print to Sara's statement.

The second group of interviewees were women currently working in television production who have children, mainly under the age of ten. They chiefly worked for large commercial companies rather than the BBC because the move towards freelance working has been more marked in the former. They tended to be employed on contract and were usually involved in the production rather than technical side of programme making.

Finally I interviewed a number of women who were not programme- makers but who have some direct contact with those working in television, either through a personnel role or in terms of trade union representation.

A divergence of opinion existed even within this small sample and noticeably respondents did not necessarily receive support from their female colleagues, even those who also had children. All the women felt that it was an important issue that should be addressed but there was a level of acceptance rather than a demand for changes to their working conditions. There were, however, certain themes which emerged from the interviews.

There was general agreement that a very particular culture exists within television which is demanding and has a high expectation of commitment. While some thought it was particularly *macho* others felt it centred more on a 'young people' culture of both sexes. The consensus was that the culture was not conducive to the demands of family life. One of the most obvious indications of this culture is the long and irregular working hours worked. Although television, by its very nature, will never involve merely working nine-to-five, there was doubt as to whether long hours were always essential or simply perceived as an indication of commitment. The long hours culture was seen as damaging to both family life and to the health and productive capacity of the employee.

In an increasingly freelance workforce, the question of commitment was one of the central concerns for the respondents. Anxious to maintain employment and in order that their commitment could not be questioned, those with children who were not their own boss tended to over-compensate in their work. One example was that when children were ill, the women would not admit that this was the reason for their absence. They were anxious to conceal any sign that they were not in control of both areas of their life, work and home. The women stressed the importance of reliable childcare to the smooth running of their lives. Any sign of a lack of control or organisation, they felt, would be a sign of weakness which could subsequently be used against them, particularly when it came to renewing a contract.

Although some companies did provide a financial contribution to childcare, the actual day to day planning and organisation was something the women did as individuals without any backup from their employer. The ultimate nightmare for many seemed to be a breakdown in their childcare arrangements. However, such a crisis was not something which they could share with their employer but rather something which was their responsibility alone.

Perhaps because of the absence of this support from their employers the women stressed the value of a supportive partner. Whether the partner worked in the industry or not was not the central issue. What was considered more important was some regularity in their working hours. In general, care of children outside working hours tended to be shared. This is one of the more positive aspects to emerge from this research.

In common with the changing structure of the industry, the women interviewed had a variety of employment patterns although those who were employed tended to be on contract. Freelance working did not seem to bring any benefits such as flexibility whereas the disadvantages such as insecurity and a lack of eligibility for particular benefits were emphasised. In a market where there are increasing numbers of young people, a career break was viewed as imprudent. The experience was that if you were absent from the employment market for more than a few months, it would be very difficult to break back into the industry.

There seems to be almost a climate of fear existing partly because of the manner of recruitment. The vast majority of freelances (48 per cent according to the BFI tracking study) find work through personal contacts. This situation shows how important it is to maintain and cultivate these contacts in order to ensure continued employment. Some women were also concerned not to be identified since they felt that this might prejudice their future employment.

There has been a considerable growth in the number of independent production companies with contradictory repercussions for working mothers. The two women I interviewed who had started their own companies seemed to be in a much more advantageous position with regard to their family responsibilities. They were able to structure their work around their position as mothers and impose certain parameters to their work such as not filming abroad.

However it was conceded that tight budgets would make it difficult to institute all the benefits they might like for their staff. The establishment of equal opportunities within this type of company was regarded as the responsibility of the owner and although both women expressed a desire to follow good working practices in this area, it is debatable whether that intention is the case in other independent companies. The monitoring of equal opportunities within the independent sector seems to be one which has received little attention and is fairly low on the agenda.

Although job-share/part-time working was, in general, viewed favourably by the respondents it did not seem to be common practice. The one woman who did work part-time found it invaluable but although it was easily organised , there was an expectation that she should be 'more grateful'. This raised the question of how committed companies are to what, in other industries, would be a normal working practice. There were restrictions by management on the types of programmes where work could be job-share or part-time and it was argued that the production process could make it difficult to operate .

While employers might appear theoretically sympathetic to working mothers, evidence suggested that in practice this was not always the case. This was not necessarily through any discriminatory attitude but because of the financial pressures all companies face. It was also suggested by one Head of Personnel that it was not sufficiently high a priority to merit any attention.

Unlike most other industries television does not seem to have embraced alternative working practices. The one woman who had managed to obtain part-time employment considered herself 'lucky', and it was through necessity rather than it being presented as an option available for everyone. In this area management seemed inflexible. Because of the growing pool of potential workers, television bosses are currently able to pick and choose who they will employ. This combined with the sharp decline in union power means that they do not have to offer incentives in order to attract staff and tend to be reactive rather than proactive when it comes to equal opportunities.

Those women in a producer/researcher role did feel restricted in their promotion prospects since they considered advancement would mean working even longer hours. Yet all argued that becoming a mother had in fact improved how they performed at work. Time management was emphasised as a valuable skill they had learned and several felt that they had become more focused in how they addressed their work. They also emphasised the contribution they could make as mothers to the programmes in which they were involved, both through the contacts they had made through their children and the change it had made to each as an individual.

In an increasingly competitive market, one strategy proposed was that women should use these skills as a selling point to their benefit. All the women felt that the issue of working mothers in television was highly important but the stress and frenetic nature of their own lives left little room for collective action.

The women interviewed, particularly those working at a programme-making level, felt powerless to combat these difficulties. In most cases they had been working in television all their lives. It was a job they enjoyed, found challenging and there were more opportunities becoming available for women through, for example, the BBC policy of setting targets for the employment of women. However, because of their working conditions some were questioning whether they could continue their career and most had certainly found areas of conflict between their working and domestic lives.

Without a concerted campaign to improve their working conditions, the situation for working mothers within the British television industry seems bleak. More and more young people are opting for media courses and pursuing a career in television. Although there are more job opportunities within the industry, the absence of a defined wage structure means that those who are young (and childless) will often accept a lower rate of pay. This can only contribute to a more 'competitive' employment market.

Strategies for Change
Several organisations are actively putting forward proposals to improve working conditions. The principal trade union in broadcasting, BECTU, is still a major

consultative body over such issues as equal opportunities and training. Jane Paul, BECTU's Equality Officer, states that the union's real concern with regard to all its members is the long and erratic hours they work. The union is pressing for more predictable working hours and adequately protected rest time within the period of a member's contract. The union argues that its members' health is being put at risk through long hours. BECTU is aiming to persuade commissioning editors and broadcasters to accept some responsibility with regard to long hours. It is also working with PACT (Producers Alliance for Cinema and Television) to ensure that budgets take account of health and safety during productions.

Strategies are also being put forward by BECTU at a regional level. One proposal is for a levy to be paid by independent producers into a central fund. This could then finance childcare allowances for freelance members. The union acknowledges that having a specific amount written into each programme budget might discourage employers from taking on working mothers.

The group *Women in Film and Television* also highlights the long hours culture as being the worst obstacle for parents in the industry. Following an open forum on Working Parents held in October 1995, the organisation issued a list of ideas for further action. While recognising budgetary limitations, it suggested that everyone, where possible, should be encouraged to go home at a reasonable time and that breakfast and evening meetings should be discouraged. The forum also suggested that employers should value the particular skills and experience of each employee. *Women in Film and Television* also proposes that those companies who take positive steps to become 'family-friendly' should receive a 'kite-mark' which could bring positive publicity for the particular company and make it more attractive to prospective employees.

The campaign, *Opportunity 2000*, which aims to improve women's employment opportunities in the private and public sector asserts that 'British business is not taking full advantage of the economic potential of women in the workforce'.[7] It argues that, by adopting women-friendly initiatives, employers are able to retain their staff. This may seem irrelevant in an increasingly freelance workforce but research has indicated that there may be a skill shortage in certain areas of the television industry in the near future.[8] If an employer is able to offer incentives such as flexible working arrangements then it will be in a better position to select its employees.

Some of the strategies for change are not directed specifically at the television industry but reflect a growing concern that working hours in Britain tend to be longer than anywhere in Europe, and are increasing. The organisation, *Parents at Work*, in their report *Time, Work and the Family* indicated that almost two-thirds of those surveyed worked longer than their contracted hours and a similar number felt that they did not see enough of their children. The survey concluded that while many employers are getting good value for money from their working mothers women talk of the stress of the juggling act or tug of war between work and family life. One of its recommendations is that organisations should consider the adverse effects of long hours such as stress-related ill-health and reductions in productivity. The report points out that not only can long hours be detrimental to an employee's well-being but it can also be damaging for the employer if its pool of skilled labour becomes depleted.[9]

While the British government remains resistant to any enforced reduction in working hours, the European Community has identified inequality within broadcasting as a situation which must change. In a guide to good practice issued in 1991 several strategies are recommended. With particular reference to work and the family, it is proposed that flexible working should be encouraged and that employers should provide assistance with childcare. It is also argues that: 'A surprising range of jobs [within television] can be shared'. The report also advocates career breaks and parental leave with a guaranteed return to work. The section concludes that: 'Organisations which promote the right working conditions will attract and retain the best staff'.[10]

It is this economic argument more than any other which is likely to prove the most attractive to employers and bring about change within the British television and encourage more working mothers to remain active within the industry.

Notes and References

1. Langham, J., *Lights, Camera, Action!: Careers In Film, Television and Video*, British Film Institute (London: 1993), p.x

2. Woolf, M. & Holly, S., *Employment Patterns and Training Needs 1993/4* (Freelance and Set Crafts Research), Skillset, (London: 1994) and *Employment Patterns and Training Needs 1993/4* (Women Freelances), Skillset (London: 1994) p.iv.

3. Commission of the European Community, *Equal Opportunities for European Broadcasting: A Guide to Good Practice*, p. 14

4. *Television Tracking Study The First Year: An Interim Report*, British Film Institute, (London: 1995).

5. Brown, M., 'Media women work too hard to have children', *Independent*, 5 December 1994, p.7.

6. See Ramsden, S., 'Problems when baby comes too', *Broadcast*, 15 September 1995.

7. Bargh, L., *Opportunity 2000*, Business in the Community, (London 1991)

8. Langham, *op. cit.*, p. 51.

9. Parents at Work, 1995, *Time, Work & the Family*, (London: 1995).

10. Commission of the European Community, *Equal Opportunities in European Broadcasting: A Guide to Good Practice*, (EEC 1991), pp. 13 &14.

Additional Bibliography

Ariel, 10 May 1995 , 'Birt signs up to 25 nation women's charter', p.3.

Arthurs, J., 1994, 'Women and Television' in Hood, S. (ed), *Behind the Screens – The Structure of British Television in the Nineties*, Lawrence & Wishart, (London: 1994), pp. 82-101.

Borum, B. 'Caught between the camera and the cradle', *Independent*, 27 July, 1992, p.15.

'Motherhood and TV don't mix', *Broadcast*, 1 September 1995.

Busfield, S., 'Dial M for Murder', *Broadcast*, 1 September 1995, p.15.

Coyle, A., 'Behind the Scenes' in Coyle, A. and Skinner, J. (ed), *Women and Work : Positive Action for Change*, Macmillan Education, (London: 1988) pp. 58-79.

Dougary, G., *The Executive Tart and other Myths – Media Women talk back*, Virago (London: 1994)

Independent Television Commission, 'Equal opportunities in commercial television: the ITC's annual review', *Equal Opportunity Review* No. 63, September/October, pp.24-28.

Hillier, S., 'Closing the gap', Ariel, 17 March 1992, p.13.

The *Independent*, 10 April 1991. 'Twice the input for half the job', p.17.

The *Independent*, 5 December 1994., 'Life gets tough for middle-class parents', p.13.

Innes, S., *Making It Work: Women, Change and Challenge in the 90s*, Chatto & Windus, (London: 1995)

Kenny, M., 'Absolutely fabulous – and childless', *Daily Telegraph*, 25 August 1995, p.15.

Loach, L., 'Campaigning for Change' in Baehr, H. and Dyer, G. (ed), *Boxed In : Women and Television*, Pandora, (London: 1987), pp. 55-69.

Muir, A.R., 1988, 'The Status of Women Working in Film and Television' in Gamman, L. and Marshment, M. (ed), *The Female Gaze – Women as Viewers of Popular Culture*, The Women's Press, (London: 1988), pp. 143-152.

O'Kelly, L., 'The bosses v the children: a mother's tale', *Independent*, 4 September 1991, p.19.

Thynne, J., 'TV women stay childless to achieve career success', *Daily Telegraph*, 25 August 1995.

Turner, J., 'Working towards fair play', *Broadcast*, 5 May 1995, pp. 18-19.

Turner, J., 1995, 'Women freelances: still facing barriers', *Stage, Screen, Radio*, May 1995, pp. 10-11.

Women's Broadcasting Committee, *Her Point of View*, Women's Broadcasting Committee/BECTU, (London: 1993).

Media Studies

Playground or passport?

Peter M.Lewis
Middlesex University

T his brief comment draws on my experience of teaching media studies over the last two decades, and from discussions with friends in the media industry – the background from which I came to teach in higher education. I had worked in educational and community access television in the 1960s and 1970s and took the view that understanding the processes and methods of broadcasting was likely to produce more critical and demanding viewers and listeners and in turn improve the quality of broadcasting. Furthermore I had argued, following the Chinese proverb, that to 'do is to understand' and that therefore media study should include practice (Lewis 1970).

It was thus in a liberal arts or humanities context that I began teaching what was then called communication studies at Goldsmiths College in the 1980s. The BA was developed in a School of Art and Design. Its practice elements included film, film animation, television, and radio (which I developed) and these were eventually, and not without a struggle, recognised by the University of London as a logical extension of art practice alongside theory. A joint degree with sociology was subsequently developed.

Even then it was clear that many of our students were aiming for jobs in the industry and the launch of Channel 4 came at the right time to offer a number of them a new range of openings. We could not ignore, therefore, their vocational expectations. Although our course had no formal industry recognition, we tried to equip them with at least the basic skills that would help them get a job, while at the same time trying to get them to develop a critical analysis which would allow them to situate their work experience in a social and historical context. I imagine this was more or less the sort of background from which Michael Jackson left what was then the Polytechnic of Central London (now the University of Westminster) to join the BBC. I used to advise students not to flaunt their media studies too openly among broadcasters, for whom, as I knew, sociology is a dirty word. I hoped that the best of them would act as double agents or sleepers, lying low till they were in a position to change the world, or at least C4, like Michael Jackson.

In the 1990s, how much has changed: a political and economic climate in which the old certainties about employment have completely vanished – in academia and as well as broadcasting. It is in this contemporary context that I want to examine the place of media studies, and some of the expectations that surround the subject on the part of those who plan, teach and study the courses and the broadcasters who encounter the resulting product. These expectations, I will argue, are considerably mismatched and often totally incompatible.

The Skillset survey of media courses (Skillset 1996) has given us the national picture – some 120,000 students, counting further education, undergraduate and postgraduate sectors together, are following media studies courses. Most of these courses are not intended to be vocational: the media are studied because they are a significant part of modern life. For example, at Middlesex University where I now teach, our degree is titled `Media and Cultural Studies'. The media are seen as part of culture; cultural consumption and cultural practice include media but are wider; areas such as fashion and style, music and dance culture, and issues such as cultural identity, gender, sexuality and race are covered in the degree. I teach courses about the economic aspects of media and culture (globalisation), media practices and structures, and a course on documentary and non-fictional representation. There is a very small element of practice in the degree (I shall come back to this later) and I am trying to put radio on to the theoretical agenda of cultural studies in which it is seriously neglected.

Whether or not practice features as an element, any course with `media' in its title is extremely popular. This fact bulks large in the calculations of university planners. Universities are nowadays constrained within tight budgets. Meeting intake targets is crucial, and failure to do so is penalised in financial terms. There is therefore an increasing tendency for planning and allocation of resources (this means staff as well as budgets) to be `consumer-driven', and fluctuation in demand for places is carefully studied. Under-recruitment in a relatively unpopular subject either means job cuts, or the adoption of strategies of course development which link the unpopular courses with something the consumers must have: media studies are a prime example of the `honeypot factor' which is becoming crucial in academic planning. Undergraduate numbers alone, however, do not guarantee break-even. Links with industry, investment in certain types of hardware which attract special funding, the development of postgraduate courses and, above all, the creation of a critical mass of research and publication which will score high enough in the government Research Assessment Exercise (RAE) to win the precious funds to continue to `buy out' some staff from teaching so as to continue to research and publish – and reach at least the same score in the next RAE.

If the teachers of media studies have anything to complain about in this planning strategy, it's a complaint that echoes those made by broadcasting producers about their managements: the suits are in control, ratings (students numbers) are everything, 'we aren't being given as much time as we were in the studio/for filming/preparation/assessment', 'quality is going out of the window' etc. The numbers game has, it's true, a tendency to cut the critical frills in media studies, or in other words detach the more vocational and practical elements from the theoretical and cultural in order to offer units of teaching that can be packaged with all kinds of combinations in a modular degree scheme. Shorn of its original context, media studies becomes no more than a series of training sessions, hopefully updated to keep pace with industry changes, and with the apparatus of work placements and visiting lecturers maintaining industry contact. The goal then becomes the replication of industry standards, a recipe for stifling innovation in the long term.

The trend is assisted by the changes in the character of media employment: as more producers are made redundant or choose to go freelance, teaching is seen as a useful accompaniment to freelance work. In a syllabus governed by the outlook described above, such producer/lecturers are a godsend; indeed, they seem to continue a long-standing tradition of art school practice where the best lecturers are also practising artists. Seem to, because broadcast employment, whether institution-based or freelance, is a fearsomely time- and energy-consuming occupation, like teaching, and (also like teaching) with increasingly less time for reflection or experiment. There is a danger that such input from the industry will serve the short-term goals of a college or university, but not draw out the best from the `practising artist'. Nothing is more valuable to both parties in the media studies compact than the broadcaster who has been given the time and theoretical tools to critically reflect on some aspect of his/her work, translating experience into the kind of analysis which asks the awkward questions covered up by the daily rush to meet deadlines, questions vital to the health of broadcasting and society.

What of the main characters in this cast-list, the students or consumers themselves? It's simply stated: calculations about future jobs must underlie all their choices. That they are aiming for a university place at all means they believe a degree will help improve their long-term prospects. Most support themselves in this project by working at least part-time, some for long hours which damage their studies. As we've seen, applicants opt for media studies in large numbers. Why? Partly because, in the words of a candidate I recently asked, 'it has relevance to to-day's society'. Partly, also because whatever disclaimers are made by academic planners and lecturers, they think taking media studies will help them find a job `in the media.' To this end, they prefer courses which have an element of media practice in them. But this media Mecca is not what is was. Changes in technology and staffing patterns mean that, despite the predicted growth in channels, the future for most students is less likely to be 'employment in broadcasting', as combining a freelance existence (see the 1994 Skillset Report) with some other form of employment, or with unemployment.

I would summarise industry attitudes to media studies as follows: a concern about the standards of practical courses, exasperation with unsolicited and often inept job applications, an ambiguous attitude towards work placements and a deep suspicion of theory courses. I can understand all of these reactions and will discuss most of them as I offer some suggestions about what should be happening in university media studies.

First of all, practice: of course it is right that the industry should be concerned and, through Skillset and other validating institutions, can watch standards generally, and keep in close touch with those courses which claim to be a vocational entry point into broadcasting. But a majority of courses that offer practice do not make that claim, and indeed literally cannot afford to. Keeping up with the broadcasters is beyond the budget of most universities. Since we cannot promise to match the latest digital system, we should, I believe, be trying to give students the experience of some of the key moments in the creative process – pitching an idea, researching it, planning an item within a programme or recording a short sequence or interview, editing it to a deadline, packaging and presenting it. These processes can be experienced for radio or video/film, and it's preferable if students can get a taste of both. Writing is a fundamental skill – whether for a pitch, a job application or a scripted link: we should teach all this. I have talked in terms of broadcasting, but convergence of all forms of communication means that awareness of, if not skills in, Internet use, Website and multi-media production are part of the necessary equipment for a future communicator. I'd add that in the context I work in – mostly theory – practice along such lines is intended to enhance or explain theory. You begin to understand editorial choice when, with a razor blade in your hand, you are forced to decide what to cut out of your precious interview; news values and audience attitudes come alive when you shape a bulletin against the clock. Marketing skills – for oneself and one's ideas – are increasingly important. One university I know requires written work as an outcome of a lecture programme given over the year by a distinguished series of visitors: the students' assignment is to write to any one of the visitors asking for a job and enclosing a CV. The visitors are spared reading these efforts which get no further than the assessing tutor. A pre-condition for being able to write an effective letter of this kind is an understanding of the media landscape, of programme genres, industry structures, global trends – topics which are a common ingredient of media studies courses.

The industry attitude to work placements is ambiguous because requests for them are sometimes welcome, sometimes burdensome. Both sides have a responsibility to ensure that the conditions are not such as to exploit the student. From a vocational point of view placements are obviously extremely valuable. They gain added value if a student can be helped to make sense of the experience in a written report which either makes connections with the theoretical side of the course (for example, contextualises the work of the company that offered the placement within the media landscape), or is the product of some research carried out as part of the work (ie is useful to the `employer'). In my experience students understandably want to make the leap straight into some mainstream media company, but often the placement works better in an organisation which encourages volunteers. This might be a voluntary organisation which has nothing to do with the media and precisely for that reason might welcome someone with an investment in showing how media could further its aims; or, given my specialist interest, I look to hospital and community radio. RSLs (Restricted Service Licences) which, for a period of up to four weeks, make it possible for a group to bring together and display radio skills, are an ideal situation.

I want to end by referring to some research which shows the extent to which community radio is acting as a gateway to employment in the industry, and to suggest, in the context of our efforts to make our subject relevant, that the sector is something to which we in media studies should pay more attention. Carried out for the European Division of AMARC (the French acronym for the World Association of Community radio Broadcasters), the survey found that over 2,000 people were working in community radio in the UK, a fifth of all personnel in the radio industry. Nine out of ten community radio workers were unpaid volunteers, and over half had no previous radio experience; in the year previous to the survey, three quarters had received an average of two weeks of formal training in radio production. At a time when the effects of free market competition are weakening the training provision that used to be a traditional feature of an industry dominated by the BBC, the training contribution of community radio is increasing in significance. Temporary broadcast licences (RSLs) were identified as an important factor in both training and paid jobs for volunteers. Bradford Community radio reported that after its Festival Radio broadcast in 1992, nine of its volunteers had been offered jobs in local radio or television within a month of the transmissions ending. The UK survey was part of wider research carried out in Denmark, Germany, Italy and Ireland from which it was estimated that some 40,000 to 50,000 people were working in the community radio sector in EU countries.

Here, then, is a sector, confined in this country at present mainly to non-broadcast projects or temporary licences, but flourishing as part of the broadcasting scene in most other European countries, where the advantage is that volunteers are welcome, that training is an accepted part of the operation, and where there is an impressive record of subsequent employment in the industry. There is no space here to pursue all the implications of this conjuncture of interests, but we in the university sector should certainly consider strengthening our connections with community radio. The industry needs nursery slopes and so do our students.

References

Lewis, P. (1970) 'Not so much a programme, More a Way of Life..', *Screen*, Vol. 11, No. 4/5

Lewis, P. (1994) *Community Radio – a gateway to employment: UK report of a transnational survey of employment trends and training needs in the community radio sector*, Sheffield: AMARC-Europe; funded by the EU's FORCE programme and Sheffield TEC.

Skillset (1994) *Employment Patterns and Training Needs 1993/4*.

Skillset (1996) *Media Courses Survey and Consultation 1995/6*.